interchange
FOURTH EDITION

Jack C. Richards

Series Editor: David Bohlke

CAMBRIDGE
UNIVERSITY PRESS

Intro
STUDENT'S BOOK

CAMBRIDGE
UNIVERSITY PRESS

University Printing House, Cambridge CB2 8BS, United Kingdom

One Liberty Plaza, 20th Floor, New York, NY 10006, USA

477 Williamstown Road, Port Melbourne, VIC 3207, Australia

4843/24, 2nd Floor, Ansari Road, Daryaganj, Delhi – 110002, India

79 Anson Road, #06–04/06, Singapore 079906

Cambridge University Press is part of the University of Cambridge.

It furthers the University's mission by disseminating knowledge in the pursuit of education, learning and research at the highest international levels of excellence.

www.cambridge.org
Information on this title: www.cambridge.org/9781107614956

First published 2005
20 19 18 17 16 15 14 13 12 11

Printed in Dubai by Oriental Press

A catalog record for this publication is available from the British Library

ISBN 978-1-107-64866-1 Intro Student's Book with Self-study DVD
ISBN 978-1-107-68031-9 Intro Student's Book A with Self-study DVD
ISBN 978-1-107-61155-9 Intro Student's Book B with Self-study DVD
ISBN 978-1-107-64871-5 Intro Workbook
ISBN 978-1-107-67020-4 Intro Workbook A
ISBN 978-1-107-61537-3 Intro Workbook B
ISBN 978-1-107-64011-5 Intro Teacher's Edition with Assessment Audio CD/CD-ROM
ISBN 978-1-107-61034-7 Intro Class Audio CDs
ISBN 978-1-107-61495-6 Intro Full Contact with Self-study DVD-ROM
ISBN 978-1-107-68000-5 Intro Full Contact A with Self-study DVD-ROM
ISBN 978-1-107-69456-9 Intro Full Contact B with Self-study DVD-ROM

For a full list of components, visit www.cambridge.org/interchange

Art direction, book design, layout services, and photo research: Integra
Audio production: CityVox, NYC
Video production: Nesson Media Boston, Inc.

Welcome to *Interchange Fourth Edition*, the world's most successful English series!

Interchange offers a complete set of tools for learning how to communicate in English.

Student's Book
with **NEW Self-study DVD-ROM**

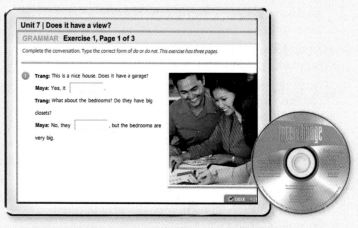

- **Complete video program** with additional **video exercises**

- Additional **vocabulary**, **grammar, speaking, listening**, and **reading** practice
- Printable **score reports** to submit to teachers

Available online

Interchange Arcade

- **Free** self-study website
- **Fun**, interactive, self-scoring activities
- Practice **vocabulary**, **grammar**, **listening**, and **reading**
- **MP3s** of the class audio program

Online Workbook

- A variety of **interactive activities** that correspond to each Student's Book lesson
- **Instant feedback** for hundreds of activities
- **Easy to use** with clear, easy-to-follow instructions
- Extra **listening practice**
- Simple tools for teachers to **monitor progress** such as scores, attendance, and time spent online

Author's acknowledgments

A great number of people contributed to the development of *Interchange Fourth Edition*. Particular thanks are owed to the reviewers using *Interchange*, *Third Edition* in the following schools and institutes – their insights and suggestions have helped define the content and format of the fourth edition:

Ian Geoffrey Hanley, **The Address Education Center**, Izmir, Turkey

James McBride, **AUA Language Center**, Bangkok, Thailand

Jane Merivale, **Centennial College**, Toronto, Ontario, Canada

Elva Elena Peña Andrade, **Centro de Auto Aprendizaje de Idiomas**, Nuevo León, Mexico

José Paredes, **Centro de Educación Continua de la Escuela Politécnica Nacional** (CEC-EPN), Quito, Ecuador

Chia-jung Tsai, **Changhua University of Education**, Changhua City, Taiwan

Kevin Liang, **Chinese Culture University**, Taipei, Taiwan

Roger Alberto Neira Perez, **Colegio Santo Tomás de Aquino**, Bogotá, Colombia

Teachers at **Escuela Miguel F. Martínez**, Monterrey, Mexico

Maria Virgínia Goulart Borges de Lebron, **Great Idiomas**, São Paulo, Brazil

Gina Kim, **Hoseo University**, Chungnam, South Korea

Heeyong Kim, Seoul, South Korea

Elisa Borges, **IBEU-Rio**, Rio de Janeiro, Brazil

Jason M. Ham, **Inha University**, Incheon, South Korea

Rita de Cássia S. Silva Miranda, **Instituto Batista de Idiomas**, Belo Horizonte, Brazil

Teachers at **Instituto Politécnico Nacional**, Mexico City, Mexico

Victoria M. Roberts and Regina Marie Williams, **Interactive College of Technology**, Chamblee, Georgia, USA

Teachers at **Internacional de Idiomas**, Mexico City, Mexico

Marcelo Serafim Godinho, **Life Idiomas**, São Paulo, Brazil

J. Kevin Varden, **Meiji Gakuin University**, Yokohama, Japan

Rosa Maria Valencia Rodríguez, Mexico City, Mexico

Chung-Ju Fan, **National Kinmen Institute of Technology**, Kinmen, Taiwan

Shawn Beasom, **Nihon Daigaku**, Tokyo, Japan

Gregory Hadley, **Niigata University of International and Information Studies**, Niigata, Japan

Chris Ruddenklau, **Osaka University of Economics and Law**, Osaka, Japan

Byron Roberts, **Our Lady of Providence Girls' High School**, Xindian City, Taiwan

Simon Banha, **Phil Young's English School**, Curitiba, Brazil

Flávia Gonçalves Carneiro Braathen, **Real English Center**, Viçosa, Brazil

Márcia Cristina Barboza de Miranda, **SENAC**, Recife, Brazil

Raymond Stone, **Seneca College of Applied Arts and Technology**, Toronto, Ontario, Canada

Gen Murai, **Takushoku University**, Tokyo, Japan

Teachers at **Tecnológico de Estudios Superiores de Ecatepec**, Mexico City, Mexico

Teachers at **Universidad Autónoma Metropolitana–Azcapotzalco**, Mexico City, Mexico

Teachers at **Universidad Autónoma de Nuevo León**, Monterrey, Mexico

Mary Grace Killian Reyes, **Universidad Autónoma de Tamaulipas**, Tampico Tamaulipas, Mexico

Teachers at **Universidad Estatal del Valle de Ecatepec**, Mexico City, Mexico

Teachers at **Universidad Nacional Autónoma de Mexico – Zaragoza**, Mexico City, Mexico

Teachers at **Universidad Nacional Autónoma de Mexico – Iztacala**, Mexico City, Mexico

Luz Edith Herrera Diaz, Veracruz, Mexico

Seri Park, **YBM PLS**, Seoul, South Korea

Self-assessment charts revised by Alex Tilbury

Grammar plus written by Karen Davy

Plan of Intro Book

Titles/Topics	Speaking	Grammar
UNIT 1 PAGES 2–7		
It's nice to meet you. Alphabet; greetings and leave-takings; names and titles of address; numbers 0–10, phone numbers, and email addresses	Introducing yourself and friends; saying hello and good-bye; asking for names and phone numbers	Possessive adjectives *my, your, his, her*; the verb *be*; affirmative statements and contractions
UNIT 2 PAGES 8–13		
What's this? Possessions, classroom objects, personal items, and locations in a room	Naming objects; asking for and giving the locations of objects	Articles *a, an*, and *the; this/these, it/they*; plurals; yes/no and *where* questions with *be*; prepositions of place: *in, in front of, behind, on, next to*, and *under*
PROGRESS CHECK PAGES 14–15		
UNIT 3 PAGES 16–21		
Where are you from? Cities and countries; adjectives of personality and appearance; numbers 11–103 and ages	Talking about cities and countries; asking for and giving information about place of origin, nationality, first language, and age; describing people	The verb *be*: affirmative and negative statements, yes/no questions, short answers, and Wh-questions
UNIT 4 PAGES 22–27		
Whose jeans are these? Clothing; colors; weather and seasons	Asking about and describing clothing and colors; talking about the weather and seasons; finding the owners of objects	Possessives: adjectives *our* and *their*, pronouns, names, and *whose*; present continuous statements and yes/no questions; conjunctions *and, but*, and *so*; placement of adjectives before nouns
PROGRESS CHECK PAGES 28–29		
UNIT 5 PAGES 30–35		
What are you doing? Clock time; times of the day; everyday activities	Asking for and telling time; asking about and describing current activities	Time expressions: *o'clock, A.M., P.M., noon, midnight, in the morning/ afternoon/evening, at 7:00/night/ midnight*; present continuous Wh-questions
UNIT 6 PAGES 36–41		
My sister works downtown. Transportation; family relationships; daily routines; days of the week	Asking for and giving information about how people go to work or school; talking about family members; describing daily and weekly routines	Simple present statements with regular and irregular verbs; simple present yes/no and Wh-questions; time expressions: *early, late, every day, on Sundays/weekends/ weekdays*
PROGRESS CHECK PAGES 42–43		
UNIT 7 PAGES 44–49		
Does it have a view? Houses and apartments; rooms; furniture	Asking about and describing houses and apartments; talking about the furniture in a room	Simple present short answers; *there is, there are; there's no, there isn't a, there are no, there aren't any*
UNIT 8 PAGES 50–55		
What do you do? Jobs and workplaces	Asking for and giving information about work; giving opinions about jobs; describing workday routines	Simple present Wh-questions with *do* and *does*; placement of adjectives after *be* and before nouns
PROGRESS CHECK PAGES 56–57		

Titles/Topics	Speaking	Grammar
UNIT 9 PAGES 58–63		
Do we need any eggs? Basic foods; breakfast foods; meals	Talking about food likes and dislikes; giving opinions about healthy and unhealthy foods; talking about foods you have and need; describing eating habits	Count and noncount nouns; *some* and *any*; adverbs of frequency: *always, usually, often, sometimes, hardly ever, never*
UNIT 10 PAGES 64–69		
What sports do you play? Sports; abilities and talents	Asking about free-time activities; asking for and giving information about abilities and talents	Simple present Wh-questions; *can* for ability; yes/no and Wh-questions with *can*
PROGRESS CHECK PAGES 70–71		
UNIT 11 PAGES 72–77		
What are you going to do? Months and dates; birthdays, holidays, festivals, and special days	Asking about birthdays; talking about plans for the evening, weekend, and other occasions	The future with *be going to*; yes/no and Wh-questions with *be going to*; future time expressions
UNIT 12 PAGES 78–83		
What's the matter? Parts of the body; health problems and advice; medications	Describing health problems; talking about common medications; giving advice for health problems	*Have* + noun; *feel* + adjective; negative and positive adjectives; imperatives
PROGRESS CHECK PAGES 84–85		
UNIT 13 PAGES 86–91		
You can't miss it. Stores and things you can buy there; tourist attractions	Talking about stores and other places; asking for and giving directions	Prepositions of place: *on, on the corner of, across from, next to, between;* giving directions with imperatives
UNIT 14 PAGES 92–97		
Did you have fun? Weekends; chores and fun activities; vacations; summer activities	Asking for and giving information about weekend and vacation activities	Simple past statements with regular and irregular verbs; simple past yes/no questions and short answers
PROGRESS CHECK PAGES 98–99		
UNIT 15 PAGES 100–105		
Where did you grow up? Biographical information; years; school days	Asking for and giving information about date and place of birth; describing school experiences and memories	Statements and questions with the past of *be*; Wh-questions with *did, was,* and *were*
UNIT 16 PAGES 106–111		
Can she call you later? Locations; telephone calls; invitations; going out with friends	Describing people's locations; making, accepting, and declining invitations; making excuses	Prepositional phrases; subject and object pronouns; invitations with *Do you want to…?* and *Would you like to…?*; verb + *to*
PROGRESS CHECK PAGES 112–113		
GRAMMAR PLUS PAGES 132–151		

Pronunciation/Listening	Writing/Reading	Interchange Activity
Sentence stress Listening for people's food preferences	Writing about mealtime habits "Eating for Good Luck": Reading about foods people eat for good luck in the new year	"Snack survey": Taking a survey about snacks you eat and comparing answers PAGE 123
Pronunciation of *can* and *can't* Listening for people's favorite sports to watch or play; listening to people talk about their abilities	Writing questions about sports "An Interview with Shawn Johnson": Reading about the life of an Olympic athlete	"Hidden talents": Finding out more about your classmates' hidden talents PAGE 124
Reduction of *going to* Listening to people talk about their evening plans	Writing about weekend plans "What Are You Going to Do on Your Birthday?": Reading about birthday customs in different places	"Guessing game": Making guesses about a classmate's plans PAGE 125
Sentence intonation Listening to people talk about health problems; listening for medications	Writing advice for health problems "10 Simple Ways to Improve Your Health": Reading about ways to improve your health	"Helpful advice": Giving advice for some common problems PAGE 126
Compound nouns Listening to people talk about shopping; listening to directions	Writing directions "Edinburgh's Royal Mile": Reading about popular tourist attractions in Edinburgh, Scotland	"Giving directions": Asking for directions in a neighborhood PAGES 127, 128
Simple past *-ed* endings Listening to people talk about their past summer activities	Writing about last weekend "Did You Have a Good Weekend?": Reading about four people's weekend experiences	"Past and present": Comparing your classmates' present lives with their childhoods PAGE 129
Negative contractions Listening for places and dates of birth	Writing questions about a young person's life "Turning Pain to Gain": Reading about a young woman's life	"Life events": Making a time line of important events in your life PAGE 130
Reduction of *want to* and *have to* Listening to phone conversations; listening to voice-mail messages	Writing about weekend plans "Around Los Angeles: This Weekend": Reading about events on a web page	"Let's make a date!": Making plans with your classmates PAGE 131

1 It's nice to meet you.

1 **CONVERSATION** *My name is Jennifer Miller.*

A Listen and practice.

Michael: Hello. My name is Michael Ota.
Jennifer: Hi. My name is Jennifer Miller.
Michael: It's nice to meet you, Jennifer.
Jennifer: Nice to meet you, too.
Michael: I'm sorry. What's your last name again?
Jennifer: It's Miller.

first names	last names
↓	↓
Jennifer	Miller
Michael	Ota

B **PAIR WORK** Introduce yourself to your partner.

2 **SNAPSHOT**

 Listen and practice.

Taylor Lautner

Popular Names in the U.S.
for Both Males and Females

Taylor Jordan Casey Jamie Riley
Jessie Hayden Peyton Quinn Rory

Taylor Swift

Source: www.babynames1000.com

Circle the names you know.
What are some popular names for males in your country? for females?
What names are popular for both males and females?

3 GRAMMAR FOCUS

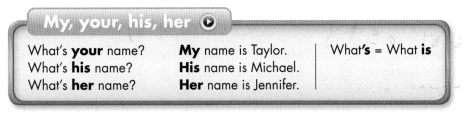

My, your, his, her ⊙

What's **your** name?   **My** name is Taylor.   What's = What **is**
What's **his** name?   **His** name is Michael.
What's **her** name?   **Her** name is Jennifer.

A Complete the conversations. Use *my*, *your*, *his*, or *her*.

1. A: Hello. What's ......*your*...... name?
   B: Hi. *S*.................... name is Antonio.
      What's ....*your*.... name?
   A: *my*........ name is Nicole.

2. A: What's ....*your*.... name?
   B: ......*my*...... name is Michael.
   A: And what's ......*your*...... name?
   B: ......*my*...... name is Jennifer.

B **PAIR WORK** Practice the conversations with a partner.

4 SPELLING NAMES

A ⊙ Listen and practice.

A B C D E F G H I J K L M N O P Q R S T U V W X Y Z
a b c d e f g h i j k l m n o p q r s t u v w x y z

B ⊙ **CLASS ACTIVITY** Listen and practice. Then practice with your own names. Make a list of your classmates' names.

A: What's your name?
B: My name is Sarah Conner.
A: Is that S-A-R-A-H?
B: Yes, that's right.
A: How do you spell your last name? C-O-N-N-O-R?
B: No, it's C-O-N-N-E-R.

> <u>My Classmates</u>
> Sarah Conner
> Jennifer Miller

5 LISTENING *First names*

⊙ How do you spell the names? Listen and check (✓) the correct answers.

1. ☑ Kara   2. ☑ Mark   3. ☑ Shawn   4. ☑ Sophia
   ☐ Cara   ☐ Marc   ☐ Sean   ☐ Sofia

6 WORD POWER *Titles*

A ▶ Listen and practice.

Miss Ito	(single females)	**Ms.** Chen	(single or married females)
Mrs. Morgan	(married females)	**Mr.** Garcia	(single or married males)

[handwritten annotations: solteros *over "single females";* mujer, soltera o casada *over "single or married females";* casadas *under "married females";* hombres *under "single or married males"]*

B ▶ Listen and write the titles.

1. ....*Mr.*.... Lopez   2. ....*Mrs.*.... Smith   3. ....*Ms.*.... Kim   4. ....*Ms.*.... Anderson

7 SAYING HELLO

A ▶ Listen and practice.

B CLASS ACTIVITY Go around the class. Greet your classmates formally (with titles) and informally (without titles).

CONVERSATION *He's over there.*

A ▶ Listen and practice.

Jennifer: Excuse me. Are you
           Steven Carson?
David: No, I'm not. He's over there.
Jennifer: Oh, I'm sorry.

Jennifer: Steven? This is your book.
Steven: Oh, thank you. You're in my
         class, right?
Jennifer: Yes, I am. I'm Jennifer Miller.

Steven: Hey, David, this is Jennifer.
        She's in our math class.
David: Hi, Jennifer.
Jennifer: Hi, David. Nice to meet you.

B **GROUP WORK** Greet a classmate. Then introduce him or her to another classmate.

"Hey, Ming, this is . . ."

9 GRAMMAR FOCUS

The verb be ▶

I'm Jennifer Miller.	**Are you** Steven Carson?	**I'm** = I am
You're in my class.	Yes, **I am**.	You're = You are
She's in our class. (**Jennifer is** in our class.)	No, **I'm not**.	He's = He is
He's over there. (**Steven is** over there.)		She's = She is
It's Miller. (**My last name is** Miller.)	How **are you**?	It's = It is
	I'm fine.	

A Complete the conversation with the correct words in parentheses. Then practice with a partner.

David: Hello, Jennifer. How ....*are*.... (is / are) you?
Jennifer: ....*I'm*.... (She's / I'm) fine, thanks.
      ....*It's*.... (I'm / It's) sorry – what's your name again?
David: ....*He's*.... (He's / It's) David – David Medina.
Jennifer: That's right! David, this ....*is*.... (is / am) Sarah Conner.
    ....*She's*.... (She's / He's) in our math class.
David: Hi, Sarah. ....*It's*.... (I'm / It's) nice to meet you.
Sarah: Hi, David. I think ....*you're*.... (you're / I'm) in my English class, too.
David: Oh, right! Yes, I ....*am*.... (are / am).

B Complete the conversations. Then practice in groups.

Nicole: Excuse me. __Are__ you Steven Carson?
David: No, __I'm__ not. My name __is__ David Medina. Steven __His__ over there.
Nicole: Oh, sorry.

Nicole: __are__ you Steven Carson?
Steven: Yes, I __am__.
Nicole: Hi. __are__ Nicole Johnson.
Steven: Oh, __you're__ in my math class, right?
Nicole: Yes, I __am__.
Steven: __HI__ nice to meet you.

C **CLASS ACTIVITY** Write your name on a piece of paper. Put the papers in a bag. Then take a different paper. Find the other student.

A: Excuse me. Are you Jin-sook Cho?
B: No, I'm not. She's over there.
A: Hi. Are you Jin-sook Cho?
C: Yes, I am.

10 PRONUNCIATION *Linked sounds*

Listen and practice. Notice the linked sounds.

I'm Antonio.   She's over there.   You're in my class.

11 PERSONAL INFORMATION

A Listen and practice.

0	1	2	3	4	5	6	7	8	9	10
zero (oh)	one	two	three	four	five	six	seven	eight	nine	ten

B **PAIR WORK** Practice these phone numbers and email addresses. Then listen and check your answers.

Allison Parker
402-555-2301 (work phone)
646-486-1004 (cell phone)
aparker1@cup.org (email address)

at   dot

KENJI MORI
212-924-1764 (home phone)
643-555-2285 (cell phone)
kenjimori09@cambridge.org (email address)

"Her name is Allison Parker. Her work phone number is four-oh-two, five-five-five, two-three-oh-one. Her cell . . ."

12 LISTENING *A class list*

A Jennifer and Michael are making a list of classmates' phone numbers and email addresses. Listen and complete the list.

Name	☎ Phone number	@ Email address
David Medina	212-555-1937	
Sarah Conner		
Steven Carson		
Nicole Johnson		

B CLASS ACTIVITY Make a list of your classmates' names, phone numbers, and email addresses.

A: What's your name?
B: I'm Anna Silva.

A: And what's your phone number?
B: It's 201-555-2491.

13 INTERCHANGE 1 *Famous classmates*

Meet some "famous classmates." Go to Interchange 1 on page 114.

14 SAYING GOOD-BYE

A ▶ Listen and practice.

B CLASS ACTIVITY Go around the room. Say good-bye to your classmates and teacher.

2 What's this?

▶ Listen and practice.

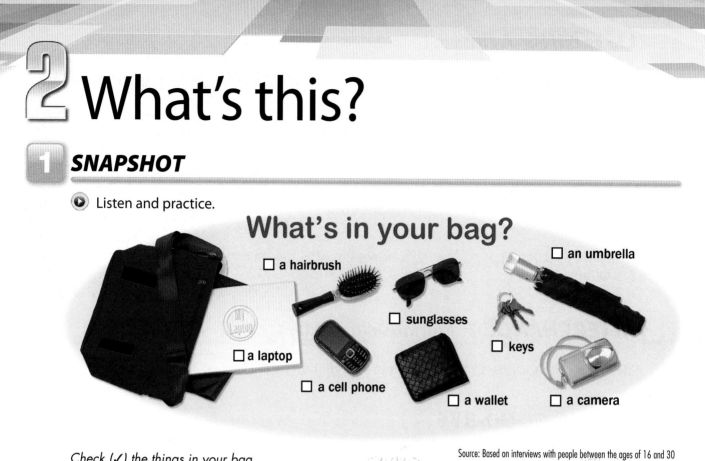

What's in your bag?

☐ a hairbrush
☐ an umbrella
☐ a laptop
☐ sunglasses
☐ a cell phone
☐ keys
☐ a wallet
☐ a camera

Check (✓) the things in your bag.
What other things are in your bag?

Source: Based on interviews with people between the ages of 16 and 30

2 ARTICLES *Classroom objects*

A ▶ Listen. Complete these sentences with *a* or *an*.

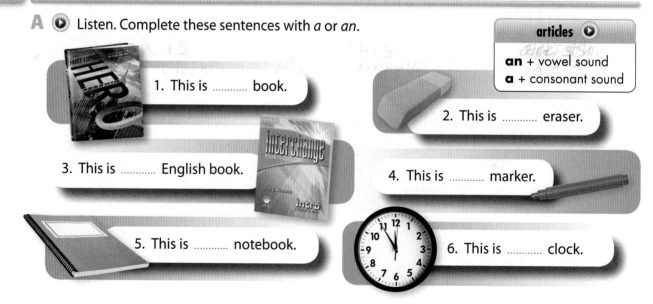

articles ▶
an + vowel sound
a + consonant sound

1. This is .... book.

2. This is .... eraser.

3. This is .... English book.

4. This is .... marker.

5. This is .... notebook.

6. This is .... clock.

B PAIR WORK Find and spell these things in your classroom.

board	desk	eraser	pen	wall
book bag	dictionary	map	pencil	wastebasket
chair	door	notebook	table	window

A: This is a board.
B: How do you spell *board*?
A: B-O-A-R-D.

8

3 CONVERSATION It's ... interesting.

▶ Listen and practice.

Wendy: Wow! What are these?
Helen: They're earrings.
Wendy: Oh, cool! Thank you, Helen.
They're great!
Helen: You're welcome.
Rex: Now open this box!
Wendy: OK. Uh, what's this?
Rex: It's a scarf.
Wendy: Oh. It's ... interesting.
Thank you, Rex. It's very nice.

4 PRONUNCIATION Plural -s endings

A ▶ Listen and practice. Notice the pronunciation of the plural **-s** endings.

s = /z/		s = /s/		(e)s = /ɪz/	
earring	earring**s**	desk	desk**s**	pencil case	pencil case**s**
phone	phone**s**	laptop	laptop**s**	class	class**es**
book bag	book bag**s**	wastebasket	wastebasket**s**	box	box**es**

B Say the plural forms of these nouns. Then complete the chart.

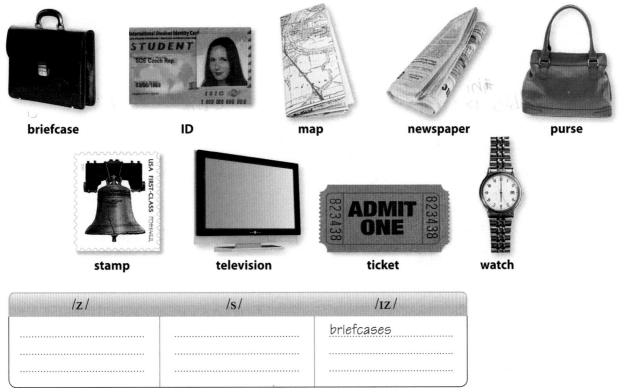

briefcase   ID   map   newspaper   purse

stamp   television   ticket   watch

/z/	/s/	/ɪz/
		briefcases

C ▶ Listen and check your answers.

GRAMMAR FOCUS

This/these, it/they; plurals

This is a clock.

These are clocks.

What's **this**?
It's an earring.

What **are these**?
They're earrings.

It**'s** = It is
They**'re** = They are

Complete these conversations. Then practice with a partner.

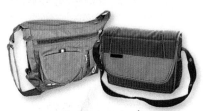

1. A: What _are these_ ?
   B: _They're keys._ .

2. A: What_'s this_ ?
   B: _this is a map_ .

3. A: What _are these_ ?
   B: _they're purses_

4. A: What _this is_ ?
   B: _this is a clock_ .

5. A: What _it this_ ?
   B: _It's an umbrella_ .

6. A: What _are these_ ?
   B: _It's an glasses_

WHAT'S THIS CALLED?

A Listen and practice.

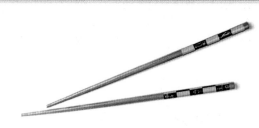

A: What's this called in English?
B: I don't know.
C: It's a credit card.
A: How do you spell that?
C: C-R-E-D-I-T C-A-R-D.

A: What are these called in English?
B: I think they're called chopsticks.
A: How do you spell that?
B: C-H-O-P-S-T-I-C-K-S.

B GROUP WORK Choose four things. Put them on a desk.
Then ask about the name and spelling of each thing.

7 CONVERSATION *Oh, no!*

▶ Listen and practice.

Kate: Oh, no! Where are my car keys?
Joe: I don't know. Are they in your purse?
Kate: No, they're not.
Joe: Maybe they're on the table in the restaurant.

Server: Excuse me. Are these your keys?
Kate: Yes, they are. Thank you!
Server: You're welcome. And is this your wallet?
Kate: Hmm. No, it's not. Where's your wallet, Joe?
Joe: It's in my pocket. . . . Wait a minute! That *is* my wallet!

8 GRAMMAR FOCUS

Yes/No and where questions with be ▶

Is this your wallet? Yes, **it is**. / No, **it's not**.	**Where's** your wallet? **It's** in my pocket.
Are these your keys? Yes, **they are**. / No, **they're not**.	**Where are** my keys? **They're** on the table.

A Complete these conversations. Then practice with a partner.

1. A: ....Is.... this your umbrella?
   B: No, ...It's.... not.
   A: ..I are.. these your keys?
   B: Yes, ..they.. are. Thanks!

2. A: Where ..are.. my glasses?
   B: Are ..these.. your glasses?
   A: No, they're ..not.. .
   B: Wait! ..are.. they in your pocket?
   A: Yes, ..they.. are. Thanks!

3. A: Where ..s this.. your sunglasses?
   B: ..they are.. on the table.
   A: No, ..they're.. not. They're *my* sunglasses!
   B: You're right. My sunglasses ..they are.. in my purse.

4. A: ..It's.. this my pen?
   B: No, ..It's.. not. It's *my* pen.
   A: Sorry, ..this.. is my pen?
   B: ..It's.. on your desk.
   A: Oh, you're right!

B GROUP WORK Put three of your things in a bag. Then choose three different things. Find the owner of each thing.

A: Is this your pen, Yuko?
B: No, it's not.

A: Are these your keys, Sergio?
C: Let me see. Yes, they are.

9 WORD POWER Prepositions; article the

A ▶ Listen and practice.

Where are **the** keys?
The keys are in **the** box.

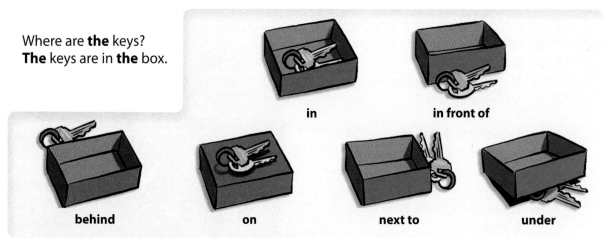

in   in front of

behind   on   next to   under

B ▶ Complete these sentences. Then listen and check your answers.

1. The books are _in the_
   book bag .

2. The cell phone is ....
   ....

3. The map is ....
   ....

4. The chair is ....
   ....

5. The wallet is ....
   ....

6. The sunglasses are ....
   ....

C PAIR WORK Ask and answer questions about the pictures in part B.

A: Where are the books?
B: They're in the book bag.

10 LISTENING Kate's things

▶ Listen. Where are Kate's things? Match the things with their locations.

1. earrings ....d....
2. watch ....
3. sunglasses ....
4. camera ....

a. under the table
b. in front of the television
c. on the chair
d. in her purse

11 WHERE ARE JOE'S THINGS?

PAIR WORK Now help Joe find his things. Ask and answer questions.

briefcase   cell phone   newspaper   umbrella
camera   glasses   notebook   wallet

A: Where's his briefcase?
B: It's on the table.

12 INTERCHANGE 2 *Find the differences*

Compare two pictures of a room. Go to Interchange 2 on page 115.

Units 1–2 Progress check

SELF-ASSESSMENT

How well can you do these things? Check (✓) the boxes.

I can	Very well	OK	A little
Introduce myself and other people (Ex. 1)	☐	☐	☐
Say hello and good-bye (Ex. 1)	☐	☐	☐
Exchange contact information, e.g., phone numbers (Ex. 2)	☐	☐	☐
Understand names for everyday objects and possessions (Ex. 3)	☐	☐	☐
Ask and answer questions about where things are (Ex. 4, 5)	☐	☐	☐

1 HOW ARE YOU?

A Complete the conversation. Use the sentences and questions in the box.

Matt: Hi. How are you?
Nicki: I'm fine, thanks. ....
Matt: Pretty good, thanks. ....
Nicki: And I'm Nicki White.
Matt: ....
Nicki: Nice to meet you, too. ....
Matt: Yes, I am.
Nicki: ....
Matt: See you in class.

> My name is Matt Carlson.
> Oh, are you in my English class?
> How about you?
> ✓ Hi. How are you?
> It's nice to meet you, Nicki.
> Well, have a good day.

B **PAIR WORK** Practice the conversation from part A. Use your own information. Then introduce your partner to a classmate.

"Malena, this is my friend. His name is Tetsu. . . ."

2 IS YOUR PHONE NUMBER . . . ?

CLASS ACTIVITY Write your phone number on a piece of paper. Then put the papers in a bag. Take a different paper and find the owner. Write his or her name on the paper.

A: Ali, is your phone number 781-555-1532?
B: No, it's not. Sorry!
A: Mila, is your . . . ?

LISTENING *What's this? What are these?*

 Listen to the conversations. Number the pictures from 1 to 6.

WHAT'S WRONG WITH THIS ROOM?

A What's wrong with this room? Make a list. Find 10 things.

The chair is on the desk.

B PAIR WORK Ask and answer *Where* questions about the picture.

A: Where's the chair?
B: It's on the desk.

YES OR NO GAME

Write five yes/no questions about the picture in Exercise 4. Three have "yes" answers, and two have "no" answers. Then ask a partner the questions.

A: Is the chair behind the clock?
B: No, it isn't.

WHAT'S NEXT?

Look at your Self-assessment again. Do you need to review anything?

3 Where are you from?

SNAPSHOT

 Listen and practice.

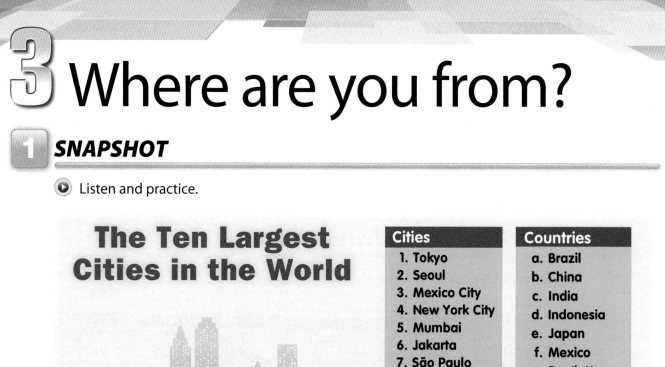

The Ten Largest Cities in the World

(based on population in the metropolitan area)

Cities
1. Tokyo
2. Seoul
3. Mexico City
4. New York City
5. Mumbai
6. Jakarta
7. São Paulo
8. Delhi
9. Osaka
10. Shanghai

Countries
a. Brazil
b. China
c. India
d. Indonesia
e. Japan
f. Mexico
g. South Korea
h. the U.S.

Answers: 1.e 2.g 3.f 4.h 5.c 6.d 7.a 8.c 9.e 10.b

Source: www.worldatlas.com

Match the cities with the countries. Then check your answers at the bottom of the Snapshot. What other large cities are in each country? What large cities are in your country?

2 CONVERSATION *Are you from Seoul?*

A Listen and practice.

Tim: Are you from California, Jessica?
Jessica: Well, my family is in California now, but we're from South Korea originally.
Tim: Oh, my mother is Korean – from Seoul! Are you from Seoul?
Jessica: No, we're not. We're from Daejeon.
Tim: So is your first language Korean?
Jessica: Yes, it is.

B Listen to Jessica and Tim talk to Tony, Natasha, and Monique. Check (✓) True or False.

WELCOME NEW STUDENTS

	True	False
1. Tony is from Italy.	☐	☐
2. Natasha is from New York.	☐	☐
3. Monique's first language is English.	☐	☐

GRAMMAR FOCUS

Negative statements and yes/no questions with be

I'm not from New York.	**Are you** from California?	
You're not late.	**Am I** early?	
She's not from Russia.	**Is she** from Brazil?	
He's not from Italy.	**Is he** from Chile?	Yes,
It's not English.	**Is it** Korean?	
We're not from Japan.	**Are you** from China?	
You're not early.	**Are we** late?	
They're not in Mexico.	**Are they** in Canada?	

	I am.		I'm	not.
	you are.		you're	not.
	she is.		she's	not.
Yes,	he is.	No,	he's	not.
	it is.		it's	not.
	we are.		we're	not.
	you are.		you're	not.
	they are.		they're	not.

We**'re** = We are

A Complete the conversations. Then practice with a partner.

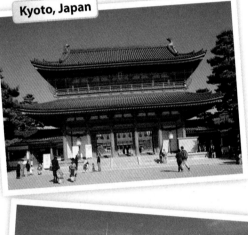
Kyoto, Japan

1. A: Hiroshi, ...*are*........ you and Maiko from Japan?
   B: Yes, we ....
   A: Oh? .... you from Tokyo?
   B: No, ... not. .... from Kyoto.

2. A: .... Laura from the U.S.?
   B: No, ... not. She's from the U.K.
   A: .... she from London?
   B: Yes, she .... But her parents are from Italy. .... not from the U.K. originally.
   A: .... Laura's first language Italian?
   B: No, ... not. .... English.

Lima, Peru

3. A: .... Selina and Carlos from Mexico?
   B: No, ... not. .... from Brazil.
   A: .... you from Brazil, too?
   B: No, ... not. I'm from Peru.
   A: So, ... your first language Spanish?
   B: Yes, it ....

B Match the questions with the answers. Then practice with a partner.

1. Are you and your family from Canada? ....*d*....
2. Is your first language English? ....
3. Are you Japanese? ....
4. Is Mr. Ho from Hong Kong? ....
5. Is your mother from the U.S.? ....

a. No, he's not. He's from Singapore.
b. Yes, she is. She's from California.
c. No, it's not. It's Japanese.
d. No, we're not. We're from Australia.
e. Yes, we are. We're from Kyoto.

C **PAIR WORK** Write five questions like the ones in part B. Then ask and answer your questions with a partner.

PRONUNCIATION *Syllable stress*

A ▶ Listen and practice. Notice the syllable stress.

●●	○●	●○○	○●○
China	Japan	Canada	Morocco
Turkey	Brazil	Mexico	Malaysia
....	....	....	....
....	....	....	....

B ▶ What is the syllable stress in these words? Add the words to the chart in part A. Then listen and check.

English	Spanish	Arabic	Korean
Mexican	Honduras	Chinese	Peru

C **GROUP WORK** Are the words in part A countries, nationalities, or languages? Make a chart and add more words.

Countries	Nationalities	Languages
China	Chinese	Chinese
Mexico	Mexican	Spanish

5 WHERE ARE THEY FROM?

A Where are these people from? Check (✓) your guesses.

Penelope Cruz	**Robert Pattinson**	**Haru Nomura**	**Cate Blanchett**	**Javier Hernández**
☐ Mexico	☐ the U.S.	☐ South Korea	☐ Australia	☐ Brazil
☐ France	☐ the U.K.	☐ Japan	☐ New Zealand	☐ Mexico
☐ Spain	☐ Canada	☐ China	☐ South Africa	☐ Chile

B **PAIR WORK** Compare your guesses. Then check your answers at the bottom of the page.

A: Is Penelope Cruz from Mexico?
B: No, she's not.
A: Is she from France?

Answers: 1. Spain 2. the U.K. 3. Japan 4. Australia 5. Mexico

6 CONVERSATION *He's cute.*

▶ Listen and practice.

Emma: Who's that?

Jill: He's my brother.

Emma: Wow! He's cute. What's his name?

Jill: James. We call him Jim.

Emma: Oh, how old is he?

Jill: He's twenty-one years old.

Emma: What's he like? Is he nice?

Jill: Yes, he is – and he's very smart, too!

Emma: And who's that?

Jill: My sister Tammy. She's only twelve.
She's the baby of the family.

7 NUMBERS AND AGES

A ▶ Listen and practice.

11 eleven	**21** twenty-one	**40** forty
12 twelve	**22** twenty-two	**50** fifty
13 thirteen	**23** twenty-three	**60** sixty
14 fourteen	**24** twenty-four	**70** seventy
15 fifteen	**25** twenty-five	**80** eighty
16 sixteen	**26** twenty-six	**90** ninety
17 seventeen	**27** twenty-seven	**100** one hundred
18 eighteen	**28** twenty-eight	**101** one hundred (and) one
19 nineteen	**29** twenty-nine	**102** one hundred (and) two
20 twenty	**30** thirty	**103** one hundred (and) three

B ▶ Listen and practice. Notice the word stress.

thirteen – thirty   fourteen – forty   fifteen – fifty   sixteen – sixty

C **PAIR WORK** Look at the people in Jill's family for one minute.
Then close your books. How old are they? Tell your partner.

A. Helen – 76   **B.** Howard – 52   **C.** Jackie – 49   **D.** Megan – 23   **E.** Tim and Tom – 14

Wh-questions with be

What's your name?
My name is Jill.
Where are you from?
I'm from Canada.
How are you today?
I'm just fine.

Who's that?
He's my brother.
How old is he?
He's twenty-one.
What's he like?
He's very nice.

Who are they?
They're my classmates.
Where are they from?
They're from Rio.
What's Rio like?
It's very beautiful.

Who**'s** = Who is

A Complete the conversations with Wh-questions.
Then practice with a partner.

1. A: Look! Who's that .... ?
   B: Oh, he's a new student.
   A: .... ?
   B: I think his name is Ming.
   A: Ming? .... ?
   B: He's from China.

2. A: Serhat, ... ?
   B: I'm from Turkey – from Istanbul.
   A: .... ?
   B: Istanbul is very old and beautiful.
   A: .... ?
   B: My last name is Erdogan.

3. A: Hi, John. .... ?
   B: I'm just fine. My friend Teresa is here
      this week – from Argentina.
   A: Oh, cool. .... ?
   B: She's really friendly.
   A: .... ?
   B: She's twenty-eight years old.

B **PAIR WORK** Write five Wh-questions about your partner and five Wh-questions
about your partner's best friend. Then ask and answer the questions.

Partner	Partner's best friend
Where are you from?	Who's your best friend?

9 WORD POWER Descriptions

A ▶ Listen and practice.

a. pretty
b. handsome
c. good-looking

d. talkative
e. quiet
f. funny

g. serious
h. shy
i. short

j. tall
k. friendly
l. heavy

m. thin

B PAIR WORK Complete the chart with words from part A. Add two more words to each list. Then describe your personality and appearance to a partner.

Personality			Appearance		
talkative	....	....	pretty	....	....
....	....	....	....	....	....
....	....	....	....	....	....

"I'm funny, smart, and very handsome."

10 LISTENING Who's that?

▶ Listen to three descriptions. Check (✓) the two correct words for each description.

1. Elena is . . .	☐ short	☐ pretty	☐ friendly
2. Marco is . . .	☐ tall	☐ nice	☐ shy
3. Andrew is . . .	☐ talkative	☐ funny	☐ friendly

11 INTERCHANGE 3 Board game

Play a board game with your classmates. Go to Interchange 3 on page 118.

4 Whose jeans are these?

WORD POWER *Clothes*

A ▶ Listen and practice.

CLOTHES FOR WORK

- tie
- shirt
- belt
- scarf
- blouse
- skirt
- jacket
- pants
- suit
- coat
- shoes
- high heels
- raincoat
- dress

CLOTHES FOR LEISURE

- hat
- sweater
- cap
- T-shirt
- shorts
- gloves
- jeans
- socks
- boots
- sneakers
- pajamas
- swimsuits

B Complete the chart with words from part A.

Clothes for warm weather	Clothes for cold weather
....	....
....	....
....	....
....	....

C **PAIR WORK** Look around the classroom. What clothes do you see? Tell a partner.

"I see jeans, a sweater, boots, and . . ."

2 COLORS

A ▶ Listen and practice.

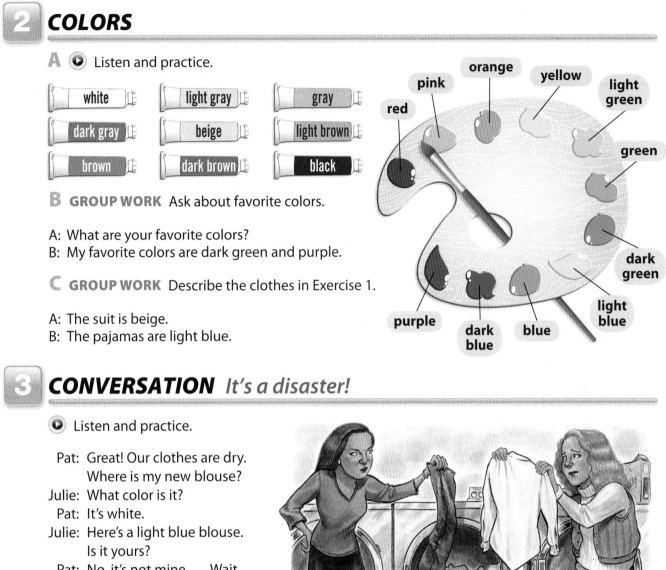

white   light gray   gray

dark gray   beige   light brown

brown   dark brown   black

red   pink   orange   yellow   light green   green   dark green   light blue   blue   dark blue   purple

B **GROUP WORK** Ask about favorite colors.

A: What are your favorite colors?
B: My favorite colors are dark green and purple.

C **GROUP WORK** Describe the clothes in Exercise 1.

A: The suit is beige.
B: The pajamas are light blue.

3 CONVERSATION *It's a disaster!*

▶ Listen and practice.

Pat: Great! Our clothes are dry. Where is my new blouse?
Julie: What color is it?
Pat: It's white.
Julie: Here's a light blue blouse. Is it yours?
Pat: No, it's not mine. . . . Wait. It *is* mine. It's a disaster!
Julie: Oh, no! *All* our clothes are light blue.
Pat: Here's the problem. It's these new blue jeans. Whose jeans are these?
Julie: Uh, they're mine. Sorry.

4 PRONUNCIATION *The letters s and sh*

A ▶ Listen and practice. Notice the pronunciation of **s** and **sh**.

1. **s**uit   **s**ocks   **s**carf
2. **sh**irt   **sh**orts   **sh**oes

B Read the sentences. Pay attention to the pronunciation of **s** and **sh**.

1. This is **S**andra's new **sh**irt.
2. These are **S**am's purple **sh**oes!
3. Where are my **sh**oes and **s**ocks?
4. My **sh**orts and T-**sh**irts are blue!

5 GRAMMAR FOCUS

Possessives ▶

Adjectives	Pronouns	Names	
my	**mine**	**Pat's** blouse	/s/
your	**yours**	**Julie's** jeans	/z/
These are **his** socks.	These socks are **his**.	**Rex's** T-shirt	/ɪz/
her	**hers**		
our	**ours**	**Whose** blouse is this? It's **Pat's**.	
their	**theirs**	**Whose** jeans are these? They're **Julie's**.	

A Complete the conversations with the correct words in parentheses. Then practice with a partner.

1. A: Hey! These aren't ......our...... (our / ours) clothes!
   B: You're right. .... (Our / Ours) are over there.

2. A: These aren't .... (my / mine) gloves. Are
      they .... (your / yours)?
   B: No, they're not .... (my / mine). Ask Sally. Maybe
      they're .... (her / hers).

3. A: .... (Whose / Yours) T-shirts are these? Are they
      Julie's and Pat's?
   B: No, they're not .... (their / theirs) T-shirts. But
      these socks are .... (their / theirs). And these
      shorts are .... (your / yours).

B **CLASS ACTIVITY** Put one of your things in a box. Then choose a different thing from the box. Go around the class and find the owner.

A: Diego, is this watch yours?
B: No, it's not mine. Maybe it's Rex's.

6 LISTENING *His shirt is green.*

A ▶ Listen to someone describe these clothes. Number the pictures from 1 to 6.

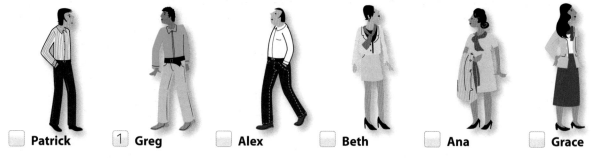

| Patrick | 1 Greg | Alex | Beth | Ana | Grace |

B **PAIR WORK** Now talk about the people. What colors are their clothes?

A: What color is Patrick's shirt?
B: It's green and white.

7 SNAPSHOT

▶ Listen and practice.

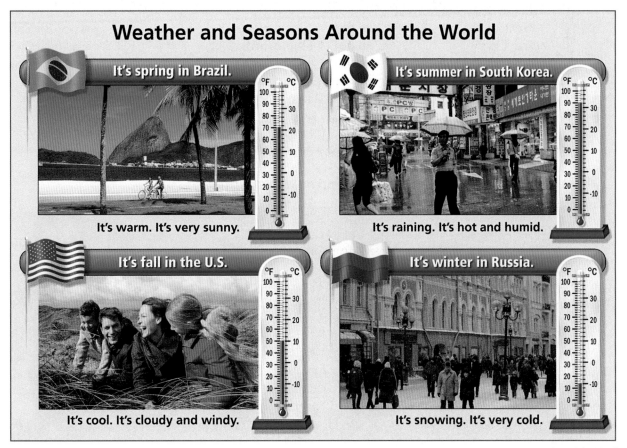

Weather and Seasons Around the World

It's spring in Brazil.
It's warm. It's very sunny.

It's summer in South Korea.
It's raining. It's hot and humid.

It's fall in the U.S.
It's cool. It's cloudy and windy.

It's winter in Russia.
It's snowing. It's very cold.

Source: *Yahoo! Travel*

What season is it now?
What's the weather like today?
What's your favorite season?

8 CONVERSATION *It's really cold!*

▶ Listen and practice.

Pat: Oh, no!
Julie: What's the matter?
Pat: It's snowing! And it's windy, so it's really cold.
Julie: Are you wearing your gloves?
Pat: No, I'm not. They're at home.
Julie: What about your scarf?
Pat: It's at home, too.
Julie: Well, you're wearing your coat.
Pat: But my coat isn't very warm. And I'm not wearing boots!
Julie: Let's take a taxi.
Pat: Good idea!

Whose jeans are these? ■ 25

Present continuous statements; conjunctions ▶

I'm		I'm not	OR:		Conjunctions
You**'re**		You**'re not**	You **aren't**		It's snowing, **and** it's windy.
She**'s wearing** shoes.		She**'s not**	She **isn't wearing** boots.		It's sunny, **but** it's cold.
We**'re**		We**'re not**	We **aren't**		It's windy, **so** it's very cold.
They**'re**		They**'re not**	They **aren't**		
It**'s snowing**.		It**'s not**	It **isn't raining**.		

A Complete these sentences. Then compare with a partner.

My name is Claire. I __'m wearing__ a green suit today. I _____ high heels, too. It's raining, but I _____ a raincoat.

It's very hot today. Toshi and Noriko _____ shorts and T-shirts. It's really sunny, so they _____ sunglasses.

Phil _____ a suit today – he _____ pants and a jacket. He _____ a light blue shirt, but he _____ a tie.

It's cold today, but Kathy _____ a coat. She _____ gloves and a hat. She _____ boots. She _____ sneakers.

Present continuous yes/no questions

Are you **wearing** gloves?	Yes, I **am**.	No, I**'m not**.
Is she **wearing** boots?	Yes, she **is**.	No, she**'s not**./No, she **isn't**.
Are they **wearing** sunglasses?	Yes, they **are**.	No, they**'re not**./No, they **aren't**.

B **PAIR WORK** Ask and answer these questions about the people in part A.

1. Is Claire wearing a green suit?
2. Is she wearing a raincoat?
3. Is she wearing high heels?
4. Are Toshi and Noriko wearing swimsuits?
5. Are they wearing jackets?
6. Are they wearing sunglasses?

7. Is Phil wearing brown pants?
8. Is he wearing a blue shirt?
9. Is he wearing a tie?
10. Is Kathy wearing boots?
11. Is she wearing a coat?
12. Is she wearing a hat and gloves?

A: Is Claire wearing a green suit?
B: Yes, she is. Is she wearing a raincoat?
A: No, she's not. OR No, she isn't.

C Write four more questions about the people in part A. Then ask a partner the questions.

adjective + noun

My suit is black.
I'm wearing a **black suit**.

10 LISTENING *He's wearing a T-shirt!*

A ▶ Listen. Write the names **Bruce, Beth, Jon, Anita,** and **Nick** in the correct boxes.

				Bruce

B **GROUP WORK** Ask questions about the people in the picture.

A: Is Bruce wearing a light brown jacket?
B: Yes, he is.
C: Is he wearing a tie?

C **GROUP WORK** Write five questions about your classmates. Then ask and answer the questions.

> Are Sonia and Paulo wearing jeans?
> Is Paulo wearing a red shirt?

11 INTERCHANGE 4 *Celebrity fashions*

What are your favorite celebrities wearing? Go to Interchange 4 on pages 116–117.

Units 3–4 Progress check

How well can you do these things? Check (✓) the boxes.

I can	Very well	OK	A little
Ask and answer questions about countries of origin, nationalities, and languages (Ex. 1)	☐	☐	☐
Understand descriptions of people (Ex. 2)	☐	☐	☐
Ask and answer questions about people's appearance and personality (Ex. 2, 5)	☐	☐	☐
Ask and answer questions about people's possessions (Ex. 3)	☐	☐	☐
Talk and write about my and other people's favorite things (Ex. 4)	☐	☐	☐
Ask and answer questions about what people are wearing (Ex. 5)	☐	☐	☐

1 INTERVIEW

Match the questions with the answers. Then ask and answer the questions with a partner. Answer with your own information.

1. Are you from Malaysia? ...h...
2. Where are you and your family from? ....
3. What is your hometown like? ....
4. Is English your first language? ....
5. Who is your best friend? ....
6. Are your classmates Brazilian? ....
7. How old is your best friend? ....
8. Is our teacher from the U.S.? ....

a. It's very beautiful.
b. Yes, she is.
c. We're from Mexico.
d. My best friend is Kevin.
e. Yes, they are.
f. No, it's not. It's Spanish.
g. He's nineteen.
h. No, I'm not. I'm from Thailand.

2 LISTENING Who's that?

A ▶ Listen to four conversations. Check (✓) the correct description for each person. You will check more than one adjective.

1. Min-ho	☐ tall	☐ short	☐ funny	☐ friendly	☐ talkative	☐ quiet
2. Ryan	☐ tall	☐ short	☐ funny	☐ serious	☐ friendly	☐ shy
3. Angela	☐ thin	☐ heavy	☐ pretty	☐ shy	☐ nice	☐ friendly
4. Helen	☐ thin	☐ heavy	☐ quiet	☐ shy	☐ serious	☐ funny

B Write five yes/no questions about the people in part A. Then ask a partner the questions.

> Is Min-ho friendly?
>
> Is Ryan tall?

3 WHOSE CLOTHES ARE THESE?

CLASS ACTIVITY Draw three pictures of clothes on different pieces of paper. Then put the papers in a bag. Take three different papers, go around the class, and find the owners.

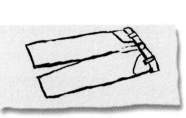

A: Gina, is this your cap?
B: No, it's not mine. Maybe it's Emi's.

A: Young-woo, are these your pants?
B: Yes, they're mine. Thanks!

4 MY FAVORITE THINGS

A Write your favorite things in the chart. Then ask a partner about his or her favorite things. Write them in the chart.

Favorite	Me	My partner
1. season	....	....
2. color	....	....
3. clothes	....	....

B Compare answers. What's the same? What's different? Write sentences.

> Summer is my favorite season, and it's Kyle's favorite season. That's the same.
> My favorite color is blue, but Kyle's favorite color is brown, so that's different.

5 GUESS THE CLASSMATE

GROUP WORK Think of a student in the class. Your classmates ask yes/no questions to guess the student.

A: I'm thinking of a student in this class.
B: Is it a man?
A: Yes, it is.
C: Is he short?
A: No, he isn't.
D: Is he wearing blue jeans?

WHAT'S NEXT?

Look at your Self-assessment again. Do you need to review anything?

5 What are you doing?

1 ## SNAPSHOT

 Listen and practice.

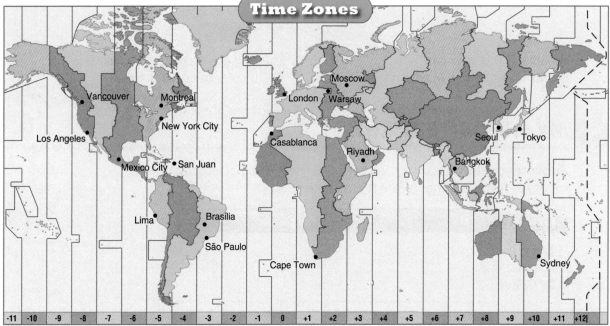

Time Zones

Vancouver • Montreal • New York City • Los Angeles • Mexico City • San Juan • Lima • Brasília • São Paulo • Cape Town • London • Casablanca • Moscow • Warsaw • Riyadh • Bangkok • Seoul • Tokyo • Sydney

| -11 | -10 | -9 | -8 | -7 | -6 | -5 | -4 | -3 | -2 | -1 | 0 | +1 | +2 | +3 | +4 | +5 | +6 | +7 | +8 | +9 | +10 | +11 | +12 |

Source: Time Service Department, U.S. Naval Observatory

Which cities are in the same time zones?
Which cities are in your time zone?

2 CONVERSATION *What time is it there?*

 Listen and practice.

Debbie: Hello?
  John: Hi, Debbie. This is John.
      I'm calling from Australia.
Debbie: Australia?
  John: I'm at a conference in Sydney.
      Remember?
Debbie: Oh, right. What time is it there?
  John: It's 10:00 P.M. And it's four o'clock
      there in Los Angeles. Right?
Debbie: Yes – four o'clock in the morning!
  John: 4:00 A.M.? Oh, I'm really sorry.
Debbie: That's OK. I'm awake . . . now.

30

What time is it? ▶

It's one **o'clock**.

It's one-oh-five.
It's five **after** one.

It's one-fifteen.
It's **a quarter after** one.

It's one-thirty.

It's one-forty.
It's twenty **to** two.

It's one forty-five.
It's **a quarter to** two.

A **PAIR WORK** Look at these clocks. What time is it?

1. 2. 3. 4. 5. 6.

A: What time is it?
B: It's twenty after two. OR It's two-twenty.

Is it A.M. or P.M.? ▶

It's seven (o'clock)
in the morning.
It's 7:00 A.M.

It's twelve (o'clock).
It's 12:00 P.M.
It's **noon**.

It's four (o'clock)
in the afternoon.
It's 4:00 P.M.

It's seven (o'clock)
in the evening.
It's 7:00 P.M.

It's ten (o'clock) **at night**.
It's 10:00 P.M.

It's twelve (o'clock) **at night**.
It's 12:00 A.M.
It's **midnight**.

B **PAIR WORK** Say each time a different way.

1. It's nine o'clock in the evening. *"It's 9:00 P.M."*
2. It's eight o'clock in the morning.
3. It's twelve o'clock at night.
4. It's three in the afternoon.
5. It's 3:00 A.M.
6. It's 6:00 P.M.
7. It's 4:00 P.M.
8. It's 12:00 P.M.

4 LISTENING *It's 4:00 P.M. in Vancouver.*

▶ Tracy and Eric are calling friends in different parts of the world. Listen. What time is it in these cities?

City	Time
Vancouver	4:00 p.m.
Bangkok	....
London	....
Tokyo	....
São Paulo	....

5 CONVERSATION *I'm really hungry!*

▶ Listen and practice.

Steve: Hi, Mom.
Mom: What are you doing, Steve?
Steve: I'm cooking.
Mom: Why are you cooking now? It's two o'clock in the morning!
Steve: Well, I'm really hungry!
Mom: What are you making?
Steve: Pizza.
Mom: Oh? What kind?
Steve: Cheese and mushroom.
Mom: That's my favorite! Now I'm getting hungry. Let's eat!

6 PRONUNCIATION *Rising and falling intonation*

A ▶ Listen and practice. Notice the intonation of the yes/no and Wh-questions.

Is she getting up? ↗
Are they sleeping?

What's she doing? ↘
What are they doing?

B ▶ Listen to the questions. Draw a rising arrow (↗) for rising intonation and a falling arrow (↘) for falling intonation.

1. ↗ ....   2. ....   3. ....   4. ....   5. ....   6. ....

Los Angeles   4:00 A.M.

What's Victoria **doing**?
She**'s sleeping** right now.

Mexico City   6:00 A.M.

What's Marcos **doing**?
It's 6:00 A.M., so he**'s getting up.**

New York City   7:00 A.M.

What are Sue and Tom **doing**?
They**'re having** breakfast.

Brasília   9:00 A.M.

What's Célia **doing**?
She**'s going** to work.

London   12:00 noon

What are Jim and Ann **doing**?
It's noon, so they**'re eating** lunch.

Moscow   3:00 P.M.

What's Andrei **doing**?
He**'s working.**

Bangkok   7:00 P.M.

What's Permsak **doing**?
He**'s eating** dinner right now.

Tokyo   9:00 P.M.

What's Hiroshi **doing**?
He**'s checking** his email.

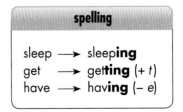

Your city   00:00

What are you **doing**?
It's . . . . I**'m** . . .

A **PAIR WORK** Ask and answer the questions about the pictures.

1. Who's sleeping now?
2. Who's having breakfast?
3. Where's Andrei working?
4. Where's Hiroshi checking his email?
5. What's Célia wearing?
6. What's Marcos wearing?
7. Why is Marcos getting up?
8. Why are Jim and Ann having lunch?

spelling	
sleep	→ sleep**ing**
get	→ ge**tt**ing (+ *t*)
have	→ hav**ing** (– *e*)

B **GROUP WORK** Write five more questions about the pictures.
Then ask and answer your questions in groups.

WORD POWER Activities

A ▶ Listen and practice. *"She's playing tennis."*

play tennis	ride a bike	run	swim
take a walk	dance	drive	watch a movie
shop	read	study	watch television

B PAIR WORK Ask and answer questions about the pictures in part A.

A: Is she playing soccer?
B: No, she's not.
A: What's she doing?
B: She's playing tennis.

C ▶ What's Mary doing? Listen to the sounds and number the actions from 1 to 8.

☐ dancing	☐ eating dinner	☐ riding a bike	☐ swimming
[1] driving	☐ playing tennis	☐ shopping	☐ watching television

9 # INTERCHANGE 5 *What's wrong with this picture?*

What's wrong with this picture? Go to Interchange 5 on page 119.

10 **READING** ▶

Friends Across a Continent

Skim the conversation. Write the name of the correct person under each picture.

Meg Martin and Kathy O'Brien chat online almost every day. Meg is an exchange student from the U.S. She's studying in Mexico. Kathy is in the U.S.

megm: Hi, there!

kathyo: Hi, Meg!

megm: What are you doing?

kathyo: I'm sitting on my bed with my laptop. I'm doing my homework.

megm: What are you working on?

kathyo: I'm writing an essay for Spanish class. :) Where are you?

megm: I'm in a café with my friend Carmen. I'm having coffee, and she's talking on the phone outside. How is your family?

kathyo: They're all fine! My father's watching a baseball game with his friends. My mother is out shopping.

megm: Where's your brother?

kathyo: John's playing soccer in the park. Oh, wait. My phone is ringing. My mother's calling me. I have to go! Bye!

megm: OK! Bye!

_____

_____

A Read the conversation. Who is doing these things? Complete the sentences.

1. .... is writing an essay.
2. .... is having coffee.
3. .... is talking on the phone.
4. .... is watching a baseball game.
5. .... is shopping.
6. .... is playing soccer.

B **PAIR WORK** Imagine you are texting or chatting online. Where are you? Who are you communicating with? Write a short conversation.

What are you doing? ▪ **35**

6 My sister works downtown.

1 SNAPSHOT

▶ Listen and practice.

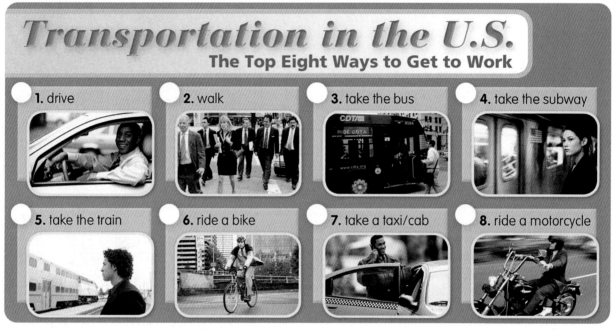

Transportation in the U.S.
The Top Eight Ways to Get to Work

1. drive
2. walk
3. take the bus
4. take the subway
5. take the train
6. ride a bike
7. take a taxi/cab
8. ride a motorcycle

Source: U.S. Census Bureau

Check (✓) the kinds of transportation you use.
What are some other kinds of transportation?

2 CONVERSATION *Nice car!*

▶ Listen and practice.

Ashley: Nice car, Jason! Is it yours?
Jason: No, it's my sister's. She has a new job, and she drives to work.
Ashley: Is her job here in the suburbs?
Jason: No, it's downtown.
Ashley: My parents work downtown, but they don't drive to work. They use public transportation.
Jason: The bus or the train?
Ashley: The train doesn't stop near our house, so they take the bus.

3 WORD POWER *Family*

A ▶ **PAIR WORK** Complete the sentences about the Carter family. Then listen and check your answers.

1. Anne is Paul's ......*wife*...... .
2. Jason and Emily are their ....
3. Paul is Anne's ....
4. Jason is Anne's ....
5. Emily is Paul's ....
6. Jason is Emily's ....
7. Emily is Jason's ....
8. Paul and Anne are Jason's ....

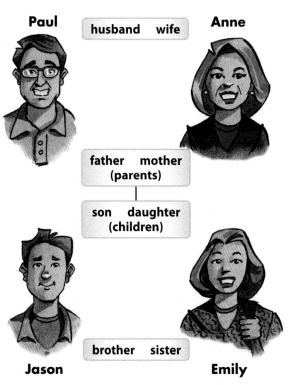

Paul   husband   wife   **Anne**

father   mother
(parents)

son   daughter
(children)

brother   sister

Jason   **Emily**

kids	=	children
mom	=	mother
dad	=	father

B **PAIR WORK** Who are the people in your family? What are their names?

"My mother's name is Angela. My brothers' names are David and Daniel."

4 GRAMMAR FOCUS

Simple present statements ▶

I	**walk**	to school.	I	**don't live**	far from here.	**don't** = do not
You	**ride**	your bike to school.	You	**don't live**	near here.	**doesn't** = does not
He	**works**	near here.	He	**doesn't work**	downtown.	
She	**takes**	the bus to work.	She	**doesn't drive**	to work.	
We	**live**	with our parents.	We	**don't live**	alone.	
They	**use**	public transportation.	They	**don't need**	a car.	

A Paul Carter is talking about his family. Complete the sentences with the correct verb forms. Then compare with a partner.

1. My family and I ......*live*........ (live / lives) in the suburbs. My wife and I
   .... (work / works) near here, so we .... (walk / walks)
   to work. Our daughter Emily .... (work / works) downtown,
   so she .... (drive / drives) to work. Our son ....
   (don't / doesn't) drive. He .... (ride / rides) his bike to school.

2. My parents .... (live / lives) in the city. My mother
   .... (take / takes) a train to work. My father is retired,
   so he .... (don't / doesn't) work now. He also ....
   (use / uses) public transportation, so they .... (don't / doesn't)
   need a car.

verb endings: *he, she, it*	
walk	⟶ walk**s**
ride	⟶ ride**s**
study	⟶ stud**ies**
watch	⟶ watch**es**

B Ashley is talking about her family and her friend Jason.
Complete the sentences. Then compare with a partner.

1. My parents ......*have*...... (have / has) a house in the suburbs. My mom
   and dad .... (go / goes) downtown to work. My parents are very
   busy, so I .... (do / does) a lot of work at home.

2. My brother doesn't live with us. He .... (have / has) an apartment in
   the city. He .... (go / goes) to school all day, and he .... (do / does)
   his homework at night.

3. I .... (have / has) a new friend. His name is Jason. We ....
   (go / goes) to the same school, and sometimes we .... (do / does)
   our homework together.

C **PAIR WORK** Tell your partner about your family.

"I have one brother and two sisters. My brother is a teacher.
He has a car, so he drives to work."

5 PRONUNCIATION *Third-person singular -s endings*

 Listen and practice. Notice the pronunciation of the **-s** endings.

s = /s/	s = /z/	(e)s = /ɪz/	irregular
take take**s**	drive drive**s**	dance dance**s**	do do**es**
sleep sleep**s**	study stud**ies**	watch watch**es**	have ha**s**

6 CONVERSATION *I get up at noon.*

▸ Listen and practice.

Jack: Let's go to the park on Sunday.
Amy: OK, but let's go in the afternoon.
    I sleep late on weekends.
Jack: What time do you get up on Sundays?
Amy: At ten o'clock.
Jack: Oh, that's early. On Sundays,
    I get up at noon.
Amy: Really? Do you eat breakfast then?
Jack: Sure. I have breakfast every day.
Amy: Then let's meet at this restaurant at
    one o'clock. They serve breakfast all day!

Simple present questions ▶

Do you **get up** early?	**What time do** you **get up**?
No, I **get up** late.	At ten o'clock.
Does he **eat** lunch at noon?	**What time does** he **have** dinner?
No, he **eats** lunch at one o'clock.	At eight o'clock.
Do they **take** the bus to class?	**When do** they **take** the subway?
No, they **take** the subway.	On Tuesdays and Thursdays.

A Complete the questions with *do* or *does*.

1. ......*Do*...... you get up early on weekdays?
2. What time .... you go home on Fridays?
3. .... your father work on weekends?
4. .... your mother cook every day?
5. .... your parents read in the evening?
6. When .... your parents shop?
7. .... you check your email at night?
8. What time .... you have dinner?
9. When .... you study?
10. .... your best friend drive to class?
11. What time .... your father get up?

time expressions	
early	**in** the morning
late	**in** the afternoon
every day	**in** the evening
at 9:00	**on** Sundays
at noon / midnight	**on** weekdays
at night	**on** weekends

B **PAIR WORK** Ask and answer the questions from part A. Use time expressions from the box.

A: Do you get up early on weekdays?
B: Yes. I get up at seven o'clock.

C Unscramble the questions to complete the conversations. Then ask a partner the questions. Answer with your own information.

1. A: *Do you check your email every day*................... ?
    you / every day / check your email / do
   B: Yes, I check my email every day.

2. A: .... ?
    you / what time / lunch / do / eat
   B: At 1:00 P.M.

3. A: .... ?
    at / start / does / eight o'clock / this class
   B: No, this class starts at nine o'clock.

4. A: .... ?
    study / you / English / do / when
   B: I study English in the evening.

5. A: .... ?
    on weekends / you and your friends / do / play sports
   B: Yes, we play soccer on Saturdays.

8 **LISTENING** *Marsha's weekly routine*

▶ Listen to Marsha talk about her weekly routine.
Check (✓) the days she does each thing.

	Monday	Tuesday	Wednesday	Thursday	Friday	Saturday	Sunday
get up early	☐	☐	☐	☐	☐	☐	☐
go to work	☐	☐	☐	☐	☐	☐	☐
exercise	☐	☐	☐	☐	☐	☐	☐
see friends	☐	☐	☐	☐	☐	☐	☐
see family	☐	☐	☐	☐	☐	☐	☐
study	☐	☐	☐	☐	☐	☐	☐

9 **MY ROUTINE**

A What do you do every week? Write things in the chart.

⊙ ◯ ◯			Calendar			
Sunday	**Monday**	**Tuesday**	**Wednesday**	**Thursday**	**Friday**	**Saturday**

◀ Day　Week　Month　▶

B **GROUP WORK** Discuss your weekly routines. Ask and
answer questions.

A: I go to bed late on Fridays.
B: What do you do on Friday nights?
A: I see my friends. We watch television or play
   video games.
C: On Fridays, I study in the evening. I see my friends
   on the weekend.

10 **INTERCHANGE 6** *Class survey*

Find out more about your classmates. Go to Interchange 6 on page 120.

Interviews | **The Bulletin** | Home | News | Photos | Log In

What's your schedule like?

Look at the pictures and the labels. Who gets up early? Who gets up late?

Student reporter Mike Starr talks to people on the street about their schedules.

Brittany Davis
College Student

Mike: What's your schedule like?
Brittany: My classes start at 8:00 A.M., so I get up at 7:00 and take the bus to school.
MS: When do your classes end?
BD: They end at noon. Then I have a job at the library.
MS: So when do you study?
BD: My only time to study is in the evening, from eight until midnight.

Justin Reid
City Tour Guide

Mike: What's your schedule like?
Justin: I get up at 6:15 A.M. and start work at 9:00.
MS: And what do you do before work?
JR: I go for a run at 6:30 A.M., and then I have breakfast at 7:00.
MS: And after work?
JR: I finish at 6:00 P.M., and I have dinner downtown.
MS: Do you work every day?
JR: No, I work on Fridays, Saturdays, and Sundays.

Maya Choo
Rock Musician

Mike: What's your schedule like?
Maya: Well, I work at night. I go to work at 10:00 P.M., and I play until 3:00 A.M.
MS: What do you do after work?
MC: I have dinner at 3:30 or 4:00. Then I take a taxi home.
MS: What time do you go to bed?
MC: I go to bed at 5:00 in the morning.

A Read the article. Then number the activities in each person's schedule from 1 to 5.

Brittany Davis

.... a. She goes to class.
.... b. She takes the bus.
.... c. She works.
.... d. She studies.
...1... e. She gets up.

Justin Reid

.... a. He has breakfast.
.... b. He starts work.
.... c. He eats dinner.
.... d. He gets up.
.... e. He goes for a run.

Maya Choo

.... a. She has dinner.
.... b. She finishes work.
.... c. She goes to bed.
.... d. She goes to work.
.... e. She goes home.

B Write five sentences about your schedule. Are you an "early bird" or a "night owl"? Compare with a partner.

early bird | night owl

My sister works downtown. ■ **41**

Units 5–6 Progress check

SELF-ASSESSMENT

How well can you do these things? Check (✓) the boxes.

I can	Very well	OK	A little
Understand times and descriptions of activities (Ex. 1)	☐	☐	☐
Ask and answer questions about present activities (Ex. 2)	☐	☐	☐
Talk about personal routines (Ex. 3)	☐	☐	☐
Ask and answer questions about routines (Ex. 4)	☐	☐	☐
Ask and answer questions about people's lifestyles and appearance (Ex. 5)	☐	☐	☐

1 LISTENING *Around the world*

 It's 9 A.M. in Los Angeles. Vanessa is calling friends around the world. Listen to the conversations and complete the chart.

	City	Time	Activity
1. Sarah	New York	....	....
2. Manuel	....	....	....
3. Bob	....	....	....

2 ON VACATION

Student A: Imagine your classmates are on vacation. Student B calls you. Ask questions about your classmates.

Student B: Imagine you are on vacation with your classmates. Call Student A. Answer Student A's questions about your classmates.

A: Hello?
B: Hi, it's . . . . I'm on vacation in . . .
A: In . . . ? Wow! What are you doing?
B: . . .
A: Who are you with?
B: . . .
A: What's he/she doing?
B: . . .
A: Well, have fun. Bye!

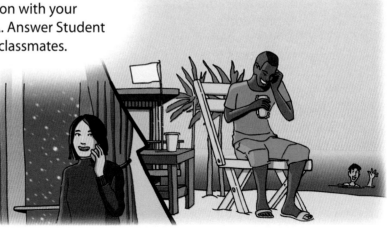

3 MY DAILY ROUTINE

A Choose one day of the week and write it in the blank.
What do you do on this day? Complete the chart.

Day	
In the morning	....
In the afternoon	....
In the evening	....
At night	....

B **PAIR WORK** Tell your partner about your routine.

A: On Saturdays, I exercise in the morning. I play soccer with my friends.
B: What time do you play?
A: We play at 10:00.

4 LIFESTYLE SURVEY

A Answer the questions in the chart. Check (✓) Yes or No.

	Yes	No	Name
1. Do you live with your parents?	☐	☐	....
2. Do both your parents work?	☐	☐	....
3. Do you watch television at night?	☐	☐	....
4. Do you eat dinner with your family?	☐	☐	....
5. Do you stay home on weekends?	☐	☐	....
6. Do you work on Saturdays?	☐	☐	....

B **CLASS ACTIVITY** Go around the class and find classmates with the same answers.
Write their names in the chart. Try to write a different name on each line.

5 WHO IS IT?

GROUP WORK Think of a famous person. Your classmates
ask yes/no questions to guess the person.

Is it a man? a woman?   Is he/she tall? short?
Does he/she live in . . . ?   Does he/she wear glasses?
Is he/she a singer? an actor?

WHAT'S NEXT?

Look at your Self-assessment again. Do you need to review anything?

7 Does it have a view?

▶ Listen and practice.

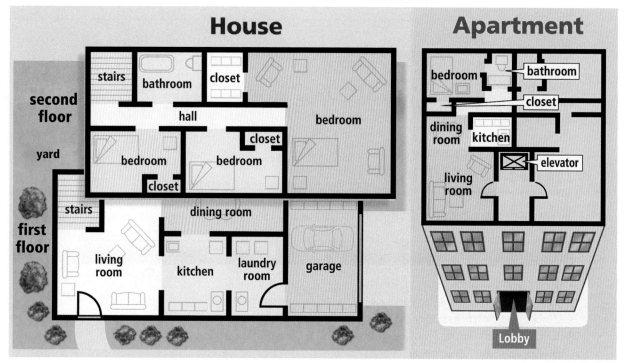

House

second floor

yard

first floor

stairs | bathroom | closet

hall

bedroom

closet

bedroom | bedroom

closet

stairs | dining room

living room | kitchen | laundry room | garage

Apartment

bedroom | bathroom

closet

dining room | kitchen

elevator

living room

Lobby

Source: www.floorplanner.com

What rooms are in houses in your country? What rooms are in apartments?
What rooms are in your house or apartment?

2 CONVERSATION *My new apartment*

▶ Listen and practice.

Linda: Guess what! I have a new apartment.
Chris: That's great! What's it like?
Linda: It's really nice.
Chris: Is it very big?
Linda: Well, it has a big living room, a bedroom, a bathroom, and a kitchen.
Chris: Nice! Do you live downtown?
Linda: No, I don't. I live near the university.
Chris: Does it have a view?
Linda: Yes, it does. It has a great view of another apartment building!

44

GRAMMAR FOCUS

Simple present short answers

Do you **live** in an apartment?
Yes, I **do**. / No, I **don't**.
Do the bedrooms **have** windows?
Yes, they **do**. / No, they **don't**.

Does Chris **live** in a house?
Yes, he **does**. / No, he **doesn't**.
Does the house **have** a yard?
Yes, it **does**. / No, it **doesn't**.

A Complete the conversation. Then practice with a partner.

Linda: ....*Do*........ you ......*live*...... in an apartment?
Chris: No, I .... I .... in a house.
Linda: .... it .... a yard?
Chris: Yes, it ....
Linda: That sounds nice. .... you .... alone?
Chris: No, I .... I .... with my family.
Linda: .... you .... any brothers or sisters?
Chris: Yes, I .... I .... four sisters.
Linda: Really? .... your house .... many bedrooms?
Chris: Yes, it .... It .... four.
Linda: .... you .... your own bedroom?
Chris: Yes, I .... I'm really lucky.

B **PAIR WORK** Read the conversation in part A again. Ask and answer these questions about Chris.

1. Does he live in an apartment?
2. Does his house have a yard?
3. Does he live alone?
4. Does he have his own room?

C **PAIR WORK** Write five questions to ask your partner about his or her home. Then ask and answer the questions.

4 LISTENING *It has just one room.*

Listen to four people describe their homes. Number the pictures from 1 to 4.

5 WORD POWER Furniture

A ▶ Listen and practice.

armchairs	**stove**	**curtains**	**pictures**	**bed**
table	**coffee table**	**microwave oven**	**refrigerator**	**lamps**
sofa	**desk**	**bookcase**	**dresser**	**chairs**
mirror	**rug**	**TV**	**cupboards**	

B Which rooms have the things in part A? Complete the chart.

Kitchen	table stove
Dining room	table
Living room	
Bedroom	

C **GROUP WORK** What furniture is in your house or apartment? Tell your classmates.

"My living room has a sofa, a rug, and a TV. . . ."

6 CONVERSATION *There aren't any chairs.*

▶ Listen and practice.

Chris: This apartment is great.
Linda: Thanks. I love it, but I really need some furniture.
Chris: What do you need?
Linda: Oh, I need lots of things. There are some chairs in the kitchen, but there isn't a table.
Chris: And there's no sofa here in the living room.
Linda: And there aren't any chairs. There's only this lamp.
Chris: So let's go shopping next weekend.

7 GRAMMAR FOCUS

There is, there are ▶

There's a bed in the bedroom.	**There are some** chairs in the kitchen.	There**'s** = There is
There's no sofa in the bedroom.	**There are no** chairs in the living room.	
There isn't a table in the kitchen.	**There aren't any** chairs in the living room.	

A Look at the picture of Linda's apartment. Complete the sentences. Then practice with a partner.

1. ....*There's no*.... dresser in the bedroom.
2. .... chairs in the kitchen.
3. .... TV in the living room.
4. .... refrigerator.

5. .... rugs on the floor.
6. .... curtains on the windows.
7. .... mirror in the bedroom.
8. .... books in the bookcase.

B Write five sentences about things you have or don't have in your classroom. Then compare with a partner.

> There are 10 desks in the classroom.

8 INTERCHANGE 7 *Find the differences*

Compare two apartments. Go to Interchange 7 on page 121.

9 PRONUNCIATION *Words with th*

A ▶ Listen and practice. Notice the pronunciation of /θ/ and /ð/.

/ð/   /θ/   /ð/   /ð/   /θ/   /θ/
There are **th**irteen rooms in **th**is house. **The** house has **th**ree ba**th**rooms.

B **PAIR WORK** List other words with /θ/ and /ð/. Then use them to write four funny sentences. Read them aloud.

> On Thursdays, their mother and father think for thirteen minutes.

10 LISTENING *Furniture is expensive!*

▶ Listen to Chris and Linda talk in a furniture store.
What does Linda like? Check (✓) the things.

☐ armchairs   ☐ a sofa   ☐ a rug   ☐ lamps
☐ a bookcase   ☐ a mirror   ☐ a coffee table   ☐ curtains

11 MY DREAM HOME

A Write a description of your dream home.

What is your dream home like?
Where is it?
What rooms does it have?
What things are in the rooms?
Does it have a view?

> My dream home is a loft in a big city. There is one large living room with a lot of windows. There are two bedrooms and . . .

B **PAIR WORK** Ask your partner about his or her dream home.

A: Does it have a view?
B: Yes, it has a very nice view of the forest. . . .

loft

cabin

villa

beach house

Unusual Homes

Scan the article. Where are the lofts? Where does Dan Phillips build houses?

🏠 Shusaku Arakawa and Madeline Gins are famous designers. Their nine lofts near Tokyo, Japan, are very colorful. The apartments are blue, pink, red, yellow, and other bright colors. Inside, the walls are colorful, too. The floors go up and down, and some rooms are round. The windows have strange shapes, so there are no curtains. There are small doors to the outside. Inside, there aren't any closets. The bookcase is in the middle of the living room.

🏠 Dan Phillips likes to help people. He builds houses for artists and other low-income people in Huntsville, Texas, in the United States. One house, the "tree house," is in a large tree in the forest. It has windows on the floor! It also has a small kitchen. The bed is on the upstairs floor. There is a wood-burning stove from an old ship in the living room. Phillips teaches people how to build houses with recycled materials.

A Read the article. What's in each home? Complete the chart.

bed on the upstairs floor   bookcase   closets
✓colorful walls   windows on the floor   wood-burning stove

Arakawa and Gins's lofts	Dan Phillips's tree house
1. There are _colorful walls_ .	4. There are _windows on the floor_
2. There aren't any _closets_ .	5. There is a _bed on the upstairs floor_
3. There is a _bookcase_ in the middle of the living room.	6. There is a _wood-burning stove_

B **GROUP WORK** Talk about these questions.

1. Imagine you are painting your house. What colors do you use? Why?
2. Imagine you are building a house. Do you use new materials or recycled materials? Why?

What do you do?

el Poder dela Palabra *qué haces*

WORD POWER Jobs

trabajes

A ▶ Match the jobs with the pictures. Then listen and practice.

a. accountant	e. electrician	i. painter	m. salesperson
b. bellhop	f. front desk clerk	j. plumber	n. security guard
c. cashier	g. nurse	✓k. police officer	o. taxi driver
d. doctor	h. office manager	l. receptionist	p. vendor

1. k   2. o   3. P

4. j   5. e   6. l

7. h   8. a   9. L

10. F   11. b

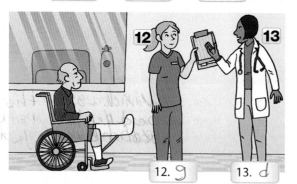

12. g   13. d

14. m   15. C   16. n

B **PAIR WORK** Ask questions about the people in part A. What are their jobs?

A: What's her job?
B: She's a police officer.

THE WORKPLACE

A **PAIR WORK** Who works in these places? Complete the chart with jobs from Exercise 1. Add one more job to each list.

A: A doctor works in a hospital.
B: A nurse works in a hospital, too.

In a hospital	In an office	In a store	In a hotel
doctor	accountant	Salesperson	Front desk clerk
nurse	receptionist	cashier	bellhop

B **CLASS ACTIVITY** Ask and answer *Who* questions about jobs. Use these words.

wears a uniform	sits all day	talks to people	works hard
stands all day	handles money	works at night	makes a lot of money

A: Who wears a uniform?
B: A police officer wears a uniform.
C: And a security guard . . .

3 ## CONVERSATION *He works in a hotel.*

▶ Listen and practice.

Rachel: Where does your brother work?
Angela: In a hotel.
Rachel: Oh, really? My brother works in a hotel, too. He's a front desk clerk.
Angela: How does he like it?
Rachel: He hates it. He doesn't like the manager.
Angela: That's too bad. What hotel does he work for?
Rachel: The Plaza.
Angela: That's funny. My brother works there, too.
Rachel: Oh, that's interesting. What does he do?
Angela: Actually, he's the manager!

Y de Hecho

4 GRAMMAR FOCUS

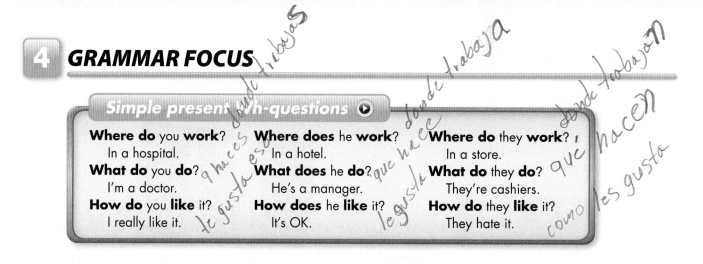

Where do you **work**?	**Where does** he **work**?	**Where do** they **work**?
In a hospital.	In a hotel.	In a store.
What do you **do**?	**What does** he **do**?	**What do** they **do**?
I'm a doctor.	He's a manager.	They're cashiers.
How do you **like** it?	**How does** he **like** it?	**How do** they **like** it?
I really like it.	It's OK.	They hate it.

A Complete these conversations. Then practice with a partner.

1. A: ___What___ does your sister ___do___ ?
   B: My sister? She's a nurse.
   A: ___How___ does she ___like___ it?
   B: It's difficult, but she loves it.

2. A: ___where's___ does your brother ___work___ ?
   B: In a hotel. He's a front desk clerk.
   A: Oh? ___really___ does he ___like___ it?
   B: He doesn't really like it.

3. A: ___where___ do your parents ___like___ their jobs?
   B: Oh, I guess they like them.
   A: I don't remember. ___where___ do they ___work___ ?
   B: In an office in the city.

4. A: ___what___ do you ___do___ ?
   B: I'm a student.
   A: I see. ___How___ do you ___like___ your classes?
   B: They're great. I like them a lot.

B **PAIR WORK** Ask questions about these people.
Where do they work? What do they do? How do they like it?

David

Laura

Brian and Jessica

A: Where does David work?
B: He works in . . .

5 PRONUNCIATION *Reduction of do*

 Listen and practice. Notice the reduction of **do**.

Where **do you** work?   Where **do they** work?

What **do you** do?   What **do they** do?

6 SNAPSHOT

▶ Listen and practice.

What do you do? What's your job like?

I'm a server in a coffee shop. It's easy, but boring. I don't like my job much.

aburrido

I'm a firefighter. It's exciting and very dangerous, but I like my job a lot.

Peligroso

I'm a social worker. It's difficult and really stressful, but I love my job.

safe "seguro"

I'm a florist. My job isn't very exciting, but it's pretty relaxing. I like my job OK.

Source: www.careercast.com

Who likes his or her job? Who doesn't? Why or why not?
How do they describe their jobs? Write one more adjective for each job.

7 CONVERSATION *Please be careful!*

▶ Listen and practice.

Richard: Hey, Stephanie. I hear you have a new job.
Stephanie: Yes. I'm teaching math at Lincoln High School.
Richard: How do you like it?
Stephanie: It's great. The students are terrific. How are things with you?
Richard: Not bad. I'm a window washer now, you know.
Stephanie: Really? How do you like it?
Richard: It's a stressful job. And it's pretty dangerous.
Stephanie: Please be careful!

8 LISTENING *It's pretty boring.*

▶ Listen to four people talk about their jobs. Complete the chart with the correct jobs and adjectives.

	What do you do?	What's it like?
1. Monica	Hospital	exitan
2. Hye-soon	manager	dificult
3. Kirk	stores	boring.
4. Philip	florist	It's easy

GRAMMAR FOCUS

> ## Placement of adjectives ▶
>
> | **be + adjective** | **adjective + noun** |
> | --- | --- |
> | A doctor's job **is stressful**. | A doctor has **a stressful job**. |
> | A window washer's job **is dangerous**. | A window washer has **a dangerous job**. |

A Write each sentence a different way. Then compare with a partner.

1. A doctor's job is interesting. _A doctor has an interesting job._
2. A police officer's job is dangerous. _Police officer has a dangerous job_
3. A teacher's job is stressful. _teacher's has a stressfu_
4. A plumber has a boring job. _a Plumber's job is a boring_
5. An electrician has a difficult job. _an electrician job is difficult_
6. A vendor has an easy job. _a vendor job is easy_

B **GROUP WORK** Write one job for each adjective.
Do your classmates agree?

flight attendant

1. exciting _flight attendant_	4. boring _Service_
2. easy _Florist_	5. difficult _Police Officc_
3. dangerous _window washer_	6. relaxing _Teacher_

A: A flight attendant has an exciting job.
B: I don't agree. A flight attendant's job is boring.
C: I think . . .

10 INTERCHANGE 8 *The perfect job*

What do you want in a job? Go to Interchange 8 on page 122.

11 WORKDAY ROUTINES

GROUP WORK Ask three classmates about their jobs (or their friends' or family members' jobs). Then tell the class.

Ask about a classmate
Do you have a job?
Where do you work?
What do you do, exactly?
Is your job interesting?
What time do you start work?
When do you finish work?
Do you like your job?
What do you do after work? . . .

Ask about a classmate's friend or family member
Tell me about your . . .
Where does he/she work?
What does he/she do, exactly?
Is his/her job difficult?
What time does he/she start work?
When does he/she finish work?
Does he/she like his/her job?
What does he/she do after work? . . .

JOB *Profiles*

Look at the photos. Which jobs look interesting? Why?

dog groomer

Lots of **Marco Mendez**'s friends walk on four legs. He makes these furry friends beautiful. Marco is a professional dog groomer. He likes his job a lot because it's never boring. Each dog has a different personality. What's his favorite kind of dog? He's not telling!

wedding planner

Lila Martin goes to nice restaurants, eats cake, listens to bands – and gets paid for it! Lila is a wedding planner. She chooses the place, the food, and the music for people's weddings. It's stressful because everything needs to be perfect!

video game designer

Hal Garner has his dream job. He plays video games all day long! Hal is a game designer for a large video game company. He makes new games and tests them. It's always exciting, and he almost always wins!

baker

Junko Watanabe has a sweet life. She makes bread, cookies, and cakes in her neighborhood bakery. Junko really likes her job. Her salary isn't great, but the customers love her cakes and cookies, so she's happy.

A Read the article. Who says these things? Write your guesses.

1. "I go to work very early in the morning." *wedding planner*
2. "I know every restaurant in town." *baker*
3. "After work, I need to take a bath!" *dog groomer*
4. "I sit down all day long!" *video game designer*

B Write a short description of a job, but don't write the name of the job. Then read it to the class. Your classmates guess the job.

Units 7–8 Progress check

How well can you do these things? Check (✓) the boxes.

I can	Very well	OK	A little
Ask and answer questions about living spaces (Ex. 1)	☐	☐	☐
Talk about rooms and furniture (Ex. 1)	☐	☐	☐
Ask and answer questions about work (Ex. 2)	☐	☐	☐
Understand descriptions of jobs (Ex. 3)	☐	☐	☐
Give and respond to opinions about jobs (Ex. 4)	☐	☐	☐

1 A NEW APARTMENT

A Imagine you are moving into this apartment. What things are in the rooms? Draw pictures. Use the furniture in the box and your own ideas.

bed	desk	lamp	sofa
chairs	dresser	mirror	table

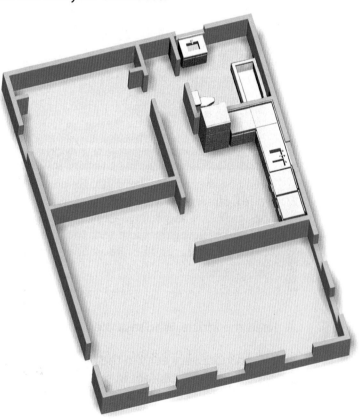

B **PAIR WORK** Ask questions about your partner's apartment.

A: I'm moving into a new apartment!
B: That's great! Where is it?
A: . . .
B: What's it like? Does it have many rooms?
A: Well, it has . . .
B: Does the . . . have . . . ?
A: . . .
B: Do you have a lot of furniture?
A: Well, there's . . . in the . . .
   There are some . . . in the . . .
B: Do you have everything you need for the apartment?
A: No, I don't. There's no . . .
   There isn't any . . .
   There aren't any . . .
B: OK. Let's go shopping this weekend!

2 WHERE DOES HE WORK?

A Complete the conversations with Wh-questions.

1. A: <u>Where does your father work</u> ?
    B: My father? He works in a store.
    A: .... ?
    B: He's a salesperson.
    A: .... ?
    B: He likes his job a lot!

2. A: .... ?
    B: I'm an accountant.
    A: .... ?
    B: I work in an office.
    A: .... ?
    B: It's OK. I guess I like it.

B **PAIR WORK** Your partner asks the questions in part A.
Answer with your own information.

3 LISTENING *Where do they work?*

▶ Listen to Linda, Kyle, and Wendy talk about their jobs.
Check (✓) the correct answers.

	Where do they work?		What do they do?	
1. Linda	☐ office ☐ store		☐ receptionist ☐ doctor	
2. Kyle	☐ hospital ☐ school		☐ nurse ☐ teacher	
3. Wendy	☐ hotel ☐ office		☐ manager ☐ bellhop	

4 AN INTERESTING JOB

GROUP WORK What do you think of these jobs?
Give your opinions.

farmer   bus driver   architect   hairstylist

A: I think a farmer has a boring job.
B: I don't really agree. I think a farmer's job is relaxing.
C: Well, I think a farmer's job is difficult. . . .

WHAT'S NEXT?

Look at your Self-assessment again. Do you need to review anything?

9 Do we need any eggs?

WORD POWER *Foods*

A ▶ Listen and practice.

Food Guidelines

For good health, eat a lot of grains, vegetables, and fruit. Eat some dairy, meat, and other protein. Eat a little fat and oils.

Fruit

Vegetables
- lettuce
- carrots
- broccoli

blueberries

apples
oranges
lemons
tomatoes
potatoes
bananas
onions
kiwis

Meat and other proteins
- chicken
- eggs
- beans
- fish
- nuts
- beef

Grains
- pasta
- rice
- crackers
- noodles
- bread
- cereal

Corn Flakes

yogurt
oil
milk
cream
cheese
butter

Dairy

Fats and Oils

B What foods do you like? What foods don't you like? Make a list. Then tell a partner.

A: I like rice, noodles, and oranges. I don't like fish, cheese, and carrots.
B: I like . . .

I like	I don't like
rice	fish
noodles	cheese
oranges	carrots

2 CONVERSATION *How about some sandwiches?*

▶ Listen and practice.

Adam: What do you want for the picnic?
Amanda: Hmm. How about some sandwiches?
Adam: OK. We have some chicken, but we don't have any bread.
Amanda: And we don't have any cheese.
Adam: Do we have any lettuce?
Amanda: Let's see. . . . No, we need some.
Adam: Let's get some tomatoes, too.
Amanda: OK. And let's buy some potato salad.
Adam: All right. Everyone likes potato salad.

3 GRAMMAR FOCUS

Count and noncount nouns; some and any ▶

Count nouns	Noncount nouns
an egg → egg**s**	bread
a sandwich → sandwich**es**	lettuce
Do we need **any** eggs? *many*	Do we need **any** bread? *much*
Yes. Let's get **some** (eggs).	Yes. Let's get **some** (bread).
No. We do**n't** need **any** (eggs).	No. We do**n't** need **any** (bread).

A Complete the conversation with *some* or *any*.

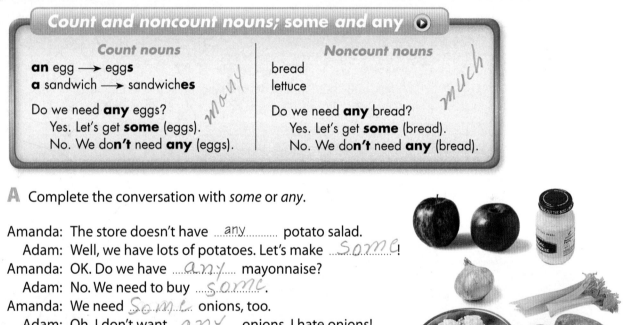

Amanda: The store doesn't have ......*any*...... potato salad.
Adam: Well, we have lots of potatoes. Let's make ......*some*......!
Amanda: OK. Do we have ....*any*.... mayonnaise?
Adam: No. We need to buy ....*some*.....
Amanda: We need ..*some*.. onions, too.
Adam: Oh, I don't want ....*any*.... onions. I hate onions!
Amanda: Then let's get ....*some*.. celery.
Adam: No. I don't want ....*any*.... celery in my potato salad.
But let's put ....*some*.. apples in it.
Amanda: Apples in potato salad? That sounds awful! *of ool*

B Complete the chart with foods from Exercise 1. Then compare with a partner.

Count		Noncount		
eggs	*beans*	cream		*oil*
Tomatoes	*nuts*	*fish*	*pasta*	
Potatoes		*bread*	*milk*	*yogurt*
Lemons		*rice*	*oil*	
apples		*butter*	*cereal*	

4 PRONUNCIATION *Sentence stress*

A ▶ Listen and practice. Notice the stressed words.

A: Do we need any eggs?

B: Yes. We need some eggs.

A: Do we need any lettuce?

B: No. We don't need any lettuce.

B **PAIR WORK** Ask *Do we need . . . ?* questions about the food in the picture. Then look at your shopping list and answer.

A: Do we need any oranges?

B: Yes. We need some oranges. Do we need any lettuce?

A: Let's see. . . . No. We don't need any lettuce.

Shopping list

oranges	onions
tomatoes	broccoli
celery	kiwis
potatoes	apples

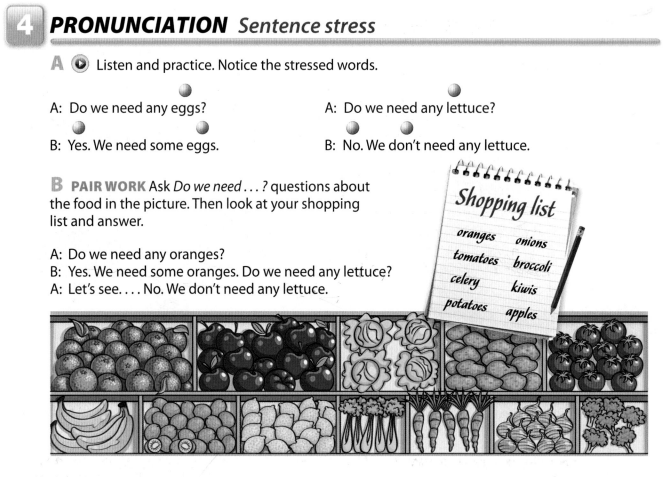

5 SNAPSHOT

▶ Listen and practice.

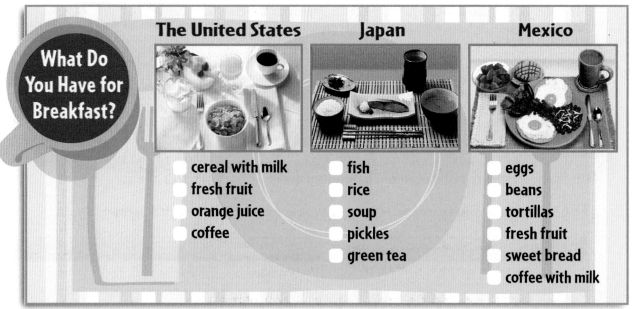

What Do You Have for Breakfast?

The United States
- cereal with milk
- fresh fruit
- orange juice
- coffee

Japan
- fish
- rice
- soup
- pickles
- green tea

Mexico
- eggs
- beans
- tortillas
- fresh fruit
- sweet bread
- coffee with milk

Source: www.about.com

What do you have for breakfast? Check (✓) the foods.
What else do you have for breakfast?

6 CONVERSATION *Fish for breakfast?*

▶ Listen and practice.

Sarah: Let's have breakfast together on Sunday.
Kumiko: OK. Come to my house. My family always
has a Japanese-style breakfast on Sundays.
Sarah: Really? What do you have?
Kumiko: We usually have fish, rice, and soup.
Sarah: Fish for breakfast? That's interesting.
Kumiko: Sometimes we have a salad, too.
And we always have green tea.
Sarah: Well, I never eat fish for breakfast,
but I like to try new things.

↘probar

7 GRAMMAR FOCUS

Adverbs of frequency ▶

		Do you **ever** have fish for breakfast?		always	siempre
	always	Yes, I **always** do.	**100%**	usually	usualmente
	usually	**Sometimes** I do.		often	seguido
	often	No, I **never** do.		sometimes	a veces
I	sometimes eat breakfast.			hardly ever	casi nunca
	hardly ever			never	nunca
	never		**0%**		

Sometimes I eat breakfast.

A Put the adverbs in the correct places. Then practice
with a partner.

            usually
A: What do you have for breakfast? (usually)
B: Well, I have coffee and cereal. (often)
A: Do you eat breakfast at work? (ever)
B: I have breakfast at my desk. (sometimes)
A: Do you eat rice for breakfast? (usually)
B: No, I have rice. (hardly ever)

B Unscramble the sentences.

1. I / have breakfast / on / never / weekends   *I never have breakfast on weekends.*
2. work / I / snacks / eat / at / hardly ever   *I hardly ever eat snacks at work*
3. eat / for / pasta / dinner / sometimes / I   *I sometimes eat pasta for dinner*
4. have / I / dinner / with / often / family / my   *I often*

C Rewrite the sentences from part B with your own information.
Then compare with a partner.

A: I always have breakfast on weekends.
B: I hardly ever have breakfast on weekends. I usually get up late.

8 LISTENING *Really? Never?*

A ▶ Paul and Megan are talking about food.
How often does Megan eat these foods?
Listen and check (✓) Often, Sometimes, or Never.

	Often	Sometimes	Never
pasta	✓	☐	☐
hamburgers	☐	☐	✓
fish	☐	✓	☐
eggs	☐	✓	☐
broccoli	✓	☐	☐

B **GROUP WORK** Do you ever eat the foods
in part A? Tell your classmates.

A: I often eat pasta.
B: Really? I never eat pasta.
C: Well, I . . .

9 MEALTIME HABITS

A Add two questions about mealtime habits to the chart. Then ask two people
the questions. Write their names and complete the chart.

	Name:	Name: ....
1. Do you always eat breakfast?	....	....
2. What time do you usually eat lunch?	....	....
3. Do you ever eat cereal for dinner?	....	....
4. Do you ever go to a restaurant for breakfast?	....	....
5. What's something you never eat for lunch?	....	....
6. What do you usually drink with dinner?	....	....
7. .... ?	....	....
8. .... ?	....	....

A: Manuel, do you always eat breakfast?
B: No, I hardly ever do.

B **CLASS ACTIVITY** Tell your classmates about your partners' mealtime habits.

"Manuel hardly ever eats breakfast. But he always eats lunch and dinner. . . ."

10 INTERCHANGE 9 *Snack survey*

Complete a snack survey. Go to Interchange 9 on page 123.

EATING for GOOD LUCK

Look at the pictures. On special occasions, do you ever eat any of these foods?

On New Year's Day, many people eat special foods for good luck in the new year.

Some Chinese people eat tangerines and oranges. "Tangerine" sounds like "luck" and "orange" sounds like "wealth" in the Mandarin language.

In Greece and some other Mediterranean countries, people eat pomegranates. Pomegranates bring wealth in the new year.

In Spain and some Latin American countries, people eat 12 grapes at midnight on New Year's Eve – one grape for good luck in each month of the new year.

At the end of the year in Sweden, people eat rice pudding with an almond inside. Everyone tries to find the almond for good luck in the new year.

On New Year's Day in South Korea, people eat *dduk guk* – soup with rice cakes – for strength and health in the new year.

Some Americans from southern states eat black-eyed peas and rice with collard greens. The black-eyed peas are like coins, and the greens are like dollar bills.

A Read the article. Then correct these sentences.

1. In Mandarin, the word "tangerine" sounds like "~~wealth~~." [luck]
2. Greeks eat pomegranates. Pomegranates bring health.
3. People in Spain eat 12 grapes, one grape for good luck in each hour of the day.
4. Swedish people eat rice pudding with money inside.
5. Koreans eat soup with chocolate cake for strength and health.
6. Some Americans eat black-eyed peas. Black-eyed peas are like dollar bills.

B **GROUP WORK** Do you eat anything special on New Year's Day for good luck? Do you do anything special? Tell your classmates.

Do we need any eggs? ▪ **63**

10 What sports do you play?

1 SNAPSHOT

▶ Listen and practice.

Sports Seasons in the U.S. and Canada

In the spring, people...
- play golf
- play soccer
- play basketball

In the summer, people...
- play baseball
- play volleyball
- go swimming

In the fall, people...
- play football
- go bike riding
- go hiking

In the winter, people...
- play hockey
- go ice-skating
- go snowboarding

Source: Adapted from *ESPN Information Please Sports Almanac*

What sports are popular in your country? Check (✓) the sports.
Do you like sports? What sports do you play or watch?

2 CONVERSATION *I love sports.*

▶ Listen and practice.

Lauren: So, Justin, what do you do in your free time?
Justin: Well, I love sports.
Lauren: Really? What sports do you like?
Justin: My favorites are hockey, baseball, and soccer.
Lauren: Wow, you're a really good athlete! When do you play all these sports?
Justin: Oh, I don't play these sports.
Lauren: What do you mean?
Justin: I just watch them on TV!

Simple present Wh-questions ▶

What sports do you play?	I play **hockey and baseball**.
Who do you play baseball **with**?	I play **with some friends from work**.
Where do you play?	We play **at Hunter Park**.
How often do you practice?	We practice **once or twice a week**.
When do you practice?	We practice **on Sundays**.
What time do you start?	We start **at ten o'clock in the morning**.

A Complete the conversations with the correct Wh-question words. Then practice with a partner.

1. A: I watch sports on TV every weekend.
   B: Really? ...... *What sports* ...... do you like to watch?
   A: Soccer. It's my favorite!
   B: ...... *when* ...... do you usually watch soccer?
   A: On Sunday afternoons.
   B: And ...... *where* ...... do you usually watch it? At home?
   A: No, at my friend's house. He has a really big TV!

2. A: ...... *how often* ...... do you go bike riding?
   B: Oh, about once a month.
   A: I love to go bike riding. I go every Saturday.
   B: Really? ...... *What time* ...... do you go?
   A: Usually at about one o'clock.
   B: Oh, yeah? ...... *who often* ...... do you usually go with?
   A: My sister. Come with us next time!

B Complete the conversation with Wh-questions. Then compare with a partner.

A: *What sports do you like* ?
B: I like a lot of sports, but I really love volleyball!
A: *who do you play with* ?
B: I usually play with my sister and some friends.
A: *when do you practice* ?
B: We practice on Saturdays.
A: *what time do you start* ?
B: We start at about noon.
A: *where do you play* ?
B: We usually play in our yard, but sometimes we play at the beach.

C **PAIR WORK** Ask your partner five questions about sports or other activities. Then tell the class.

A: What sports do you like?
B: I don't like sports very much.
A: Oh? What do you like to do in your free time?

4 LISTENING *What sports do you like?*

▶ Listen to the conversations about sports.
Complete the chart.

	Favorite sport	Do they play or watch it?	
		Play	**Watch**
1. Casey	golf	✓	☐
2. John	baseball	✓	☐
3. Sue	basketball	☐	✓
4. Henry	hockey	✓	✓

5 FREE-TIME ACTIVITIES

A Add one question about free-time activities to the chart. Then ask two people the questions. Write their names and complete the chart.

	Name: Jonathan	Name:
1. What sports do you like?	bike riding	
2. What sports do you dislike?	volleyball	
3. What do you do on Sundays?	visit family	
4. What do you like to do in the summer?	walk in the night	
5. How often do you play video games?	never	
6. ....?		

A: Jae-hoon, what sports do you like?
B: I like a lot of sports. My favorites are soccer and baseball.

B CLASS ACTIVITY Tell your classmates about your partners' free-time activities.

6 CONVERSATION *I can't sing.*

▶ Listen and practice.

Kayla: Oh, look. There's a talent contest on Saturday. Let's enter.
Philip: I can't enter a talent contest. What can I do?
Kayla: You can sing really well.
Philip: Oh, thanks. . . . Well, you can, too.
Kayla: Oh, no. I can't sing at all – but I can play the piano.
Philip: So maybe we *can* enter the contest.
Kayla: Sure. Why not?
Philip: OK. Let's practice tomorrow!

GRAMMAR FOCUS

Can *for ability* ▶

								What **can** I do?
I			you		I			You **can** sing.
You			I		you			
He	**can**	sing very well.	**Can**	he	sing?	Yes,	he	**can**.	Who **can** sing?
She	**can't**	sing at all.		she		No,	she	**can't**.	Philip **can**.
We			we		we			
They			they		they			

A Kayla is talking about things she can and can't do. Complete these sentences.

1. I ....can't.... draw.

2. I ...Can.... fix cars.

3. I ..can't... sing.

4. I ..can't.. ice-skate at all.

5. I ..Can.... play the piano.

6. I ...Can.... act.

B PAIR WORK Ask and answer questions about the pictures in part A.

A: Can Kayla draw?
B: No, she can't.

C GROUP WORK Can your classmates do the things in part A? Ask and answer questions.

"Can you draw, Pedro?"

8 PRONUNCIATION Can *and* can't

A ▶ Listen and practice. Notice the pronunciation of **can** and **can't**.

/kən/   /kænt/
I **can** play the piano.   I **can't** sing at all.

B PAIR WORK Your partner reads a sentence for each number. Check (✓) the sentence you hear.

1. ☐ I can sing.   2. ☐ I can act.   3. ☐ I can dance.   4. ☐ I can swim.
   ☐ I can't sing.   ☐ I can't act.   ☐ I can't dance.   ☐ I can't swim.

LISTENING *I can do that!*

Listen to three people talk about their abilities. Check (✓) the things they can do well.

1. Craig	✓	☐	☐	☐	✓	☐	☐	☐
2. Julie	☐	☐	☐	☐	☐	✓	✓	☐
3. Rob	☐	✓	☐	✓	☐	☐	☐	✓

10 WORD POWER

A Complete the word map with abilities and talents from the list.
Then listen and check.

✓ bake a cake
  download a video
  do yoga
  fix a car
  play chess
  play the violin
  ride a horse
  sing English songs
  snowboard ɔ
  tell good jokes ч
  upload photos
  write poems

Musical or artistic
write poems
sing english songs
play the violin

Athletic
ride a horse
do yoga
snowboard

Abilities and talents

Technical or mechanical
fix a car
download a video
upload photos.

Other
bake a cake
tell good jokes
play chess

B **GROUP WORK** Who can do the things in part A?
Make a list of guesses about your classmates.

A: Who can bake a cake?
B: I think Sophie can.
C: Who can download . . . ?

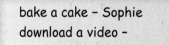

bake a cake – Sophie
download a video –

C **CLASS ACTIVITY** Go around the room and check your guesses.

A: Sophie, can you bake a cake?
B: Yes, I can.

11 INTERCHANGE 10 *Hidden talents*

Learn more about your classmates' hidden talents. Go to Interchange 10 on page 124.

An interview with Shawn Johnson

How often do you think professional athletes practice?

Get a sneak peek inside the life of this U.S. gold medal–winning Olympic gymnast!

Where are you from?

Des Moines, Iowa. I live there now.

Who do you train with?

A lot of people think I have a private coach. But I train with 13 other girls at the gym!

How often do you practice?

Most athletes train about 45 hours a week. But my parents want me to have a "normal life." I train about 25 hours a week. I usually work out four hours a day during the week, and five to six hours on Saturdays. I don't practice on Sundays.

What do you eat to stay healthy?

I have to watch my diet to be a healthy gymnast. But I don't get stressed about it.

What are your favorite foods?

Chicken and steak kebabs, peaches and cream, and corn on the cob.

What do you do when you're not training?

I love to ride horses and spend time with my friends.

What do you do for good luck?

I always travel with my blankets. But I don't believe in good-luck charms!

Who are your biggest fans?

My mom, dad, and of course my coach!

A Read the interview. Then check (✓) the correct answers to the questions.

1. Who does Shawn train with?
   a. ☐ just her coach   b. ✓ other gymnasts
2. How often does she practice?
   a. ✓ 25 hours a week   b. ☐ 45 hours a week
3. How much does she train on Saturdays?
   a. ☐ four hours   b. ✓ five to six hours
4. What does she like to do in her free time?
   a. ☐ eat in restaurants   b. ✓ ride horses and be with friends
5. What does she travel with?
   a. ☐ a good-luck charm   b. ✓ her blankets

B **GROUP WORK** Do you think athletes have an easy life? Is playing a sport fun, or hard work? Discuss your reasons with your classmates.

Units 9–10 Progress check

SELF-ASSESSMENT

How well can you do these things? Check (✓) the boxes.

I can	Very well	OK	A little
Make and respond to suggestions (Ex. 1)	☐	☐	☐
Talk about food and drink (Ex. 1, 2)	☐	☐	☐
Ask and answer questions about eating habits (Ex. 2)	☐	☐	☐
Understand descriptions of sporting activities (Ex. 3)	☐	☐	☐
Ask and answer questions about likes and dislikes (Ex. 4)	☐	☐	☐
Talk about job abilities (Ex. 5)	☐	☐	☐

1 CLASS PICNIC

GROUP WORK Plan a class picnic. Choose two main dishes, two salads, two drinks, and two desserts. Then tell the class.

Main dishes	
Salads	
Drinks	
Desserts	

useful expressions
Do we want any . . . ?
Let's get/make some . . .
I don't want/like . . .

2 AT THE MOVIES

PAIR WORK Does your partner ever have these things at the movies? Ask questions and complete the survey.

	always	usually	sometimes	hardly ever	never
1. popcorn	☐	☐	☐	☐	☐
2. fruit	☐	☐	☐	☐	☐
3. soda	☐	☐	☐	☐	☐
4. candy	☐	☐	☐	☐	☐
5. fish	☐	☐	☐	☐	☐
6. coffee	☐	☐	☐	☐	☐

A: Do you have popcorn at the movies?
B: Yes, I always have popcorn.

3 LISTENING *What do you play?*

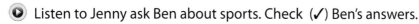

▶ Listen to Jenny ask Ben about sports. Check (✓) Ben's answers.

1. ☐ I play baseball.
   ☐ I play basketball.

2. ☐ Some friends from school.
   ☐ Some friends from work.

3. ☐ At 6:30 P.M.
   ☐ At 6:30 A.M.

4. ☐ Every day.
   ☐ Every week.

5. ☐ On the weekends.
   ☐ In the afternoons.

6. ☐ At the park.
   ☐ In the yard.

4 WHAT DO YOU LIKE?

A Complete the chart with things you love, like, and don't like.

	I love . . .	I like . . .	I don't like . . .
Sports			
Foods			
Clothes			

B **PAIR WORK** Find out what your partner loves, likes, and doesn't like. Then ask more questions with *who, where, how often,* or *when.*

A: What sports do you love?
B: I love ice-skating.
A: Who do you usually go ice-skating with?

5 JOB ABILITIES

GROUP WORK What can these people do well? Make a list.
Use the abilities in the box and your own ideas. Then tell the class.

chef

mechanic

artist   musician

bake
cook
draw
fix a car
fix a motorcycle
paint
play the piano
read music

A: A chef can cook very well.
B: A chef can also bake things, like cakes.
C: Also, a chef can . . .

WHAT'S NEXT?

Look at your Self-assessment again. Do you need to review anything?

11 What are you going to do?

1 MONTHS AND DATES

A ▶ Listen and practice the months.

Months	January July	February August	March September	April October	May November	June December

B ▶ Complete the dates. Then listen and practice.

Dates

1st	first	11th	eleventh	21st	twenty-first
2nd	second		twelfth		twenty-second
	third	13th	thirteenth	23rd	twenty-third
4th	fourth	14th	fourteenth		twenty-fourth
5th	fifth		fifteenth	25th	twenty-fifth
6th	sixth	16th	sixteenth		twenty-sixth
	seventh	17th	seventeenth	27th	twenty-seventh
8th	eighth	18th	eighteenth		twenty-eighth
9th	ninth		nineteenth	29th	twenty-ninth
	tenth	20th	twentieth		thirtieth
					thirty-first

C **CLASS ACTIVITY** Go around the room. Ask your classmates' birthdays.

A: When's your birthday?
B: It's July twenty-first. When's yours?

2 CONVERSATION *Birthday plans*

▶ Listen and practice.

Angie: Are you going to do anything exciting this weekend?
Philip: Well, I'm going to celebrate my birthday.
Angie: Oh, happy birthday! When is it, exactly?
Philip: It's August ninth – Sunday.
Angie: So what are your plans?
Philip: I'm going to go to my friend Kayla's house.
       She's going to cook a special dinner for me.
Angie: Nice! Is she going to bake a cake, too?
Philip: Bake a cake? Oh, I'm not sure.

> **The future with be going to** ▶
>
> **Are** you **going to do** anything this weekend? | Yes, I am. I**'m going to celebrate** my birthday.
> | No, I'm not. I**'m going to stay** home.
>
> **Is** Kayla **going to cook** dinner for you? | Yes, she is. She**'s going to cook** a special dinner.
> | No, she's not. She**'s going to order** takeout.
>
> **Are** your friends **going to be** there? | Yes, they are. They**'re going to stop** by after dinner.
> | No, they're not. They**'re going to be** away all weekend.

A What are these people going to do this weekend?
Write sentences. Then compare with a partner.

1. They're going to go dancing.

B **PAIR WORK** Is your partner going to do the things in part A
this weekend? Ask and answer questions.

"Are you going to go dancing this weekend?"

4 **PRONUNCIATION** *Reduction of* going to

A ▶ Listen and practice. Notice the reduction of **going to** to /gənə/.

A: Are you **going to** have a party?   A: Are you **going to** go to a restaurant?
B: No. I'm **going to** meet a friend.   B: Yes. We're **going to** go to Nick's Café.

B **PAIR WORK** Ask your partner about his or her evening plans. Try to reduce **going to**.

5 LISTENING Evening plans

A It's 5:30 P.M. What are these people's evening plans? Write your guesses in the chart.

B ▶ Listen to the interview. What are the people really going to do? Complete the chart.

Michelle Kevin Robert Jackie

Your guess	What they're really going to do
Michelle _is going to go to the gym_ .	Michelle ....
Kevin	Kevin ....
Robert	Robert ....
Jackie	Jackie ....

6 INTERCHANGE 11 Guessing game

Make guesses about your classmates' plans. Go to Interchange 11 on page 125.

7 SNAPSHOT

▶ Listen and practice.

Holidays in the United States

New Year's Day	Valentine's Day	Independence Day	Halloween	Thanksgiving	Christmas
January 1st	February 14th	July 4th	October 31st	The fourth Thursday in November	December 25th

Source: *The Concise Columbia Encyclopedia*

Do you celebrate any of these holidays?
What are some holidays in your country? What's your favorite holiday?

8 CONVERSATION *Have a good Valentine's Day.*

▶ Listen and practice.

Mona: So, Tyler, do you have any plans for Valentine's Day?
Tyler: I do. I'm going to take my girlfriend out for dinner.
Mona: Oh, really? Where are you going to eat?
Tyler: At Laguna's. It's her favorite restaurant.
Mona: How fancy! She's going to like that!
Tyler: How about you? What are you going to do?
Mona: Well, I'm not going to go to a restaurant.
       I'm going to go to a dance.
Tyler: Sounds like fun. Well, have a good
       Valentine's Day.
Mona: Thanks. You, too.

fantastic

9 GRAMMAR FOCUS

Wh-questions with be going to ▶

What are you **going to do** for Valentine's Day?

How is Mona **going to get** to the dance?

Where are Tyler and his girlfriend **going to eat**?

I**'m going to go** to a dance.
I**'m not going to go** to a restaurant.
She**'s going to drive**.
She**'s not going to take** the bus.
They**'re going to eat** at Laguna's.
They**'re not going to eat** at Nick's Café.

A Complete these conversations with the correct form of *be going to*.
Then practice with a partner.

1. A: Where ......*are*...... you .....*going to spend*..... (spend) summer vacation?
   B: My parents and I *are going* (visit) my grandparents.
2. B: Who ....*are* you ....*going to* (invite) to Thanksgiving dinner?
   A: I *going to* (ask) my family and some good friends.
3. A: What ....*are* you ....*going to* (do) for Halloween?
   B: I don't know. I *'m not going* (not do) anything special.
4. A: How ....*are* your parents ....*going to*.... (celebrate) New Year's Eve?
   B: They *are going to* (go) to their neighbor's party.
5. A: What ......*is*...... your sister ....*going to* (do) for her birthday?
   B: Her boyfriend ...*is going to* (take) her out to dinner.

B GROUP WORK Ask your classmates about their plans.
Use the time expressions in the box.

A: What are you going to do tonight?
B: I'm going to go to a party.
C: Oh, really? Who's going to be there?
B: Well, Lara and Rosa are going to come.
   But Jeff isn't going to be there. . . .

time expressions	
tonight	next week
tomorrow	next month
tomorrow afternoon	next summer
tomorrow night	next year

10 WORD POWER *Ways to celebrate*

A ▶ Listen and practice.

decorate	**eat special food**	**go to a parade**	**give gifts**
watch fireworks	**play music**	**go on a picnic**	**wear special clothes**

B **PAIR WORK** Are you going to celebrate a special day this year? Are you (or is someone you know) going to do any of the things in part A?

A: I'm going to go to a wedding next month. I'm going to wear special clothes.
B: Is it a traditional wedding?

11 HOLIDAYS AND FESTIVALS

A **PAIR WORK** Choose any holiday or festival.
Then ask and answer these questions.

What is the holiday or festival?
When is it?
What are you going to do?
Where are you going to go?
Who's going to be there?
When are you going to go?
How are you going to get there?

Cinco de Mayo in Mexico

Setsubun in Japan

A: What is the holiday or festival?
B: It's Cinco de Mayo.
A: When is it?
B: It's on May fifth.
A: What are you going to do?
B: I'm going to go to a parade. . . .

B **CLASS ACTIVITY** Tell the class about your partner's plans.

What are you going to do on *your birthday?*

Scan the article. How old is each person going to be?

Ka-mei Shi

Taipei

"Tomorrow is my sixteenth birthday. It's a special birthday, so we're going to have a family ceremony. I'm probably going to get some money in 'lucky' envelopes from my relatives. My mother is going to cook noodles – noodles are for a long life."

Elena Buenaventura

Madrid

"My twenty-first birthday is on Saturday, and I'm going to go out with some friends. To wish me a happy birthday, they're going to pull on my ear 21 times – once for each year. It's an old custom. Some people pull on the ear just once, but my friends are very traditional!"

Mr. and Mrs. Aoki

Kyoto

"My husband is going to be 60 tomorrow. In Japan, the sixtieth birthday is called *kanreki* – it's the beginning of a new life. The color red represents a new life, so children often give something red as a present. What are our children going to give him? A red hat and vest!"

Philippe Joly

Paris

"I'm going to be 30 next week, so I'm going to invite three very good friends out to dinner. In France, when you have a birthday, you often invite people out. In some countries, I know it's the opposite – people take you out."

A Read the article. Then correct these sentences.

1. To celebrate her birthday, Elena is going to pull on her friends' ears.
2. Ka-mei is going to cook some noodles on her birthday.
3. On his birthday, Mr. Aoki is going to buy something red.
4. Philippe's friends are going to take him out to dinner on his birthday.

B GROUP WORK How do people usually celebrate birthdays in your country? Do you have plans for your next birthday? How about the birthday of a friend or a family member? What are you going to do? Tell your classmates.

12 What's the matter?

WORD POWER *Parts of the body*

A ▶ Listen and practice.

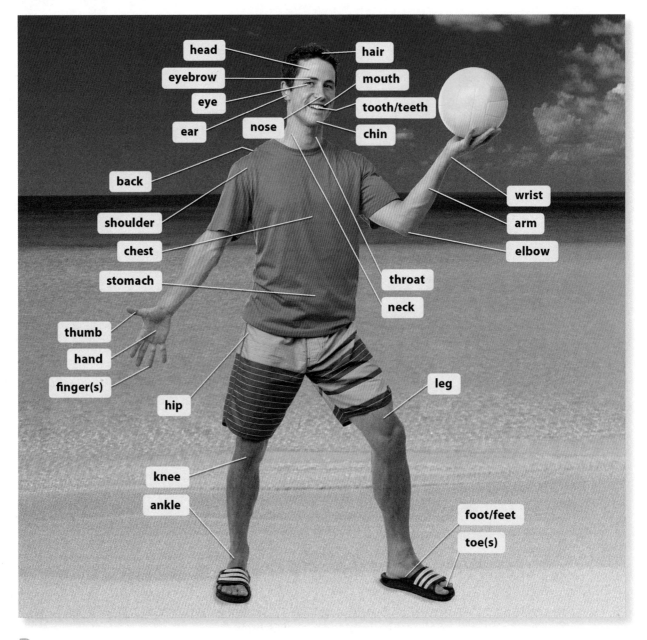

head
eyebrow
eye
ear
nose
hair
mouth
tooth/teeth
chin
back
shoulder
chest
stomach
thumb
hand
finger(s)
hip
knee
ankle
wrist
arm
elbow
throat
neck
leg
foot/feet
toe(s)

B PAIR WORK Complete these sentences.

I have one . . .   I have two . . .   I have ten . . .

A: I have one head, one nose, one mouth, one . . .
B: And I have two eyes, two ears, two elbows, two . . .

CONVERSATION *I don't feel well.*

▶ Listen and practice.

Steve: Hi, Kyle. How's it going?
Kyle: Oh, hi, Steve. Not so well, actually.
I don't feel well.
Steve: What's the matter? Hey, you don't look so good.
Kyle: I have a stomachache.
Steve: That's too bad. Do you have the flu?
Kyle: No, I just feel really sick.
Steve: Well, do you want anything? A glass of soda?
Kyle: No, but thanks anyway.
Steve: Well, I'm going to have some pizza.
Is that OK?

3 GRAMMAR FOCUS

Have + *noun;* feel + *adjective* ▶

What's the matter?	How are you?	*Negative adjectives*	*Positive adjectives*
What's wrong?	How do you feel?	horrible	fine
I have a headache.	**I feel sick.**	awful	great
I have a backache.	**I feel better.**	terrible	terrific
I have the flu.	**I don't feel well.**	miserable	fantastic

A ▶ Listen and practice. *"He has a backache."*

    a backache   an earache   a headache   a stomachache   a toothache

    a cold   a cough   a fever   the flu   dry eyes   a sore throat

B CLASS ACTIVITY Imagine you don't feel well today.
Go around the class. Find out what's wrong with your classmates.

A: How are you today, Jun?
B: I feel terrible. I have a stomachache.
A: I'm sorry to hear that.
B: How do *you* feel?

useful expressions
That's good.
I'm glad to hear that.
That's too bad.
I'm sorry to hear that.

LISTENING *What's wrong?*

A Where do these people hurt? Guess.
Write down the parts of the body.

1. Jeffrey

2. Marta

3. Ben

4. Alison

B Listen to the conversations. Check your guesses.

SNAPSHOT

Listen and practice.

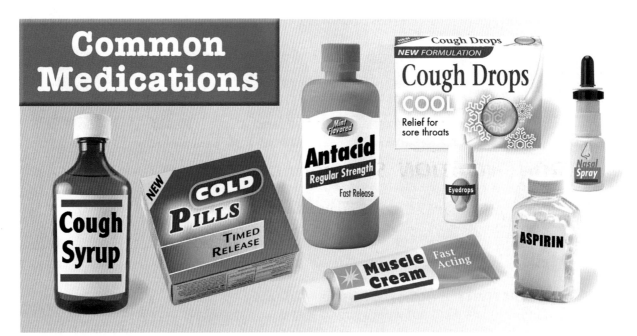

Source: Based on information from *Almanac of the American People*

What medications do you have at home?
What are these medications for?

6 CONVERSATION *Don't work too hard.*

 Listen and practice.

Dr. Young: Hello, Ms. West. How are you today?
Ms. West: Not so good.
Dr. Young: What's wrong, exactly?
Ms. West: I'm exhausted!
Dr. Young: Hmm. Why are you so tired?
Ms. West: I don't know. I just can't sleep at night.
Dr. Young: OK. Let's take a look at you.

A few minutes later

Dr. Young: I'm going to give you some pills.
Take one pill every evening after dinner.
Ms. West: OK.
Dr. Young: And don't drink coffee, tea, or soda.
Ms. West: Anything else?
Dr. Young: Yes. Don't work too hard.
Ms. West: All right. Thanks, Dr. Young.

7 LISTENING *Let's take a look.*

 Listen to Dr. Young talk to four other patients. What does she
give them? Check (✓) the correct medications.

	Cough drops	Aspirin	Cold pills	Eyedrops	Nasal spray	Muscle cream
1. Chuck	☐	☐	☐	☐	☐	☐
2. Pam	☐	☐	☐	☐	☐	☐
3. Joey	☐	☐	☐	☐	☐	☐
4. Sandra	☐	☐	☐	☐	☐	☐

8 PRONUNCIATION *Sentence intonation*

A Listen and practice. Notice the intonation in these sentences.

Take some aspirin.   Don't drink coffee.

Try these eyedrops.   Don't work too hard.

Use some muscle cream.   Don't exercise this week.

B **PAIR WORK** Practice the conversation in Exercise 6 again.
Pay attention to the sentence intonation.

What's the matter? ▪ 81

9 GRAMMAR FOCUS

> **Imperatives** ▶
>
> **Get** some rest.   **Don't stay** up late.
> **Drink** lots of juice.   **Don't drink** soda.
> **Take** one pill every evening. **Don't work** too hard.

Complete these sentences. Use the correct forms of the words in the box.

> | ✓call | stay | not go | not drink |
> |-------|------|--------|-----------|
> | see | take | ✓not worry | not eat |

1. ...._Call_........ a dentist.
2. ....._Don't worry_..... too much.
3. .... two aspirin.
4. .... to school.

5. .... in bed.
6. .... a doctor.
7. .... coffee.
8. .... any candy.

10 GOOD ADVICE?

A Write two pieces of advice for each problem.

My feet hurt.

I have a sore wrist.

I have the flu.

I can't sleep at night.

1. ....   2. ....   3. ....   4. ....
....

B GROUP WORK Act out the problems from part A. Your classmates give advice.

A: I feel awful!
B: What's the matter?
A: My feet hurt.
B: I have an idea. Take a hot bath. And don't . . .
C: Here's another idea . . .

11 INTERCHANGE 12 *Helpful advice*

Give advice for some common problems. Go to Interchange 12 on page 126.

10 Simple Ways to Improve Your Health

Believe it or not, you can greatly improve your health in 10 very simple ways.

1 Eat breakfast. Breakfast gives you energy for the morning.

2 Go for a walk. Walking is good exercise, and exercise is necessary for good health.

3 Floss your teeth. Don't just brush them. Flossing keeps your gums healthy.

4 Drink eight glasses of water every day. Water helps your body in many ways.

5 Stretch for five minutes. Stretching is important for your muscles.

6 Get enough calcium. Your bones need it. Dairy foods like yogurt, milk, and cheese have calcium.

7 Do something to challenge your brain. For example, do a crossword puzzle or read a new book.

8 Take a "time-out" — a break of about 20 minutes. Do something different. For example, get up and walk. Or sit down and listen to music.

9 Wear a seat belt. Every year, seat belts save thousands of lives.

10 Protect your skin. Use lots of moisturizer and sunscreen.

Source: *Cooking Light* ® Magazine

A Read the article. Then complete the sentences.

1. To get exercise, *go for a walk* ....
2. To help your bones, ...
3. To help your muscles, ...
4. To keep your gums healthy, ...
5. To have energy for the morning, ...
6. To challenge your brain, ...

B GROUP WORK What things in the article do you do regularly? What else do you do for your health? Tell your classmates.

Units 11–12 Progress check

SELF-ASSESSMENT

How well can you do these things? Check (✓) the boxes.

I can	Very well	OK	A little
Ask and answer questions about future plans (Ex. 1, 2)	☐	☐	☐
Use future time expressions (Ex. 2)	☐	☐	☐
Understand conversations about problems (Ex. 3)	☐	☐	☐
Talk about problems (Ex. 4)	☐	☐	☐
Ask how people are and give advice (Ex. 4)	☐	☐	☐

1 HOLIDAY SURVEY

A Complete the questions with names of different holidays.

Are you going to . . . ?	Name
eat special food on	....
give gifts on	....
have a party on	....
play music on	....
wear special clothes on	....

B CLASS ACTIVITY Are your classmates going to do the things in part A? Go around the class and find out. Try to write a different person's name on each line.

2 PLANS, PLANS, PLANS

Complete these questions with different time expressions.
Then ask a partner the questions.

1. How are you going to get home .... _tonight_ .... ?
2. What time are you going to go to bed .... ?
3. Who's going to be here .... ?
4. Where are you going to go .... ?
5. What are you going to do .... ?
6. Who are you going to eat dinner with .... ?

3 LISTENING *What's the matter?*

▶ Listen to six conversations. Number the pictures from 1 to 6.

.... This person needs some ketchup.

.... This person has a backache.

.... This person can't dance very well.

....1.... This person feels sad.

.... This person is going to ride a horse.

.... This person has the flu.

4 THAT'S GREAT ADVICE!

A Write a problem on a piece of paper. Then write advice for the problem on a different piece of paper.

| My ankle hurts. |

| Get some muscle cream. |

B **CLASS ACTIVITY** Put the papers with problems and the papers with advice in two different boxes. Then take a new paper from each box. Go around the class and find the right advice for your problem.

A: I feel terrible.
B: What's the matter?
A: My ankle hurts.
B: I can help. Get some eyedrops.
A: That's terrible advice!

A: I feel awful.
C: Why? What's wrong?
A: My ankle hurts.
C: I know! Get some muscle cream.
A: That's great advice. Thanks!

WHAT'S NEXT?

Look at your Self-assessment again. Do you need to review anything?

13 You can't miss it.

WORD POWER *Places and things*

A ▶ Where can you get these things? Match the things with the places.
Then listen and practice. *"You can buy aspirin at a drugstore."*

1. aspirin ....*b*....
2. bread ....
3. a dictionary ....
4. gasoline ....
5. a sandwich ....
6. stamps ....
7. a suit ....
8. traveler's checks ....

a. a post office

b. a drugstore

c. a gas station

d. a department store

e. a bank

f. a bookstore

g. a coffee shop

h. a supermarket

B **PAIR WORK** What else can you get or do in the places in part A?

A: You can get a magazine at a bookstore.
B: And you can send a package at the post office.

LISTENING *I need a new swimsuit.*

A ▶ Listen to the Anderson family's conversations. What do they need? Where are they going to get the things? Complete the chart.

	What	Where
1. Jean	a swimsuit	....
2. Mom	....	....
3. Dad	....	....
4. Mike	....	....

B **PAIR WORK** What do you need? Where are you going to get it? Tell your partner.

"I need a snack, so I'm going to go to a coffee shop...."

3 CONVERSATION *It's an emergency!*

▶ Listen and practice.

Man: Excuse me. Can you help me? Is there a public restroom around here?
Woman: A public restroom? Hmm. I'm sorry. I don't think so.
Man: Oh, no. My son needs a restroom – now. It's an emergency!
Woman: Oh, dear. Well, there's a restroom in the department store on Main Street.
Man: Where on Main Street?
Woman: It's on the corner of Main and First Avenue.
Man: On the corner of Main and First?
Woman: Yes, it's across from the park. You can't miss it.
Man: Thanks a lot.

4 PRONUNCIATION *Compound nouns*

A ▶ Listen and practice. Notice the stress in these compound nouns.

● post office   ● gas station   ● restroom   ● coffee shop

● drugstore   ● bookstore   ● supermarket   ● department store

B **PAIR WORK** Practice these sentences. Pay attention to the stress in the compound nouns.

There's a restroom in the drugstore.
There's a bookstore in the department store.

There isn't a post office in the supermarket.
There isn't a coffee shop in the gas station.

Prepositions of place

on	on the corner of	across from	next to	between

The department store is **on** Main Street.
It's **on the corner of** Main and First.
It's **across from** the park.

It's **next to** the bank.
The bank is **between** the department store **and** the restaurant.

A Look at the map and complete the sentences. Then compare with a partner.

1. The coffee shop is ......*on*...... Second Avenue. It's .... the shoe store.
2. The movie theater is .... Park and Main. It's .... the park.
3. The gas station is .... the parking lot. It's .... First and Center.
4. The post office is .... Center and Second. It's .... the hospital.
5. The bank is .... the restaurant and the department store. It's .... Main Street.

B **PAIR WORK** Where are these places on the map? Ask and answer questions.

the park   the drugstore   the bookstore   the hospital   the shoe store

A: Where is the park?
B: It's between Park and First, across from the department store.

6 LISTENING *Where is it?*

Look at the map in Exercise 5. Listen to four conversations. Where are the people going?

1. ....   2. ....   3. ....   4. ....

7 SNAPSHOT

Listen and practice.

Top Tourist Attractions: New York City

Grand Central Terminal

Times Square

Central Park

Rockefeller Center

The Statue of Liberty

The Empire State Building

Source: www.iloveny.com

What do you know about these places? What makes them popular?
What are some popular tourist attractions in your country?

8 CONVERSATION *Is it far from here?*

Listen and practice.

Tourist: Excuse me, ma'am. Can you help me? How do I get to St. Patrick's Cathedral?
Woman: Just walk up Fifth Avenue to 50th Street. St. Patrick's is on the right.
Tourist: Is it near Rockefeller Center?
Woman: Yes, it's right across from Rockefeller Center.
Tourist: Thank you. And where is the Empire State Building? Is it far from here?
Woman: It's right behind you. Just turn around and look up!

Directions

How do I get to Rockefeller Center?
Walk up/Go up Fifth Avenue.
Turn left on 49th Street.
It's **on the right**.

How can I get to Bryant Park?
Walk down/Go down Fifth Avenue.
Turn right on 42nd Street.
It's **on the left**.

A **PAIR WORK** Imagine you are tourists at Grand Central Terminal.
Ask for directions. Follow the arrows.

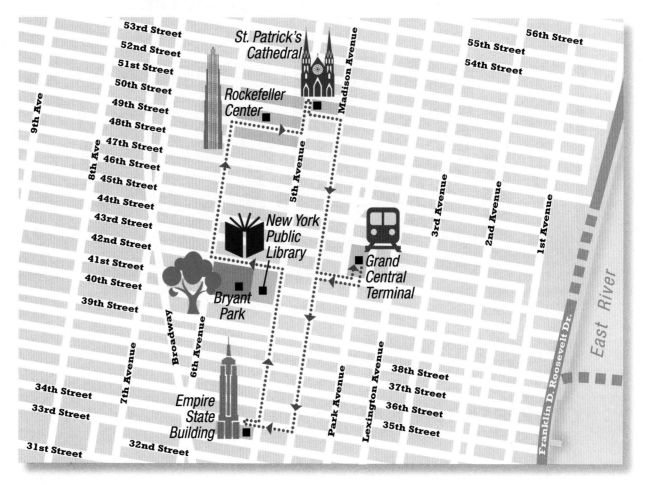

A: Excuse me. How do I get to the Empire State Building?
B: Walk up 42nd Street. Turn left on . . .

B **PAIR WORK** Ask for directions to places near your school.

A: How do I get to the train station?
B: Walk . . .

10 **INTERCHANGE 13** *Giving directions*

Student A, go to Interchange 13A on page 127; Student B, go to Interchange 13B on page 128.

·····Edinburgh's Royal Mile·····

As you read, follow the route on the map below.

1. Start your walking tour at **Edinburgh Castle**. Climb up 187 steps to the top of Castle Hill for a great view. Then take a tour of the castle.

2. Walk down the Royal Mile three blocks to **St. Giles Cathedral**. Go inside and look at the colorful windows.

3. Take a break at **Spoon Café**. Go down the Royal Mile and turn right on South Bridge. The restaurant is on the left.

4. You're almost at the **Museum of Childhood**, on the right on the Royal Mile. There's a great collection of toys, dolls, and games here.

5. Continue down the Royal Mile. Stop at the **Museum of Edinburgh** to learn about the history of Scotland's capital.

6. End your walking tour in **Holyrood Park**, right behind the museum.

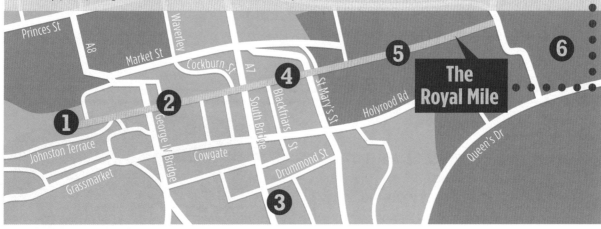

A Read the tourist information. Where can you . . . ?

1. rest and eat lunch ....
2. learn about Edinburgh's history ....
3. take a tour ....
4. see beautiful windows ....
5. see old games ....

B **PAIR WORK** Think of places in your city or town. Plan a walking tour of your town.

14 Did you have fun?

SNAPSHOT

▶ Listen and practice.

Top Eight Things People Hate to Do

1 stand in line
2 do laundry
3 travel to work
4 go to meetings
5 exercise
6 work in the yard
7 clean the house
8 open the mail

Source: Based on information from *The Book of Lists*

Do you hate to do these things?
What other things do you hate to do? Why?

CONVERSATION *I didn't study!*

▶ Listen and practice.

Jason: Hi, Amy. Did you have a
good weekend?
Amy: Well, I had a busy weekend,
so I'm a little tired today.
Jason: Really? Why?
Amy: Well, on Saturday, I exercised in
the morning. Then my roommate
and I cleaned, did laundry, and
shopped. And then I visited
my parents.
Jason: So what did you do on Sunday?
Amy: I studied for the test all day.
Jason: Oh, no! Do we have a test today?
I didn't study! I just watched
TV all weekend!

3 GRAMMAR FOCUS

Simple past statements: regular verbs ▶

							Spelling		
I	**studied**	on Sunday.	I	**didn't study**	on Saturday.	stay	→	stay**ed**	
You	**watched**	TV.	You	**didn't watch**	a movie.	watch	→	watch**ed**	
She	**stayed**	home.	She	**didn't stay**	out.	exercise	→	exercise**d**	
We	**shopped**	for groceries.	We	**didn't shop**	for clothes.	study	→	stud**ied**	
They	**exercised**	on Saturday.	They	**didn't exercise**	on Sunday.	shop	→	shop**ped**	

did**n't** = did not

A Tim is talking about his weekend. Complete the sentences. Then compare with a partner.

On Friday night, I ...<u>waited</u>... (wait) for a phone call, but my girlfriend ...<u>didn't call</u>... (not call). I just .... (stay) home and .... (watch) TV. On Saturday, I .... (visit) my friend Frank. We .... (talk) and .... (listen) to music. In the evening, he .... (invite) some friends over, and we .... (cook) a great meal. I .... (not work) very hard on Sunday. I .... (not study) at all. I just .... (walk) to the mall and .... (shop).

B Complete the sentences. Use your own information. Then compare with a partner.

1. Yesterday, I .... (watch) TV.
2. Last night, I .... (stay) home.
3. Last week, I .... (clean) the house.
4. Last month, I .... (shop) for clothes.
5. Last year, I .... (visit) a different country.

4 PRONUNCIATION Simple past -ed endings

A ▶ Listen and practice. Notice the pronunciation of **-ed**.

/t/	/d/	/ɪd/
worked	cleaned	invited
watched	stayed	visited
....	....	....
....	....	....

B ▶ Listen and write these verbs under the correct sounds.

cooked   exercised   listened   needed   shopped   waited

5 GRAMMAR FOCUS

Simple past statements: irregular verbs ▶

I **did** my homework.
I **didn't do** laundry.

You **got up** at noon.
You **didn't get up** at 10:00.

He **went** to the museum.
He **didn't go** to the library.

We **met** our classmates.
We **didn't meet** our teacher.

You **came** home late.
You **didn't come** home early.

They **had** a picnic.
They **didn't have** a party.

A ▶ Complete the chart. Then listen and check.

Present	Past	Present	Past	Present	Past
buy	bought	....	made	....	saw
....	ate	....	read /rɛd/	....	sat
....	felt	....	rode	....	took

B **PAIR WORK** Did you do the things in the pictures yesterday? Tell your partner.

"Yesterday, I did my homework. And I did laundry...."

6 LAST WEEKEND

A Write five things you did and five things you didn't do last weekend.

B **GROUP WORK** Tell your classmates about your weekend.

A: I saw a movie last weekend.
B: I didn't see a movie. But I watched TV.
C: I watched TV, too! I saw ...

Things I did	Things I didn't do
I saw a movie.	I didn't exercise.
I studied.	I didn't buy clothes.
I ...	I didn't ...

7 CONVERSATION *Did you like it?*

▶ Listen and practice.

Laura: So, did you go anywhere last summer, Erica?
Erica: Yes, I did. My sister and I went to Arizona. We saw the Grand Canyon.
Laura: Really? Did you like it?
Erica: Oh, yes. We loved it!
Laura: Did you go hiking?
Erica: No, we didn't. Actually, we rode horses. And one day we went white-water rafting on the Colorado River!
Laura: Wow! Did you have fun?
Erica: Yes, I did. But my sister didn't like the rafting very much.

8 GRAMMAR FOCUS

Simple past yes/no questions ▶

Did you **have** a good summer?
   Yes, I **did**. I **had** a great summer.
Did you **ride** a bicycle?
   No, I **didn't**. I **rode** a horse.

Did Erica **like** her vacation?
   Yes, she **did**. She **liked** it a lot.
Did Erica and her sister **go** to Colorado?
   No, they **didn't**. They **went** to Arizona.

A Complete the conversations. Then practice with a partner.

1. A: ......*Did*...... you .....*have*...... (have) a good summer?
   B: Yes, I .... I .... (have) a great summer.
   I .... (go) to the beach a lot.

2. A: .... you .... (go) anywhere last summer?
   B: No, I .... I .... (stay) here. I .... (get) a part-time job, so I .... (make) some extra money.

3. A: .... you .... (take) any classes last summer?
   B: Yes, I .... I .... (take) tennis lessons, and I .... (play) tennis every day!

4. A: .... you .... (speak) English last summer?
   B: No, I .... But I .... (read) English books and I .... (watch) English movies.

B **PAIR WORK** Ask the questions from part A. Answer with your own information.

A: Did you have a good summer?
B: Yes, I did. I went swimming every day.

9 LISTENING *I didn't go anywhere.*

▶ Listen to Andy, Gail, Patrick, and Fran. What did they do last summer? Check (✓) the correct answers.

1. Andy
2. Gail
3. Patrick
4. Fran

☐ stayed home
☐ saw movies
☐ went bike riding
☐ worked in the yard

☐ visited his brother
☐ read books
☐ went swimming
☐ got a job

☐ went to the beach
☐ watched TV
☐ played tennis
☐ painted the house

10 WORD POWER *Summer activities*

A ▶ Find two words from the list that go with each verb in the chart. Then listen and check.

camping   old friends
a class   a picnic
fun   softball
✓ a job   swimming
✓ a new bike   a trip
new people   volleyball

get	*a job*	*a new bike*
go	....	....
have	....	....
meet	....	....
play	....	....
take	....	....

B **PAIR WORK** Check (✓) six things to ask your partner. Then ask and answer questions.

Did you . . . last summer?

☐ play any sports
☐ buy anything interesting
☐ eat any new foods
☐ meet any interesting people
☐ go anywhere interesting
☐ get a job

☐ play any games
☐ read any books
☐ see any movies
☐ take any trips
☐ take any classes
☐ have fun

A: Did you play any sports last summer?
B: Yes, I did. My friends and I played basketball a lot. We . . .

C **CLASS ACTIVITY** Tell the class about your partner's summer.

"Last summer, Maria went camping with her friend Lucia. They had a lot of fun."

11 INTERCHANGE 14 *Past and present*

Are you different now from when you were a child? Go to Interchange 14 on page 129.

Did you have a good weekend? ? ?

Scan the chat room posts. Who had a terrible weekend? Who enjoyed the weekend? Who learned a lot? Who had a busy weekend?

Karen 12:45

I had a great weekend. I went to my best friend Mariela's wedding. She got married in her parents' garden. She wore a fantastic dress! Her parents served a nice meal after the ceremony. I'm really happy for her. And her new husband is really nice!

Pete 1:19

I didn't go outside all weekend. I had so much work to do! On Saturday, I studied all day. On Sunday, I did the dishes, cleaned my apartment, and did laundry. Sunday night, I watched a DVD for my history class. My weekend wasn't relaxing at all!

Lacey 2:02

I had an interesting weekend. I went camping for the first time. My friends and I drove to the campsite on Saturday. First, we put up the tent. Then we built a fire, cooked dinner, and told stories. On Sunday, we went fishing. I didn't really like camping, but I learned a lot.

Jonathan 4:57

I went to a rock concert with some friends. I had an awful time! It took three hours to drive there. I didn't like the band at all. Then on our way home, the car broke down! My parents came and got us. I finally got home at six in the morning. I'm so tired!

A Read the chat room posts. Then correct these sentences.

1. Karen got married. _Karen's best friend got married._
2. After the wedding, everyone went out to eat. ....
3. Pete studied all day on Sunday. ....
4. He watched TV Sunday night. ....
5. Lacey went camping for the third time. ....
6. Lacey liked camping a lot. ....
7. Jonathan went to a rock concert with his parents. ....
8. It took three hours to get home after the concert. ....

B GROUP WORK Do you have a story about an interesting weekend? Write four sentences about it. Then tell your classmates.

Units 13–14 Progress check

SELF-ASSESSMENT

How well can you do these things? Check (✓) the boxes.

I can	Very well	OK	A little
Understand conversations about where to get things in a town (Ex. 1)	☐	☐	☐
Ask and answer questions about where places are (Ex. 2)	☐	☐	☐
Ask for and give directions (Ex. 2)	☐	☐	☐
Talk about past activities (Ex. 3, 4)	☐	☐	☐
Ask and answer questions about past activities (Ex. 4)	☐	☐	☐

1 LISTENING What are you looking for?

▶ Listen to the conversations. What do the people need?
Where can they get or find it? Complete the chart.

What	Where
1.	....
2.	....
3.	....
4.	....

2 WHERE IS THE . . . ?

A PAIR WORK Are these places near your school? Where are they?
Ask and answer questions.

bank   coffee shop   hospital   post office
bookstore   department store   park   supermarket

A: Where is the bank?
B: It's on Second Avenue. It's across from the Korean restaurant.

B PAIR WORK Give directions from your school to the places in part A.
Your partner guesses the place.

A: Go out of the school and turn left. Walk for about three minutes. It's on
   the right, next to the drugstore.
B: It's the coffee shop.
A: That's right!

98

MY LAST VACATION

A Write four statements about your last vacation.
Two are true and two are false.

> I ate at an expensive restaurant.
> It rained all day, every day.
> I didn't go to a museum.
> I read two books.

B **PAIR WORK** Read your statements. Your partner says "True" or "False." Who has more correct guesses?

A: On my last vacation, I ate at an expensive restaurant.
B: False.
A: That's right. It's false. OR Sorry. It's true.

4 LAST WEEKEND

A Check (✓) the things you did last weekend.
Then add two more things you did.

- ☐ uploaded photos
- ☐ rode my bicycle
- ☐ cleaned the house
- ☐ played sports
- ☐ went shopping
- ☐ went to a supermarket
- ☐ met friends
- ☐ studied
- ☐ ate in a restaurant
- ☐ did laundry
- ☐ went dancing
- ☐ played video games
- ☐ talked on the phone
- ☐ saw a movie
- ☐ ....
- ☐ ....

B **PAIR WORK** Ask your partner about his or her weekend.

A: Did you upload photos last weekend, Keiko?
B: Yes, I did. I uploaded photos of my friends.
   Did you upload photos?
A: No, I didn't. . . .

C **GROUP WORK** Join another pair. Tell them about your partner's weekend.

"Keiko uploaded photos of her friends."

WHAT'S NEXT?

Look at your Self-assessment again. Do you need to review anything?

15 Where did you grow up?

1 SNAPSHOT

▶ Listen and practice.

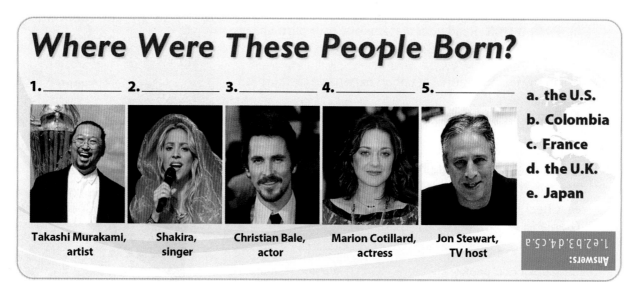

Where Were These People Born?

1._____ 2._____ 3._____ 4._____ 5._____

a. the U.S.
b. Colombia
c. France
d. the U.K.
e. Japan

Takashi Murakami, artist

Shakira, singer

Christian Bale, actor

Marion Cotillard, actress

Jon Stewart, TV host

Answers: 1.e 2.b 3.d 4.c 5.a

Source: www.biography.com

Match the people with the countries. Then check your answers at the bottom of the Snapshot. What famous people were born in your country? What do they do?

2 CONVERSATION *I was born in South Korea.*

▶ Listen and practice.

Chuck: Where were you born, Melissa?
Melissa: I was born in South Korea.
Chuck: Oh! So you weren't born in the U.S.
Melissa: No, I came here in 2005.
Chuck: Hmm. You were pretty young.
Melissa: Yeah, I was only seventeen.
Chuck: Did you go to college right away?
Melissa: No, my English wasn't very good, so I took English classes for two years first.
Chuck: Well, your English is really good now.
Melissa: Thanks. Your English is pretty good, too.
Chuck: I hope so! I was born here.

GRAMMAR FOCUS

Past of be ▶

I **was** born here.	I **wasn't** born in the U.K.	**Were** you in class yesterday?
You **were** pretty young.	You **weren't** very old.	Yes, I **was**. / No, I **wasn't**.
She **was** seventeen.	She **wasn't** in college.	**Was** your first teacher American?
We **were** at the hair salon.	We **weren't** at the café.	Yes, she **was**. / No, she **wasn't**.
They **were** born in Chile.	They **weren't** born in Peru.	**Were** your parents born in the U.S.?
		Yes, they **were**. / No, they **weren't**.

wasn**'t** = was not   weren**'t** = were not

A Melissa is talking about her family. Choose the correct verb forms. Then compare with a partner.

My family and I ......*were*...... (was / were) all born in South Korea – we .... (wasn't / weren't) born in the U.S. I .... (was / were) born in the city of Incheon, and my brother .... (was / were) born there, too. My parents .... (wasn't / weren't) born in Incheon. They .... (was / were) born in the capital, Seoul. In South Korea, my father .... (was / were) a businessman and my mother .... (was / were) a teacher.

B PAIR WORK Look at the picture below. Ask and answer these questions.

1. Was Adam on time for class yesterday?
2. Was it English class?
3. Was it a sunny day?
4. Was it 10:00?
5. Was Mrs. Carter very angry?
6. Were Cindy and Mark late to class?
7. Were they at the board?
8. Were the windows open?

A: Was Adam on time for class yesterday?
B: No, he wasn't. He was late. Was it English class?

4 PRONUNCIATION Negative contractions

A ▶ Listen and practice.

one syllable		two syllables	
aren't	don't	isn't	doesn't
weren't	can't	wasn't	didn't

B ▶ Listen and practice.

He **didn't** eat dinner because he **wasn't** hungry.
I **don't** like coffee, and she **doesn't** like tea.
This **isn't** my swimsuit. I **can't** swim.
They **weren't** here yesterday, and they **aren't** here today.

C Write four sentences with negative contractions.
Then read them to a partner.

> I didn't go because my friends weren't there.

5 CONVERSATION *I grew up in Texas.*

▶ Listen and practice.

Melissa: So, Chuck, where did you grow up?
Chuck: I grew up in Texas.
Melissa: Were you born there?
Chuck: Yeah. I was born in Dallas.
Melissa: And when did you come to Los Angeles?
Chuck: In 2000.
Melissa: How old were you then?
Chuck: I was eighteen. I went to college here.
Melissa: Oh. What was your major?
Chuck: Drama. I was an actor for five years after college.
Melissa: Really? Why did you become a hairstylist?
Chuck: Because I needed the money. And I love it. So, what do you think?
Melissa: Well, uh . . .

6 GRAMMAR FOCUS

Wh-questions with did, was, and were ▶

Where **did** you **grow up**?	I **grew up** in Texas.
What **did** your father **do** there?	He **worked** in a bank.
When **did** you **come** to Los Angeles?	I **came** to Los Angeles in 2000.
Why **did** you **become** a hairstylist?	Because I **needed** the money.
Where **were** you **born**?	I **was born** in Dallas.
When **were** you **born**?	I **was born** in 1982.
How old **were** you in 2000?	I **was** eighteen.
What **was** your major in college?	Drama. I **was** an actor for five years.

A Match the questions with the answers. Then compare with a partner.

1. Where were you born? ....*e*....
2. Where did you grow up? ....
3. How was your first day of school? ....
4. Who was your first friend in school? ....
5. What was he/she like? ....
6. Why did you take this class? ....

a. Her name was Yumiko.
b. She was really friendly.
c. I wanted to improve my English.
d. I grew up in Tokyo.
e. In Hiroshima, Japan.
f. It was a little scary.

B PAIR WORK Ask and answer the questions in part A.
Use your own information.

C GROUP WORK Ask the questions. Use a year in your answers.

1. When were you born?
2. When was your father born?
3. When was your mother born?
4. When did you turn 13?
5. When did you start high school?
6. When did you begin to study English?

saying years
1906 = nineteen oh six
1986 = nineteen eighty-six
2000 = two thousand
2001 = two thousand (and) one
2010 = two thousand (and) ten
OR twenty-ten

7 LISTENING *When was she born?*

A ▶ Listen. When were these people born?
Complete the first column of the chart.

	When were you born?	Where did you grow up?
1. Jill		
2. Roger		
3. Bianca		
4. Ahmed		

B ▶ Listen again. Where did these people grow up?
Complete the second column of the chart.

8 WORD POWER

A ▶ Complete the word map with words from the list. Then listen and check.

✓ cafeteria
classroom
college
computer lab
elementary school
high school
history
junior high school
library
math
physical education
science

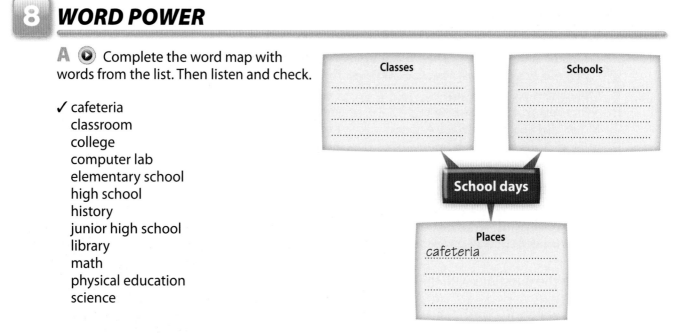

Classes
....
....
....
....

Schools
....
....
....
....

School days

Places
cafeteria
....
....
....

B PAIR WORK Find out about your partner's elementary, junior high, or high school days. Ask these questions. Then tell the class.

What classes did you take?
What was your favorite class? Why?
What classes didn't you like? Why not?
Who was your best friend?

Who was your favorite teacher? Why?
Where did you spend your free time? Why?
What was a typical day of school like?
What didn't you like about school?

"In elementary school, Dan spent his free time in the library because he liked to read. . . ."

9 WHAT DO YOU REMEMBER?

A GROUP WORK How often does this English class meet? What do you remember from your last class? Ask and answer these questions.

1. Who was in class? Who wasn't there?
2. Were you early, late, or on time?
3. Where did you sit?
4. What did you talk about?
5. What did you learn about your classmates?
6. What words did you learn?
7. Did you have any homework?
8. What did you do after class?

B CLASS ACTIVITY What does your group remember? Tell the class.

10 INTERCHANGE 15 Life events

Make a time line of your life. Go to Interchange 15 on page 130.

11 READING

Turning Pain to Gain

Scan the article. Why does Mackenzie read all the time?

Seven years ago, Mackenzie Bearup hurt her knee. She was just ten years old. A week later, the pain was still there. The pain didn't stop. Then she found out about a disease called RSD. This disease tells the brain her knee is still injured, even though it isn't. There is no cure for the pain. Her knee feels terrible all the time.

Sometimes, Mackenzie felt so awful that she stayed in bed for months. It was very difficult to walk. Her doctors tried everything: medicine, exercise, and other treatments. Nothing worked . . . except books.

Mackenzie read lots of books. The books helped her stop thinking about the pain. And she decided to help other children forget their pain, too.

She found out about a treatment center for children nearby. The center had a new library, but no books. She asked all her friends and her parents' friends to give books. Then she put ads in newspapers and made a website.

Mackenzie's goal was to give 300 books to the library. But she soon had 3,000 books, and more were on the way! Today, that number is more than 40,000. She started an organization. Sheltering Books now helps children in many states in the U.S.

Mackenzie's knee still hurts all the time. But she feels better because she's helping other kids with their pain.

A Read the article. Then write a question for each answer.

1. When did Mackenzie hurt her knee ? Seven years ago.
2. _____ ? She felt terrible.
3. _____ ? Medicine, exercise, and other treatments.
4. _____ ? They helped her forget her pain.
5. _____ ? She asked her family and friends.
6. _____ ? To give 300 books.

B Number these events in Mackenzie's life from 1 (first) to 7 (last).

_____ a. She made a website.
_____ b. She found out about RSD.
__1__ c. She hurt her knee.
_____ d. She started an organization.
_____ e. She discovered books helped her pain.
_____ f. She asked her friends for books.
_____ g. She tried lots of different treatments.

C GROUP WORK Why do you think books help people with pain? Can you think of other things that could help? Tell your classmates.

16 Can she call you later?

1 CONVERSATION *She's in a meeting.*

▶ Listen and practice.

Receptionist: Good morning. Digital Media.
Tony: Hello. Can I speak to Kathy Wilson, please?
Receptionist: I'm sorry, but she's in a meeting right now.
Tony: Oh.
Receptionist: Can I take a message?
Tony: Yes, thanks. This is her friend Tony.
Please ask her to call me at home.
Receptionist: Does she have your number?
Tony: Yes, she does.
Receptionist: OK. I'll give her your message.
Tony: Thank you so much.

2 WORD POWER *Prepositional phrases*

A ▶ Listen and practice.

at home	**at** the mall	**in** bed	**in** the shower	**on** vacation
at work	**at** the library	**in** class	**in** the hospital	**on** a trip
at school	**at** the beach	**in** Mexico	**in** a meeting	**on** his/her break

at work   in a meeting   on her break

B **PAIR WORK** Make a list of five friends and family members.
Give it to your partner. Where are these people right now?
Ask and answer questions.

A: Where's your brother right now?
B: He's on vacation. He's in Thailand.

LISTENING *I was in the shower.*

A ▶ Listen to Brian return three phone calls. Where was he? Complete the sentences.

1. He was ....*in the shower*........ .
2. He was ....
3. He was ....

B ▶ Listen again. What did the callers ask? Correct the questions.

1. Donna: "Can you please call?"
2. Jun: "Can I see your notes from class today?"
3. Ruth: "Can you study on Saturday night?"

GRAMMAR FOCUS

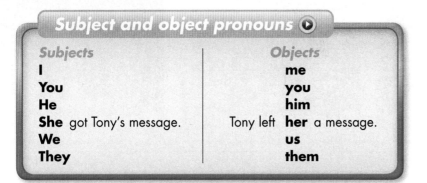

Subject and object pronouns ▶	
Subjects	**Objects**
I	**me**
You	**you**
He	**him**
She got Tony's message.	Tony left **her** a message.
We	**us**
They	**them**

A Complete the phone conversations with the correct pronouns. Then practice with a partner.

1. A: Can ....*I*........ speak with Ms. Fee, please?
   B: .... 's not here. But maybe .... can help you.
   A: Please give .... my new phone number. It's 555-2981.

2. A: Hi, this is David. Is Mr. Roberts there?
   B: .... 'm sorry, but .... 's not here right now.
      Do you want to leave a message?
   A: Yes. Please tell .... to call me at work.

3. A: Hello, this is Carol's Café. Are Kate and Joe in?
   B: No, ... 're not. Can .... help you?
   A: .... found Kate and Joe's keys. .... left .... on the table.
   B: Just bring .... the keys. I can give .... to Kate and Joe.
   A: I'm sorry, but .... can't. Can Kate and Joe call .... ?
   B: OK.

B **PAIR WORK** Roleplay this phone conversation.

Student A: "Call" your friend Calvin. He needs your new phone number.
Student B: Answer the phone. Calvin is not in. Take a message.

C **PAIR WORK** Change roles. This time give an email address.

5 SNAPSHOT

▶ Listen and practice.

Popular Activities in the U.S.

- ○ go to the movies
- ○ go to a concert
- ○ go to an amusement park
- ○ see a sports event
- ○ go to an art festival
- ○ see a play

Source: The U.S. Census Bureau

Check (✓) the activities that are popular in your country.
What other activities are popular in your country?
What are your favorite activities? Why?

6 CONVERSATION *I'd love to!*

▶ Listen and practice.

Tony: Hello?

Kathy: Hi, Tony. It's Kathy. I got your message.

Tony: Hi. Thanks for calling me back. Sorry I called you at work.

Kathy: Oh, that's OK. But I have to get back soon. What's up?

Tony: Well, do you want to see a movie with me tonight?

Kathy: Tonight? I'm sorry, but I can't. I have to work late tonight.

Tony: Oh, that's too bad. How about tomorrow night?

Kathy: Uh, . . . sure. I'd love to. What time do you want to meet?

Tony: How about around seven o'clock?

Kathy: Terrific!

7 PRONUNCIATION *Reduction of* **want to** *and* **have to**

A ▶ Listen and practice. Notice the reduction of **want to** and **have to**.

/wanə/
A: Do you **want to** go to a party with me tonight?
/hæftə/
B: I'm sorry, but I can't. I **have to** study for a test.

B **PAIR WORK** Practice the conversation in Exercise 6 again. Try to reduce **want to** and **have to**.

go to a party

8 GRAMMAR FOCUS

Invitations; verb + to ▶

Do you want to see a movie with me tonight?
 Sure. I'**d** really **like to** see a good comedy.
 I'**d like to** (see a movie), but I **have to** work late.

Would you like to go to an art festival?
 Yes, I'**d love to** (go to an art festival)!
 I'**d like to** (go), but I **need to** study.

I'**d** = I would

A Complete the invitations. Then match them with the responses.

Invitations

1. Would you ......*like to*...... go to an amusement park this weekend? ...*d*...
2. Do you .... go to a basketball game tomorrow night? ....
3. Would you .... see a play tonight? ....
4. Do you .... go swimming on Saturday? ....
5. Do you .... play soccer after school today? ....
6. Would you .... go to a hip-hop concert on Saturday night? ....

Responses

a. I'd like to, but I don't have a swimsuit!
b. I'm sorry, but I have to talk to the teacher after school.
c. I don't really like basketball. Do you want to do something else?
d. I'd like to, but I can't. I'm going to go on a trip this weekend.
e. Yes, I'd love to. It's my favorite type of music.
f. Tonight? I can't. I need to help my parents.

B **PAIR WORK** Practice the invitations from part A. Respond with your own information.

A: Would you like to go to an amusement park this weekend?
B: I'd like to, but I can't. I have to . . .

9 EXCUSES, EXCUSES!

A Do you ever use these excuses? Check (✓) Often, Sometimes, or Never. Compare with a partner.

	Often	Sometimes	Never
I have to babysit.	☐	☐	☐
I need to study for a test.	☐	☐	☐
I have to work late.	☐	☐	☐
I need to go to bed early.	☐	☐	☐
I want to visit my family.	☐	☐	☐
I have a class.	☐	☐	☐
I have a headache.	☐	☐	☐
I'm not feeling well.	☐	☐	☐
I need to do laundry.	☐	☐	☐
I already have plans.	☐	☐	☐

I have to babysit.

B Write down three things you want to do this weekend.

> I want to go to the baseball game on Saturday.

C **CLASS ACTIVITY** Go around the class and invite your classmates to do the things from part B. Your classmates respond with excuses.

A: Would you like to go to the baseball game on Saturday?
B: I'm sorry, but I can't. I need to do laundry on Saturday.

10 LISTENING *I'd love to, but . . .*

A ▶ Tony invited some people to a party. Listen to his voice-mail messages. Who can come? Who can't come? Check (✓) the correct answers.

	Can come	Can't come	Excuse
1. Roy	☐	☐	....
2. Angie	☐	☐	....
3. Brad	☐	☐	....
4. Teresa	☐	☐	....
5. Aaron	☐	☐	....

B ▶ Listen again. Why can't some people come? Write their excuses.

11 INTERCHANGE 16 *Let's make a date!*

Make a date with your classmates. Go to Interchange 16 on page 131.

Around Los Angeles *this weekend* 〈 search 〉

> *Look at the events. Which would you like to go to? Number the pictures from 1 (very interesting) to 5 (not interesting).*

HOME	EVENTS	RESTAURANTS	SHOPPING	HOTELS	CELEBRITIES	DEALS

Friday Saturday Sunday

Festivals:
Bella Via Street Painting Festival

Santa Clarita
All day
Bella Via is Italian for "beautiful street." Watch as artists turn the streets into works of art. This event features food, live music, a 5-kilometer race, and children's activities.

Music:
Concert at Hollywood Bowl

7:00 P.M. to midnight
Come hear some great music under the stars! Six terrific bands are going to get your feet moving. Sandwiches, pizza, and drinks for sale.

Movies:
Los Angeles Film Festival

Various Theaters in Westwood
Check listings for times.
Do you want to see the best North American films of the year? More than 200 films. Seats sell out fast, so get tickets now.

Art:
Fiesta Hermosa Arts and Crafts Fair

Hermosa Beach
Starts at 11:00 A.M.
Do you need to decorate your home? Visit this colorful art fair. Find paintings, crafts, and photographs. Jewelry, too! Food and live music.

Attractions:
Aquarium of the Pacific

Whale Tour
11:30 A.M. and 3:00 P.M.
Do you want to see the largest animal on the planet? Go on a boat tour and learn about the amazing blue whale. Then visit the aquarium to see thousands of beautiful fish and sea birds.

A Read the web page. Where can you do these things? Write two places.

1. buy clothes or jewelry ....
2. buy food ....
3. sit indoors ....
4. be outdoors ....
5. see a live performance ....

B GROUP WORK Where do you like to go in your city or town?
What events do you like? Tell your classmates.

Units 15–16 Progress check

SELF-ASSESSMENT

How well can you do these things? Check (✓) the boxes.

I can	Very well	OK	A little
Talk about my past (Ex. 1)	☐	☐	☐
Ask about famous people using simple past yes/no questions (Ex. 2)	☐	☐	☐
Ask and answer questions about someone's past (Ex. 2)	☐	☐	☐
Understand phone calls and leave or pass on messages (Ex. 3)	☐	☐	☐
Ask and answer questions about things I want, need, and have to do (Ex. 4)	☐	☐	☐
Make and respond to invitations (Ex. 5)	☐	☐	☐

1 INTERVIEW

A PAIR WORK Choose three years in your partner's life. Then ask your partner the questions and complete the chart.

	19____	20____	20____
How old were you in . . . ?	....	....	....
Where were your friends in . . . ?	....	....	....
What were you like in . . . ?	....	....	....

B CLASS ACTIVITY Tell the class about your partner's life.

"In 1999, Raul was four. He . . ."

2 WHO WAS HE?

GROUP WORK Think of a famous person from the past. Your classmates ask yes/no questions to guess the person.

Was he/she born in . . . ?
Was he/she a singer? an actor?
Was he/she tall? heavy? good-looking?

A: I'm thinking of a famous man from the past.
B: Was he born in the U.S.?
A: No, he wasn't.
C: Was he . . . ?

3 LISTENING *On the phone*

▶ Listen and check (✓) the best response.

1. ☐ Yes. Please tell her to call me.
   ☐ Yes. Please tell him to call me.

2. ☐ Sure. Does he have your number?
   ☐ No, sorry. He's not here right now.

3. ☐ Yes, you do.
   ☐ No, I don't.

4. ☐ I'm going to visit my parents.
   ☐ I had a terrible headache.

5. ☐ I'd love to, but I can't.
   ☐ No, I didn't go. I was at work.

6. ☐ I'm sorry. He's not here right now.
   ☐ No, Sandra is at work right now.

4 FIND SOMEONE WHO . . .

A CLASS ACTIVITY Go around the class. Ask questions to complete the chart. Try to write a different name on each line.

Find someone who . . .	Name
needs to do laundry this weekend	....
wants to go home early	....
has to babysit this week	....
wants to go shopping this weekend	....
wants to see a movie tonight	....
has to go to the doctor this week	....
needs to work this weekend	....
doesn't want to do homework tonight	....

A: Megumi, do you need to do laundry this weekend?
B: Yes, I do.

B PAIR WORK Share your answers with a partner.

5 INVITATIONS

A Make a list of five things you want to do this weekend.

B CLASS ACTIVITY Go around the class. Invite your classmates to do the things from part A. Your classmates accept or refuse the invitations.

A: Would you like to go to a museum this weekend?
B: I'm sorry, but I can't. I have to . . .

C: Do you want to go to a soccer match on Sunday?
D: Sure, I'd love to! When would you like to . . . ?

WHAT'S NEXT?

Look at your Self-assessment again. Do you need to review anything?

Interchange activities

FAMOUS CLASSMATES

A Imagine you are a famous person. Write your name, phone number, and email address on the card.

Name: Rafael Nadal
Phone: 646-555-0831
Email: rafaelnadal@cup.org

Name: ....
Phone: ....
Email: ....

B CLASS ACTIVITY Go around the class. Introduce yourself to three "famous people." Ask and answer questions to complete the cards.

A: Hi. My name is Angelina Jolie.
B: I'm Rafael Nadal. Nice to meet you, Angelina.
A: Rafael, what's your email address?
B: It's R-A-F-A-E-L N-A-D-A-L at C-U-P dot O-R-G.
A: I'm sorry. Can you repeat that?

useful expressions
I'm sorry. Can you repeat that? How do you spell that?

Name: ....
Phone: ....
Email: ....

Name: ....
Phone: ....
Email: ....

Name: ....
Phone: ....
Email: ....

MEET YOUR CLASSMATES

PAIR WORK How are the two pictures different?
Ask questions to find the differences.

A: Where are the sunglasses?
B: In picture 1, they're next to the television.
A: In picture 2, they're in front of the television.

Picture 1

Picture 2

GROUP WORK Take turns. Describe the people at the party.
Don't say the person's name. Your classmates guess the person.

A: He's wearing blue jeans, a yellow shirt, and a black jacket. Who is it?
B: Is it Daniel Radcliffe?
A: No, it isn't.
C: Is it Will Smith?
A: That's right.

B: They're wearing dresses. Who are they?
C: Are they Sandra Bullock and Cameron Diaz?
B: That's right.

Will Smith

Kristen Stewart

Daniel Radcliffe

Sandra Bullock

David Beckham

Cameron Diaz

Penelope Cruz

Jennifer Lopez

George Clooney

Robert Pattinson

Anne Hathaway

Helen Mirren

Prince William

Jackie Chan

Johnny Depp

Rain

A **PAIR WORK** Play the board game. Follow these instructions.

1. Choose a marker. Place it on **Start**.
2. Student A tosses a coin and moves one or two spaces.

   "Heads" means move two spaces.
   "Tails" means move one space.

heads   **tails**

3. Student A asks Student B a question with the words in the space.
4. Take turns. Continue until both markers are on **Finish**.

A: It's "heads." I move two spaces. What's your last name?
B: It's Lee. Now it's my turn!

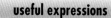

useful expressions
It's your turn.
It's my turn.
I don't know.

B **CLASS ACTIVITY** Tell the class two things about your partner.

"Ricardo is from Quito. Quito is beautiful and very exciting."

WHAT'S WRONG WITH THIS PICTURE?

GROUP WORK What's wrong with this picture? Tell your classmates.

"Ellen is swimming, but she's wearing high heels and a hat!"

A **CLASS ACTIVITY** Go around the class and find this information.
Try to write a different name on each line.

Find someone who . . .			
	Name		**Name**
gets up at 5:00 A.M. on weekdays	....	takes a bus to class	....
gets up at noon on Saturdays	....	rides a motorcycle to class	....
does homework on Sunday night	....	cooks on weekends	....
works at night	....	plays the drums	....
works on weekends	....	has two brothers	....
has a pet	....	checks email every day	....
lives in the suburbs	....	speaks three languages	....
lives alone	....	doesn't eat breakfast	....

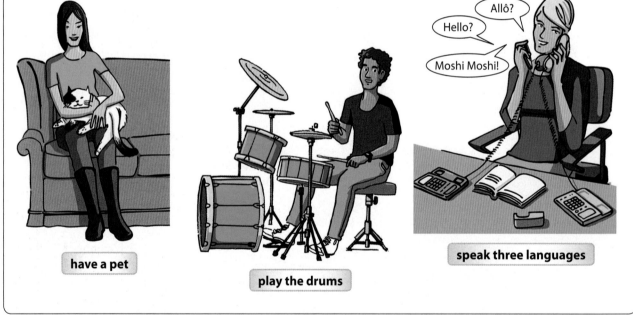

Allô?

Hello?

Moshi Moshi!

have a pet

play the drums

speak three languages

A: Do you get up at 5:00 A.M. on weekends, Jung-ho?
B: No, I get up at 7:00 A.M.
A: Do you get up at 5:00 A.M. on weekdays, Victor?
C: Yes, I get up at 5:00 A.M. every day.

B **GROUP WORK** Compare your answers.

A: Victor gets up at 5:00 A.M.
B: Maria gets up at 5:00 A.M., too.
C: Jung-ho gets up at . . .

FIND THE DIFFERENCES

A **PAIR WORK** Find the differences between Bill's apartment and Rachel's apartment.

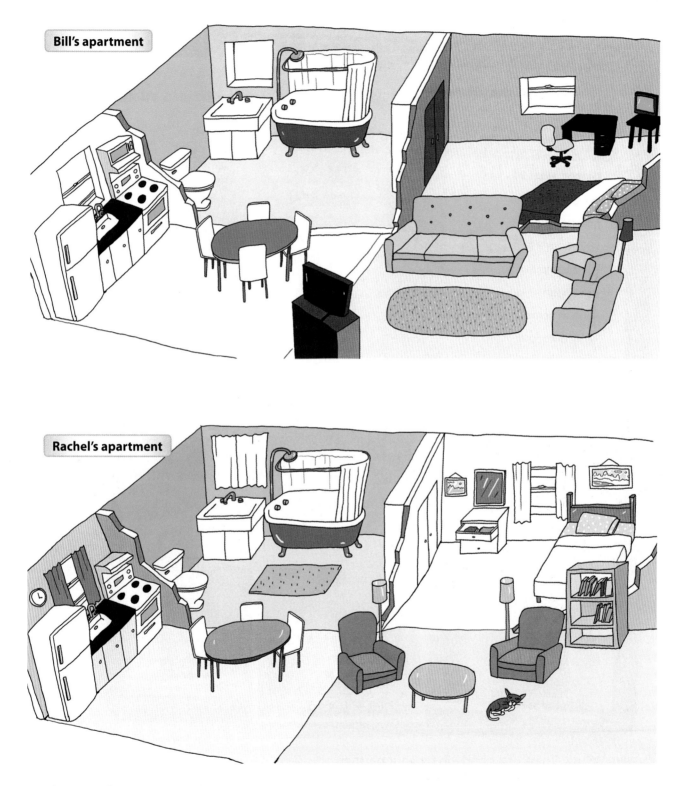

Bill's apartment

Rachel's apartment

A: There are four chairs in Bill's kitchen, but there are three chairs in Rachel's kitchen.
B: There's a sofa in Bill's living room, but there's no sofa in Rachel's living room.

B **GROUP WORK** Compare your answers.

THE PERFECT JOB

A **PAIR WORK** Imagine you're looking for a job. What do you want to do?
First, check (✓) your answers to the questions. Then ask your partner the same questions.

Do you want to . . . ?	Me		My partner	
	Yes	No	Yes	No
talk to people	○	○	○	○
help people	○	○	○	○
work from 9 to 5	○	○	○	○
use a computer	○	○	○	○
use English	○	○	○	○
work at home	○	○	○	○
work outdoors	○	○	○	○
work in an office	○	○	○	○
perform in front of people	○	○	○	○
be on TV	○	○	○	○
travel	○	○	○	○
work with a team	○	○	○	○
wear a suit	○	○	○	○
wear blue jeans	○	○	○	○
have an exciting job	○	○	○	○
have a relaxing job	○	○	○	○

work from 9 to 5

work outdoors

be on TV

perform in front of people

work with a team

B **PAIR WORK** Think of a good job for your partner.

A: You want to use English, travel, and have an exciting job.
    Do you want to be a tour guide?
B: No, a tour guide's job is very stressful.
A: Well, do you want to be . . . ?

SNACK SURVEY

A Complete the snack survey. Use these foods and other foods you know.

beef jerky

grapes

corn chips

watermelon

ice cream

cake

potato chips

candy

popcorn

pineapple

hot dogs

cookies

pizza

peanuts

chocolates

almonds

Snacks I often eat	Snacks I sometimes eat	Snacks I never eat
....	....	....
....	....	....
....	....	....
....	....	....
....	....	....
....	....	....
....	....	....

B **PAIR WORK** Compare your information.

A: I often eat watermelon.
B: I never eat watermelon. I sometimes eat popcorn.

A **CLASS ACTIVITY** Go around the class. Find someone who can and someone who can't do each thing. Try to write a different name on each line.

Names		
Can you . . . ?	**Can**	**Can't**
play two musical instruments	....	....
whistle a song	....	....
say "Hello" in three languages	....	....
swim underwater	....	....
raise one eyebrow	....	....
do a handstand	....	....
fix a computer	....	....
make your own clothes	....	....
say the alphabet backward	....	....
wiggle your ears	....	....

whistle a song   **raise one eyebrow**   **do a handstand**

make your own clothes   **say the alphabet backward**   **wiggle your ears**

A: Can you play two musical instruments?
B: Yes, I can. OR No, I can't.

B **CLASS ACTIVITY** Share your answers with the class.

"Mei-li can't play two musical instruments, but Claudia can.
She can play the violin and the piano."

C Do you have any other "hidden talents"?

A **PAIR WORK** Is your partner going to do any of these things? Check (✓) your guesses.

Is your partner going to . . . ?

	My guesses		My partner's answers	
	Yes	No	Yes	No
1. have a snack after class	☐	☐	☐	☐
2. watch TV tonight	☐	☐	☐	☐
3. go to bed late tomorrow night	☐	☐	☐	☐
4. go out with friends tomorrow night	☐	☐	☐	☐
5. go dancing this weekend	☐	☐	☐	☐
6. eat at a restaurant this weekend	☐	☐	☐	☐
7. go to the gym next week	☐	☐	☐	☐
8. buy something expensive this month	☐	☐	☐	☐
9. go on a trip next month	☐	☐	☐	☐
10. get a job next summer	☐	☐	☐	☐

B **PAIR WORK** Ask and answer questions to check your guesses.

A: Are you going to watch TV tonight?
B: Yes, I am. I'm going to watch my favorite show.

C **CLASS ACTIVITY** How many of your guesses are correct?
Who has the most correct guesses?

A PAIR WORK Imagine you have these problems. Your partner gives advice.

1. I don't have any energy. I know I need to exercise, but I don't like sports.

2. My job is very stressful. I usually work 10 hours a day and on weekends.

3. I can never get up on time in the morning. I'm always late for school.

4. I'm new in town, and I don't know any people here. How can I make some friends?

5. It's my best friend's birthday, and I don't have a gift for her. All the stores are closed!

6. I have a big test tomorrow. My family is very noisy, so I can't study!

A: I don't have any energy. . . .
B: Eat a good breakfast every day. Don't . . .

B CLASS ACTIVITY Think of a problem you have. Then tell the class. Your classmates give advice.

A: I don't understand this activity.
B: Read the instructions again.
C: Don't worry! Ask the teacher.

Student A

A **PAIR WORK** Look at the map. You are on Third Avenue between Maple and Oak Streets. Ask your partner for directions to these places. (There are no signs for these places on your map.) Then label the buildings.

garage   supermarket   flower shop

A: Excuse me. How do I get to the garage?
B: Walk down Third Avenue to . . .

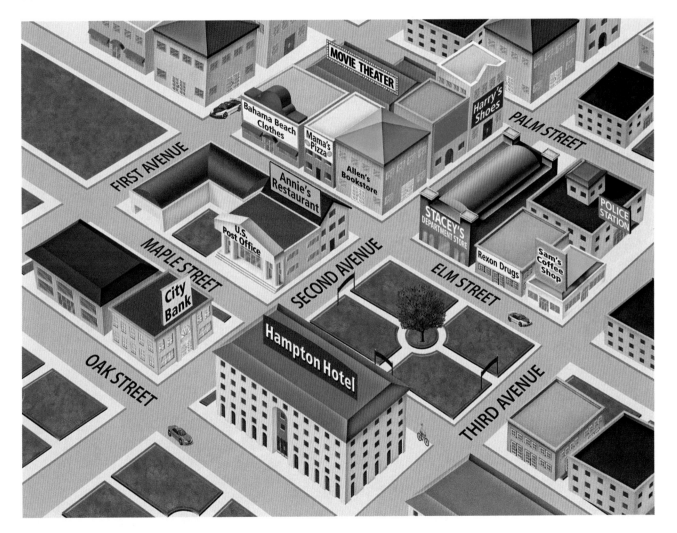

B **PAIR WORK** Your partner asks you for directions to three places. (There are signs for these places on your map.) Use the expressions in the box to give directions.

Go up/Go down . . .	It's on the corner of . . . Street	It's next to . . .
Walk up/Walk down . . .	and . . . Avenue.	It's behind . . .
Turn right/Turn left . . .	It's between . . . and . . .	It's in front of . . .
		It's across from . . .

Student B

A PAIR WORK Look at the map. You are on Third Avenue between Maple and Oak Streets. Your partner asks you for directions to three places. (There are signs for these places on your map.) Use the expressions in the box to give directions.

A: Excuse me. How do I get to the garage?
B: Walk down Third Avenue to . . .

Go up/Go down . . .	It's on the corner of . . . Street and . . . Avenue.	It's next to . . .
Walk up/Walk down . . .		It's behind . . .
Turn right/Turn left . . .	It's between . . . and . . .	It's in front of . . .
		It's across from . . .

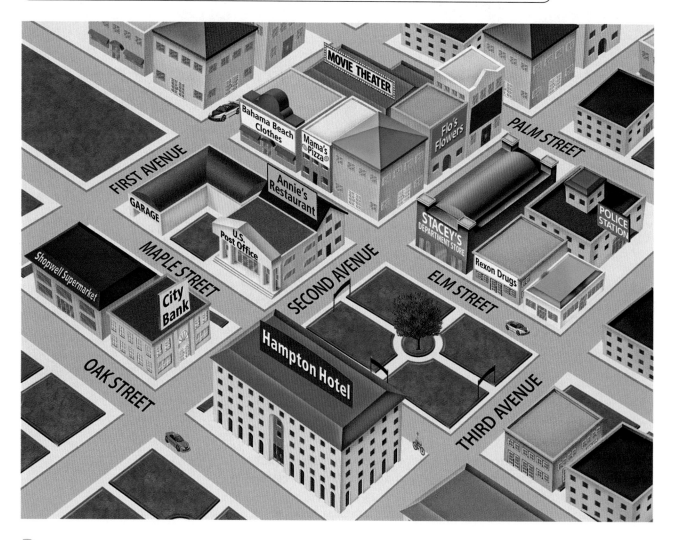

B PAIR WORK Ask your partner for directions to these places. (There are no signs for these places on your map.) Then label the buildings.

coffee shop   shoe store   bookstore

A **PAIR WORK** Ask your partner questions about his or her past and present. Check (✓) the answers.

A: Did you argue with your friends as a child?
B: Yes, I did. OR No, I didn't.

A: Do you argue with your friends now?
B: Yes, I do. OR No, I don't.

Did you ... as a child?
Do you ... now?

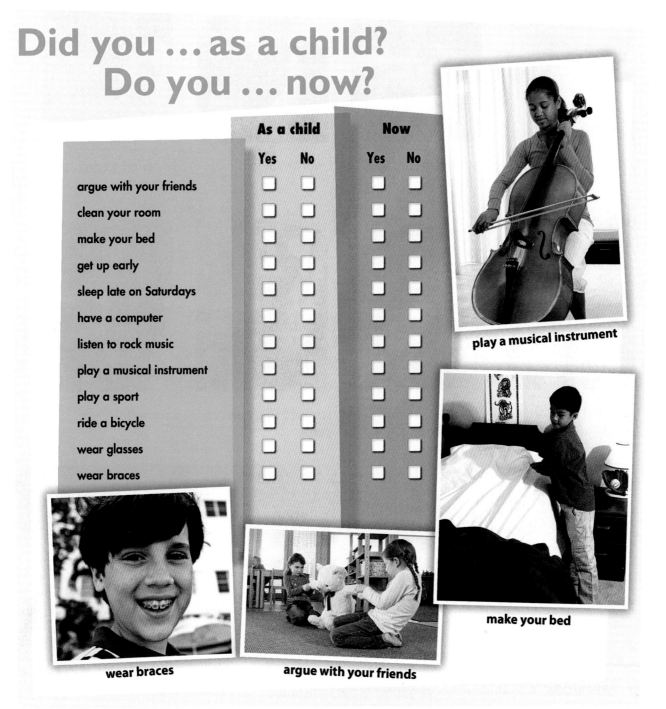

	As a child		Now	
	Yes	No	Yes	No
argue with your friends	☐	☐	☐	☐
clean your room	☐	☐	☐	☐
make your bed	☐	☐	☐	☐
get up early	☐	☐	☐	☐
sleep late on Saturdays	☐	☐	☐	☐
have a computer	☐	☐	☐	☐
listen to rock music	☐	☐	☐	☐
play a musical instrument	☐	☐	☐	☐
play a sport	☐	☐	☐	☐
ride a bicycle	☐	☐	☐	☐
wear glasses	☐	☐	☐	☐
wear braces	☐	☐	☐	☐

play a musical instrument

make your bed

wear braces

argue with your friends

B **GROUP WORK** Join another pair. Tell them about changes in your partner's life.

"Hee-jin argued with her friends as a child, but she doesn't argue with her friends now."

A What were five important events in your life? Mark the years and events on the time line. Then write a sentence about each one.

I was born . . .

I started elementary school . . .

I won an award . . .

I opened a bank account . . .

I traveled with friends . . .

I graduated from high school . . .

I moved to a new place . . .

I started college . . .

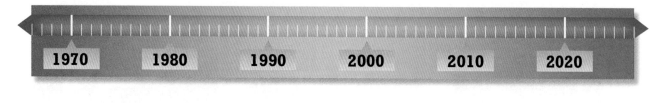

1970   1980   1990   2000   2010   2020

1. I was born in 1992.
2.
3.
4.
5.

B **PAIR WORK** Ask your partner about his or her time line.

A: What happened in 2003?
B: I moved to a new place.
A: How old were you?
B: I was twelve.

A Imagine this is next month's calendar. Write 10 plans on the calendar.
Use these expressions and your own ideas.

go to (the movies/a party)	play (basketball/video games)
go (dancing/shopping)	meet (my friend/teacher)
go (on a trip/on vacation)	have dinner with (my brother/parents)
study for (a test/an exam)	visit (my parents/grandparents)
go out with (my girlfriend/boyfriend)	see (the dentist/doctor)

SUNDAY	MONDAY	TUESDAY	WEDNESDAY	THURSDAY	FRIDAY	SATURDAY
1	2	3	4	5	6	7
8	9	10	11	12	13	14
15	16	17	18	19	20	21
22	23	24	25	26	27	28
29	30	31				

B **GROUP WORK** Look at your calendars. Agree on a date to do
something together.

A: Do you want to do something on March third?
B: I'd like to, but I can't. I'm going to play volleyball then. How about March fourth?
C: That works for me. What time?

C **GROUP WORK** Now decide what to do together. Then share your plans with the class.

A: We can all do something on March fourth. Would you like to play video games?
B: No, I don't like to play video games very much. Do you want to go to a museum?
C: Well, I really don't like museums. . . .

Grammar plus

Unit 1

1 *My, your, his, her* (page 3)

> ▶ Use *his* with males and *her* with females: **His** name is David. (NOT: ~~Her name is David.~~) **Her** name is Maria. (NOT: ~~His name is Maria.~~)

Complete the conversations with *my, your, his,* or *her*.

1. A: Hello. ....My........ name is Carlos.
   B: Hi, Carlos. What's .... last name?
   A: It's Gonzales.
   B: How do you spell .... last name? Is it G-O-N-Z-A-L-E-Z?
   A: No, it's G-O-N-Z-A-L-E-S. And what's .... name?
   B: .... name is Bill Powers. Nice to meet you.

2. A: What's Ms. Robinson's first name?
   B: .... first name is Katherine. .... nickname is Katie.
   A: I'm sorry. What's .... first name again?
   B: It's Katherine. And what's Mr. Weber's first name?
   A: .... first name is Peter.
   B: That's right. And .... nickname is Pete.

2 The verb *be* (page 5)

> ▶ In questions, the *be* verb comes before the noun or pronoun: **Is he** your teacher?
> ▶ Don't use contractions in short answers with *Yes*: Are you in my class? Yes, **I am**. (NOT: ~~Yes, I'm.~~)

Complete the conversations. Use the words in the box.

am	I'm	it's	she's
✓ are	I am	I'm not	you you're

1. A: Excuse me. ....Are........ you Patty Wilson?
   B: No, ... over there.
   A: OK. Thanks.

2. A: Hi. Are .... Patty Wilson?
   C: Yes, ...
   A: Oh, good. .... Sergio Baez. .... in my English class.
   C: Yes, I .... nice to meet you, Sergio.

Unit 2

1 *This/these; it/they; plurals* (page 10)

▶ Don't use a contraction with *What + are*: **What are** these? (NOT: ~~What're these?~~)
▶ Use *this* with singular nouns: **This** is a book. Use *these* with plural nouns: **These** are earrings.

Circle the correct words.

1. A: **What's** / **What are** these?
   B: **It's** / **They're** my **earring** / **earrings**.
2. A: **What's** / **What are** this?
   B: **It's** / **They're a** / **an** cell phone.
3. A: What's **this** / **these**?
   B: **It's** / **They're a** / **an** address book.

2 Yes/No and *where* questions with *be* (page 11)

▶ In questions with *where*, the verb comes after *Where*: **Where are** my sunglasses? (NOT: ~~Where my sunglasses are?~~)

A Match the questions with the answers.

1. Is that your wallet? ....c....   a. They're in your purse.
2. Are these your glasses? ....   b. No, it's not.
3. Where are my keys? ....   c. Oh, yes, it is!
4. Is this your pen? ....   d. It's in my pocket.
5. Where's your watch? ....   e. No, they're not.

B Complete the conversation. Use the words in the box.

are they	it is	they are	where
it	it's	this	✓ where's

A: ....Where's....... my pen?
B: I don't know. Is .... in your book bag?
A: No, ... not.
B: Is .... your pen?
A: Yes, ... Thanks! Now, ... are my keys?
B: .... on your desk?
A: Yes, ... Thank you!

Unit 2 Grammar plus ▪ 133

Unit 3

1 Negative statements and yes/no questions with *be* (page 17)

▶ Use *be* + *not* to form negative statements: Ana **isn't** a student. (NOT: ~~Ana is no a student.~~)

▶ *You* is a singular and a plural pronoun: Are **you** from Rio? Yes, **I** am./Yes, **we** are.

A Unscramble the words to write negative statements.

1. in California / not / New York City / is
   New York City is not in California.

2. London / not / from / we're
   ....

3. not / you and Tim / in my class / are
   ....

4. is / my first language / Spanish / not
   ....

5. from / my mother / not / is / Seoul
   ....

6. my keys / not / are / they
   ....

B Complete the conversations.

1. A: ....Are........... you and your family from Mexico?
   B: No, ... not. .... from Guatemala.
2. A: .... your first language English?
   B: Yes, it .... My parents .... from Australia.
3. A: .... Kenji and his friend Japanese?
   B: Yes, ... are. But .... in the U.S. now.
4. A: .... my mother and I late?
   B: No, ... not. .... early!

2 Wh-questions with *be* (page 20)

▶ Use *what* to ask about things. Use *where* to ask about places. Use *Who* to ask about people. Use *What . . . like?* to ask for a description.

▶ Use *how* to ask for a description: **How are** you today? Use *How old* to ask about age: **How old** is he?

▶ In answers about age, you can use only the number or the number + *years old*: He's **18**. OR He's **18 years old**.

Complete the questions with *how, what, where,* or *who*. Then match the questions with the answers.

1. ......Who...... is that? ...d...
2. .... is her name? ....
3. .... is she like? ....
4. .... old is she? ....
5. .... is your family from? ....
6. .... is Bangkok like? ....

a. We're from Thailand – from Bangkok.
b. She's 16.
c. Her name is Nittaya.
d. She's my sister.
e. It's really beautiful.
f. She's a little shy.

Unit 4

1 Possessives (page 24)

▶ The noun comes after a possessive adjective: This is **my** T-shirt.
▶ Don't include the noun after a possessive pronoun: This T-shirt is **mine**.
▶ *Whose* can be used with singular and plural nouns: **Whose** bag is this? **Whose** keys are these?

Complete the conversations. Use the words in the boxes. There are two extra words in each box.

his	mine	my	your	yours	✓whose

1. A: ....Whose.... jacket is this? Is it .... , Phil?
   B: No, it's not .... Ask Nick. I think it's ....

her	our	ours	your	yours

2. A: These aren't .... books. Are they .... ?
   B: No, they're not .... Maybe they're Young-min's.

her	hers	their	theirs	whose

3. A: .... sweaters are these? Are they Julie's?
   B: No, they're not .... sweaters. But these shorts are ....

2 Present continuous statements; conjunctions (page 26)

▶ The present continuous is the present of *be* + verb + *-ing*: It**'s raining**.
  She**'s wearing** shoes.
▶ The two negative contractions mean the same: **He's not/He isn't** wearing a coat. **We're not/We aren't** wearing gloves.

Change the affirmative sentences to negative sentences. Change the negative sentences to affirmative sentences.

1. Mr. and Mrs. Lee are wearing hats. Mr. and Mrs. Lee aren't wearing hats.
2. It isn't raining. ....
3. I'm wearing sunglasses. ....
4. You're wearing a new suit. ....
5. Michiko isn't wearing gloves. ....

3 Present continuous yes/no questions; adjective + noun (page 27)

▶ In questions, the present continuous is *be* + subject + verb + *-ing*: **Is** it **raining**?
  Are you **wearing** brown shoes?
▶ Adjectives can come before nouns or after the verb *be*: He's wearing a **blue hat**.
  His hat **is blue**.
▶ Adjectives don't have a plural form: a **green hat**; two **green hats**

Write questions using the words in parentheses. Then complete the responses.

1. A: Is he wearing a gray suit? (wear, gray suit)
   B: No, he ....

2. A: .... (wear, brown boots)
   B: No, we ....

3. A: .... (wear, sunglasses)
   B: Yes, I ....

4. A: .... (rain)
   B: Yes, it ....

Unit 5

1 What time is it? / Is it A.M. or P.M.? (page 31)

▶ Remember: you can say times different ways: 1:15 = *one-fifteen* OR *a quarter after one*.

Write each sentence in a different way.

1. It's a quarter to four. It's three forty-five .
2. It's 12:00 P.M. It's noon.
3. It's six-fifteen. ....
4. It's ten o'clock at night. ....
5. It's three-oh-five. ....
6. It's twenty-five to eleven. ....
7. It's one o'clock in the morning. ....
8. It's midnight. ....

2 Present continuous Wh-questions (page 33)

▶ Use the present continuous to talk about actions that are happening right now: What **are** you **doing**? I**'m talking** to you!
▶ In questions, the *be* verb comes before the subject: What **are you** doing?
▶ To form the continuous of verbs ending in –*e*, drop the *e* and add –*ing*: have → having.
▶ For verbs ending in vowel + consonant, double the consonant and add –*ing*: get → getting.

What are the people doing? Write conversations. Use the words in parentheses.

1. A: What's Steve doing? (Steve)
   B: He's watching TV. (watch TV)
2. A: .... (Jon and Megan)
   B: .... (take a walk)
3. A: .... (you)
   B: .... (write conversations)
4. A: .... (Chris)
   B: .... (call Ashley)
5. A: .... (you and Taylor)
   B: .... (shop)
6. A: .... (Sara)
   B: .... (have dinner)
7. A: .... (Victor and Sam)
   B: .... (run in the park)
8. A: .... (you and Paulo)
   B: .... (chat online)

Unit 6

1 Simple present statements (page 37) and Simple present statements with irregular verbs (page 38)

> ▶ In affirmative statements, verbs with he/she/it end in –s: He/She **walks** to school. BUT I/You/We/They **walk** to school.
>
> ▶ In negative statements, use *doesn't* with he/she/it and *don't* with all the others: He/She/It **doesn't** live here. I/You/We/They **don't** live here.
>
> ▶ Don't add –s to the verb: She **doesn't live** here. (NOT: ~~She doesn't lives here.~~)

Elena is talking about her family. Complete the sentences with the correct form of the verbs in parentheses.

My family and I ....*live*........ (live) in the city. We .... (have) an apartment on First Avenue. My sister .... (go) to school near our apartment, so she .... (walk) to school. My father .... (work) in the suburbs, so he .... (drive) to his job. My mother .... (use) public transportation – she .... (take) the bus to her office downtown. She .... (have) a new job, but she .... (not like) it very much. And me? Well, I .... (not work) far from our apartment, so I .... (not need) a car or public transportation. I .... (ride) my bike to work!

2 Simple present questions (page 39)

> ▶ In questions, use *does* with he/she/it and *do* with all the others: **Does** he/she/it get up early? **Do** I/you/we/they get up early?
>
> ▶ Don't add –s to the verb: Does she **live** alone? (NOT: ~~Does she lives alone?~~)

A Write questions to complete the conversations.

1. A: *Do you use public transportation?* ....
   B: Yes, I use public transportation.
2. A: ....
   B: No, my family doesn't eat dinner at 5:00.
3. A: ....
   B: No, my brother doesn't take the bus to work.
4. A: ....
   B: No, I don't get up late on weekends.

> ▶ Use *in* with *the morning/afternoon/evening*. Use *at* with *night*: I go to school **in** the afternoon and work **at** night.
>
> ▶ Use *at* with clock times: She gets up **at** 8:00
>
> ▶ Use *on* with days: He sleeps late **on** weekends. She has class **on** Mondays.

B Complete the conversation with *at, in,* or *on.*

A: Does your family have breakfast together ....*in*........ the morning?
B: Well, we eat together .... weekends, but .... weekdays we're all busy. My parents go to work early – .... 6:30. But we eat dinner together .... the evening, and we have a big lunch together .... Sundays. We eat .... noon. Then .... the afternoon, we play tennis or go to the movies.

Unit 7

1 Simple present short answers (page 45)

▶ Remember: I/You/We/They **do/don't**. He/She/It **does/doesn't**.

Circle the correct words.

A: **Do / Does** your family **live / lives** in an apartment?

B: No, we **don't / doesn't**. We **have / has** a house.

A: That's nice. **Do / Does** your house have two floors?

B: Yes, it **do / does**. It **have / has** four rooms on the first floor. And we **have / has** three bedrooms and a bathroom on the second floor.

A: And **do / does** you and your family **have / has** a yard?

B: Yes, we **do / does**. And how about you, Tim? **Do / Does** you **live / lives** in a house, too?

A: No, I **don't / doesn't**. My wife and I **have / has** a small apartment in the city.

B: Oh. **Do / Does** you **like / likes** the city?

A: Yes, I **do / does**. But my wife **don't / doesn't**.

2 *There is, there are* (page 47)

▶ Use *there is* with singular nouns: **There's** a bed. Use *there are* with plural nouns: **There are** two chairs.
▶ Use *some* in affirmative statements: There are **some** chairs in the kitchen. Use *any* in negative statements: There aren't **any** chairs in the bedroom.

Read the information about the Diaz family's new house. Write sentences with the phrases in the box.

there's a	there are some
there's no	there are no
there isn't a	there aren't any

1. A living room?   Yes
2. A dining room?   No
3. A dishwasher in the kitchen? No
4. A table in the kitchen?   Yes
5. Curtains on the windows?   Yes
6. Rugs on the floors?   No
7. Closets in the bedrooms?   Yes
8. Bookcases in the bedrooms?   No

1. There's a living room. ....
2. ....
3. ....
4. ....
5. ....
6. ....
7. ....
8. ....

Unit 8

1 Simple present Wh-questions (page 52)

▶ Use *What* to ask about things: **What do** you do? Use *Where* to ask about places: **Where do** you work? Use *How do/does . . . like . . . ?* to ask for an opinion: **How does** he **like** his job?

Complete the conversations.

1. A: What *does your husband do* ?
   B: My husband? Oh, he's a nurse.
   A: Really? Where .... ?
   B: He works at Mercy Hospital.
2. A: Where .... ?
   B: I work in a restaurant.
   A: Nice! What .... ?
   B: I'm a cook.
3. A: How .... ?
   B: My job? I don't really like it very much.
   A: That's too bad. What .... ?
   B: I'm a manager. I work at a clothing store.
4. A: What .... ?
   B: My brother is a doctor, and my sister is a lawyer.
   A: How .... ?
   B: They work very hard, but they love their jobs.

2 Placement of adjectives (page 54)

▶ Adjectives come after the verb *be*: A doctor's job **is stressful**. Adjectives come before nouns: A police officer has a **dangerous job**. (NOT: A police officer has a job dangerous.)
▶ Adjectives have the same form with singular or plural nouns: Firefighters and police officers have stressful jobs. (NOT . . . have stressfuls jobs.)

Use the information to write two sentences.

1. accountant / job / boring
   An accountant's job is boring.
   An accountant has a boring job.
2. salesperson / job / stressful
   ....
   ....
3. security guard / job / dangerous
   ....
   ....
4. nurse / job / exciting
   ....
   ....
5. taxi driver / job / interesting
   ....
   ....
6. electrician / job / difficult
   ....
   ....

Unit 9

1 Count and noncount nouns; *some* and *any* (page 59)

> ▶ Count nouns name things you can count: *vegetables, eggs, cookies.* Count nouns
> have a singular and plural form: *1 **book**, 2 **books**.* Noncount nouns name things
> you can't count: *water, spinach, cheese.*
> ▶ Use *some* in affirmative sentences: We have **some** chicken. Use *any* in negative
> sentences and questions: We don't have **any** bread. Do we have **any** cheese?

Complete the conversations with *some* or *any*.

1. A: What do you want for lunch?
    B: Let's make .....*some*..... sandwiches.
    A: Good idea! Do we have .... bread?
    B: I think there's .... in the refrigerator. Let me see. . . . No, I don't
       see ....
    A: Well, let's go to the store. We need .... milk, too. And do we have
       .... cheese?
    B: Yes, we do. There's .... cheese here, and there are ....
       tomatoes, too.
    A: Do we have .... mayonnaise? I love .... mayonnaise on
       my sandwiches.
    B: Me, too. But there isn't .... here. Let's buy ....
2. A: Let's make a big breakfast tomorrow morning.
    B: OK. What do we need? Are there .... eggs?
    A: There are .... , but I think we need to buy .... more.
    B: OK. And let's get .... yogurt, too. We don't have .... , and I
       love yogurt for breakfast.
    A: Me, too. Do you see .... bread in the refrigerator?
    B: Yes, there's .... in the refrigerator.
    A: Great! So we don't need to buy .... at the store.
    B: That's right. Just eggs and yogurt!

2 Adverbs of frequency (page 61)

> ▶ Adverbs of frequency usually go before the main verb: *always, almost always,
> usually, often, sometimes, hardly ever, almost never, never*: She **never plays** tennis.
> I **almost always eat** breakfast. *Sometimes* can begin a sentence: **Sometimes** I
> **eat** breakfast.

Rewrite the conversation. Add the adverbs in the correct places.

A: Where do you have lunch? (usually)　　A: Where do you usually have lunch? ....

B: I go to a restaurant near work. (often)　B: ....

A: Do you eat at your desk? (ever)　　　A: ....

B: No, I stay in for lunch. (hardly ever)　B: ....

A: And what do you have? (usually)　　A: ....

B: I have soup and a sandwich. (always)　B: ....

A: Me, too. I have a big lunch. (never)　A: ....

Unit 10

1 Simple present Wh-questions (page 65)

▶ Remember: *who = what person; where = what place; how often = what frequency; when = what days; what time = what time of day*
▶ Remember: use *do* or *does* after the question word.

Complete the questions with the correct question word and *do* or *does*. Then match the questions with the answers.

1. ....*What*.... sports ....*do*........ you like? ———— a. My father and my brother.
2. .... you go to games with? b. Usually at three o'clock.
3. .... often .... your team play? c. Baseball. I love to watch my team.
4. .... they play? d. Once a week.
5. .... they play? e. On Saturday afternoons.
6. .... time .... the games start? f. At Lincoln Park.

2 *Can* for ability (page 67)

▶ Use the base form of the verb with *can*. With third-person singular, don't add an *–s* to *can* or to the base form: She **can play** the piano. (NOT: ~~She can plays the piano.~~)

A Write sentences about the things people can and can't do. Use *can* or *can't* with *and, but,* or *or.* (✓ = can, ✗ = can't)

1. Sally: ride a bike ✓   drive a car ✗
   Sally can ride a bike, but she can't drive a car.
2. John: play the piano ✓   play the violin ✓
   ....
3. Brad and George: act ✓   sing ✗
   ....
4. Maria: snowboard ✓   ice-skate ✗
   ....
5. Justin: upload photos ✗   download a video ✗
   ....
6. Lisa: write poems ✗   tell good jokes ✓
   ....

B Look at part A. Answer the questions. Write short sentences.

1. Can Brad and George sing? No, they can't.
2. Who can tell good jokes? ....
3. Can Sally drive a car? ....
4. Can John play the piano? ....
5. Who can snowboard? ....
6. What can George do? ....

Unit 11

1 The future with *be going to* (page 73)

> ▶ Use *am/is/are* + *going to* + base form for the future: We**'re going to stay** home tonight.
>
> ▶ In questions with *be going to*, the *be* verb comes before the noun or pronoun: **Is he going to bake** me a cake?

A Complete Robert's story. Use the correct form of *be going to* and the verbs in parentheses.

Tomorrow ...*is going to be*... (be) a very exciting day. It's my birthday, and my friends and I .... (celebrate). In the morning, Scott and I .... (drive) to the beach. Our friend Sara .... (meet) us there. We .... (stay) at the beach for a few hours. Then we .... (have) lunch at my favorite restaurant. After lunch, Scott .... (go) to work, and Sara and I .... (see) a movie. After the movie, we .... (go) to our friend Charlie's house. He .... (cook) dinner for Sara and me.

B Write questions. Then look at part A and answer the questions.

1. Robert / celebrate / with his family?
   Q: *Is Robert going to celebrate with his family?* ....
   A: *No, he's going to celebrate with his friends.* ....
2. Scott and Robert / take the bus / to the beach?
   Q: ....
   A: ....
3. the friends / have lunch / at a restaurant?
   Q: ....
   A: ....
4. Sara and Robert / go to a museum?
   Q: ....
   A: ....
5. Sara and Robert / have dinner / at a restaurant?
   Q: ....
   A: ....

2 Wh-questions with *be going to* (page 75)

> ▶ Use *is* in questions with *Who* as the subject: **Who's** going to be there? (NOT: ~~Who are going to be there?~~)

Complete the conversation with the correct form of *be going to*.

A: What ....*are*.......... you ....*going to do*.... (do) this weekend?
B: I .... (have) a very busy weekend. My friend Ali .... (visit) me, and we .... (spend) the weekend in the city.
A: That's nice. .... you .... (stay) in a hotel?
B: No, we .... (stay) with our friend Donna. And Donna .... (have) a big party on Saturday night.
A: Really? And who .... (be) at the party? Do you know any of Donna's friends?
B: No, I don't. But Ali and I .... (meet) everyone on Saturday night.

Unit 12

1 *Have* + noun; *feel* + adjective (page 79)

▶ For most health problems, use *a/an*: I have **a** cold. I have **an** earache. With *flu*, use *the*: I have **the** flu. (NOT: ~~I have a flu.~~)

Complete the conversation. Use the sentences in the box.

> I think I have a fever.
> Thanks.
> I feel awful, actually.
> Yes. I'm going to call my doctor in a few minutes.
> Yes, I do. And I have a stomachache, too.
> ✓ Hi, Chris. How are you?

A: Hi, Chris. How are you?
B: I'm terrific, thanks. How about you?
A: ....
B: Oh, no! What's the matter?
A: ....
B: That's too bad. Do you have a headache?
A: ....
B: Are you going to see a doctor?
A: ....
B: Well, feel better soon.
A: ....

2 Imperatives (page 82)

▶ Use the base form of the verb in affirmative imperatives: **Go** home and **rest**, Pat.
▶ Use *don't* + base form of the verb in negative imperatives. The form doesn't change: **Don't go** to school today, Pat.

Read the situations. Give the people advice. Use the phrases in the box.

> ✓ drink coffee in the afternoon
> eat any cold food
> exercise today or tomorrow
> take an antacid
> take two aspirins
> work too hard

1. Dan can't sleep at night. Don't drink coffee in the afternoon.
2. Casey has a headache. ....
3. Kristina works 12 hours a day. ....
4. Michael has sore muscles. ....
5. Min-ho has a toothache. ....
6. Laila has an awful stomachache. ....

Unit 13

1 Prepositions of place (page 88)

> ▶ Use *on* with the names of streets and avenues: The bookstore is **on** Center Street. The theater is **on** Park Avenue.
> ▶ *Across from* is another way of saying *opposite*: The library is **across from** the theater. = The library is **opposite** the theater.

Circle the correct words.

A: Excuse me. Is there a gas station around here?
B: Yes, there is. It's **in** / **on** Third Avenue.
A: Where on Third Avenue?
B: It's **in** / **on** the corner of Center Street and Third Avenue.
A: Across **from** / **to** Stacy's Department Store?
B: Yes, that's right. It's next **to** / **from** the park.
A: Thanks. Oh, and where is the post office?
B: It's on Center Street – **between** / **next to** the hospital and the bank.
A: Great. Thanks very much.
B: You're welcome.

2 Directions (page 90)

> ▶ *Walk up/Go up* mean the same. *Walk down/Go* down also mean the same.

Bob doesn't know the city at all. Correct Bob's directions. Write the opposite of what he says.

1. Dan: How do I get to the library?
   Bob: Walk up Park Avenue.
   You: *No, don't walk up Park Avenue. Walk down Park Avenue.*
2. Dan: How can I get to the park?
   Bob: Turn right on Main Street.
   You: ....
3. Dan: How do I get to the post office?
   Bob: Go down First Avenue.
   You: ....
   Bob: It's on the left.
   You: ....

Unit 14

1 Simple past statements: regular verbs and irregular verbs (pages 93–94)

▶ Use simple past verbs to talk about the past. Regular verbs end in *–ed*: I **watched** TV last night. For verbs ending in *–e*, add *–d*: *live → lived*. For verbs ending in vowel + consonant, double the consonant and add *–ed*: shop → shopped.

▶ Use *didn't* + base form in negative statements. The form doesn't change: He **didn't shop** for groceries yesterday. (NOT: ~~He didn't shopped for groceries yesterday.~~)

Daniela wrote an email to a friend. Complete the sentences with the simple past form of the verbs in parentheses.

Hi!

I .....*didn't do*..... (not do) anything special this weekend, but I .... (have) a lot of fun. I .... (not go) out on Friday night. I .... (stay) home. I .... (clean) my room and .... (do) laundry. I .... (help) my sister with her homework, and then we .... (watch) TV. On Saturday, my friend Taylor .... (come) over. She .... (need) some new shoes, so we .... (take) the bus downtown to Harry's Shoe Store. We .... (shop) for a long time, but Taylor .... (not like) any of the shoes at Harry's. She .... (buy) some purple socks, but she .... (not buy) any shoes. On our way back to my house, we .... (stop) at the gym and .... (exercise). We .... (not exercise) very hard. I .... (invite) Taylor for dinner, and my dad .... (cook) hamburgers in the yard. After dinner, Taylor and I .... (talk) and .... (play) video games. She .... (not stay) very late – Mom .... (drive) her home at around ten. On Sunday, my whole family .... (visit) my mother's best friend and her family. They have a swimming pool, so my sister and I .... (go) swimming all afternoon.

Tell me about your weekend!

2 Simple past yes/no questions (page 95)

▶ Use *did* + base form in questions. The form doesn't change: **Did** you **have** fun yesterday? (NOT: ~~Did you had fun yesterday?~~)

Complete the conversation. Use the simple past form of the verbs in parentheses.

A: ......*Did*...... you .....*enjoy*..... (enjoy) your vacation?

B: Yes, I .... My brother and I .... (have) a great time.

A: .... you .... (take) a lot of pictures?

B: No, we .... But we .... (buy) a lot of postcards.

A: That's good. .... you .... (see) a lot of interesting things?

B: Yes, we .... And we .... (eat) a lot of new foods.

A: How about you? .... you .... (have) a good summer?

B: Well, I .... (not go) anywhere, but I .... (read) a lot of good books and .... (see) some great movies.

Unit 15

1 Past of *be* (page 101)

> Present   Past
> am/is   →   **was**
> are   →   **were**

Complete the conversations with *was, wasn't, were,* or *weren't.*

1. A: ......Were...... you here yesterday?
   B: No, I .... I .... home in bed.
   A: Oh, ... you sick?
   B: No. I .... just really tired.
2. A: Where .... you born?
   B: I .... born here in New York.
   A: Really? What about your parents? .... they born here, too?
   B: No, they .... They .... born in Brazil – in Salvador.
3. A: Where .... Yusef last week? .... he on vacation?
   B: Yes, he .... He and his best friend .... in Spain. They ....
   in Barcelona.
   A: .... it a good trip?
   B: Yes, it was. Yusef said it .... a terrific trip!

2 Wh-questions with *did, was,* and *were* (page 103)

> Don't use *did* with the past of *be*: Where **were** you last Tuesday? (NOT: ~~Where did you were last Tuesday?~~) Use *did* in simple past questions with other verbs: Where **did** you **go** last Tuesday?
> *Because* answers the question *Why?*

Complete the questions. Use the words in the box.

> ✓ how   what   where   why
> how old   when   who

1. A: ......How...... was your childhood?
   B: I had a fantastic childhood!
2. A: .... did you grow up?
   B: I grew up in Dallas, Texas.
3. A: .... were you when you started school?
   B: I think I was five.
4. A: .... did you leave home?
   B: In 2008.
5. A: .... was your best friend in high school?
   B: My best friend was a girl named Alice.
6. A: .... was your first job?
   B: I worked as a server in a restaurant.
7. A: .... did you leave Dallas?
   B: Because I wanted to live in a small city.

Unit 16

1 Subject and object pronouns (page 107)

▶ Subject pronouns usually come before verbs, and object pronouns go after verbs: **I** saw **him**, but **he** didn't see **me**.

A Complete the conversations.

1. A: Hello. Is Mr. Chin there?
   B: No, ...*he's*.... not here right now. Can .... take a message?
   A: Yes. Please tell .... to call Rob Taylor.
   B: Does .... have your number?
   A: No, but please give it to .... It's 555-0987.
2. A: Hi. This is Eliza. Is Maria home?
   B: No, ... at the mall with her brother. Their dad drove .... there this morning.
   A: Oh. Well, can I leave .... a message?
   B: Sure.
   A: Sonia and I are going to see a movie tomorrow. Maybe Maria can go with ....
   B: I can ask .... And she can call .... tonight.

2 Invitations; verb + *to* (page 109)

▶ You can use both *Do you want to . . . ?* and *Would you like to . . . ?* to invite a person to do something.
▶ Don't confuse *would like to* with *like to*. *Would like to* means the same as *want to*.
▶ *I'd (really) like to* and *I'd love to* both mean the same as *I want to*.

Rewrite the conversations. Write the sentences in a different way.

1. A: <u>Do you want</u> to see a movie tonight?
   B: Oh, I can't. I <u>need</u> to work.

   A: <u>Would you like to see a movie tonight?</u>
   B: ....

2. A: <u>Do you want</u> to play tennis on Saturday?
   B: <u>I'd love</u> to, but I <u>have</u> to help my parents.

   A: ....
   B: ....

3. A: I <u>want</u> a job at Mike's store.
   B: You <u>need</u> to speak to him.

   A: ....
   B: ....

4. A: <u>Would you like</u> to go to a party with me?
   B: <u>I want</u> to, but I can't. I <u>have</u> to study.

   A: ....
   B: ....

Grammar plus answer key

Unit 1

1 My, your, his, her

1. B: Hi, Carlos. What's **your** last name?
   A: It's Gonzales.
   B: How do you spell **your** last name?
   Is it G-O-N-Z-A-L-E-Z?
   A: No, it's G-O-N-Z-A-L-E-S. And what's **your** name?
   B: **My** name is Bill Powers. Nice to meet you.
2. A: What's Ms. Robinson's first name?
   B: **Her** first name is Katherine. **Her** nickname is Katie.
   A: I'm sorry. What's **her** first name again?
   B: It's Katherine. And what's Mr. Weber's first name?
   A: **His** first name is Peter.
   B: That's right. And his nickname is Pete.

2 The verb be

1. A: Excuse me. **Are** you Patty Wilson?
   B: No, **I'm not**. **She's** over there.
   A: OK. Thanks.
2. A: Hi. Are **you** Patty Wilson?
   C: Yes, **I am**.
   A: Oh, good. **I'm** Sergio Baez. **You're** in my English class.
   C: Yes, I **am**. **It's** nice to meet you, Sergio.

Unit 2

1 This/these; it/they; plurals

1. A: **What are** these?
   B: **They're** my **earrings**.
2. A: **What's** this?
   B: **It's a** cell phone.
3. A: What's **this**?
   B: **It's an** address book.

2 Yes/No and *where* questions with *be*

A

2. e   3. a   4. b   5. d

B

B: I don't know. Is **it** in your book bag?
A: No, **it's** not.
B: Is **this** your pen?
A: Yes, **it is**. Thanks! Now, **where** are my keys?
B: **Are they** on your desk?
A: Yes, **they are**. Thank you!

Unit 3

1 Negative statements and yes/no questions with *be*

A

2. We're not from London.
3. You and Tim are not in my class.
4. Spanish is not my first language./My first language is not Spanish.
5. My mother is not from Seoul.
6. They are not my keys.

B

1. B: No, **we're** not. **We're** from Guatemala.
2. A: **Is** your first language English?
   B: Yes, it **is**. My parents **are** from Australia.
3. A: **Are** Kenji and his friend Japanese?
   B: Yes, **they** are. But **they're / they are** in the U.S. now.
4. A: **Are** my mother and I late?
   B: No, **you're** not. **You're** early!

2 Wh-questions with *be*

2. **What** is her name? c
3. **What** is she like? f
4. **How** old is she? b
5. **Where** is your family from? a
6. **What** is Bangkok like? e

Unit 4

1 Possessives

1. A: **Whose** jacket is this? Is it **yours**, Phil?
   B: No, it's not **mine**. Ask Nick. I think it's **his**.
2. A: These aren't **our** books. Are they **yours**?
   B: No, they're not **ours**. Maybe they're Young-min's.
3. A: **Whose** sweaters are these? Are they Julie's?
   B: No, they're not **her** sweaters. But these shorts are **hers**.

2 Present continuous statements; conjunctions

2. It's raining.
3. I'm not wearing sunglasses.
4. You're not / You aren't wearing a new suit.
5. Michiko is wearing gloves.

3 Present continuous yes/no questions

1. B: No, he's **not** / he **isn't**.
2. A: Are you wearing brown boots?
   B: No, we**'re not** / we **aren't**.
3. A: Are you wearing sunglasses?
   B: Yes, I **am**.
4. A: Is it raining?
   B: Yes, it **is**.

Unit 5

1 What time is it? / Is it A.M. or P.M.?

3. It's a quarter after six.
4. It's 10:00 P.M.
5. It's five after three.
6. It's eleven thirty-five
7. It's one A.M.
8. It's 12:00 A.M.

2 Present continuous Wh-questions

2. A: What are Jon and Megan doing?
   B: They're taking a walk.
3. A: What are you doing?
   B: I'm writing conversations.
4. A: What's Chris doing?
   B: He's calling Ashley.
5. A: What are you and Taylor doing?
   B: We're shopping.
6. A: What's Sara doing?
   B: She's having dinner
7. A: What are Victor and Sam doing?
   B: They're running in the park.
8. A: What are you and Paulo doing?
   B: We're chatting online.

Unit 6

1 Simple present statements; Simple present statements with irregular verbs

My family and I **live** in the city. We **have** an apartment on First Avenue. My sister **goes** to school near our apartment, so she **walks** to school. My father **works** in the suburbs, so he **drives** to his job. My mother **uses** public transportation – she **takes** the bus to her office downtown. She **has** a new job, but she **doesn't like** it very much. And me? Well, I **don't work** far from our apartment, so I **don't need** a car or public transportation. I **ride** my bike to work!

2 Simple present questions

A

2. A: Does your family eat dinner at 5:00?
3. A: Does your brother take the bus to work?
4. A: Do you get up late on weekends?

B

B: Well, we eat together **on** weekends, but **on** weekdays we're all busy. My parents go to work early – **at** 6:30. But we eat dinner together **in** the evening, and we have a big lunch together **on** Sundays. We eat **at** noon. Then **in** the afternoon, we play tennis or go to the movies.

Unit 7

1 Simple present short answers

A: **Does** your family **live** in an apartment?
B: No, we **don't**. We **have** a house.
A: That's nice. **Does** your house have two floors?
B: Yes, it **does**. It **has** four rooms on the first floor. And we **have** three bedrooms and a bathroom on the second floor.
A: And **do** you and your family **have** a yard?
B: Yes, we **do**. And how about you, Tim? **Do you live** in a house, too?
A: No, I **don't**. My wife and I **have** a small apartment in the city.
B: Oh. **Do you like** the city?
A: Yes, I **do**. But my wife **doesn't**.

2 There is, there are

2. There's no dining room. / There isn't a dining room.
3. There's no dishwasher in the kitchen. / There isn't a dishwasher in the kitchen.
4. There's a table in the kitchen.
5. There are some curtains on the windows.
6. There are no / There aren't any rugs on the floors.
7. There are closets in the bedrooms.
8. There are no / There aren't any bookcases in the bedroom.

Unit 8

1 Simple present Wh-questions

1. A: Really? Where **does he work**?
2. A: Where **do you work**?
   B: I work in a restaurant.
   A: Nice! What **do you do**?
   B: I'm a cook.
3. A: How **do you like your job**?
   B: My job? I don't really like it very much.
   A: That's too bad. What **do you do**?
   B: I'm a manager. I work at a clothing store.
4. A: What **do your brother and sister do**?
   B: My brother is a doctor, and my sister is a lawyer.
   A: How **do they like their jobs**?

2 Placement of adjectives

2. A salesperson's job is stressful.
   A salesperson has a stressful job.
3. A security guard's job is dangerous.
   A security guard has a dangerous job.
4. A nurse's job is exciting.
   A nurse has an exciting job.
5. A taxi driver's job is interesting.
   A taxi driver has an interesting job.
6. An electrician's job is difficult.
   An electrician has a difficult job.

Unit 9

1 Count and noncount nouns; *some* and *any*

1. A: What do you want for lunch?
    B: Let's make **some** sandwiches.
    A: Good idea! Do we have **any** bread?
    B: I think there's **some** in the refrigerator. Let me see. . . . No, I don't see **any**.
    A: Well, let's go to the store. We need **some** milk, too. And do we have **any** cheese?
    B: Yes, we do. There's **some** cheese here, and there are **some** tomatoes, too.
    A: Do we have **any** mayonnaise? I love **some** mayonnaise on my sandwiches.
    B: Me, too. But there isn't **any** here. Let's buy **some**.
2. A: Let's make a big breakfast tomorrow morning.
    B: OK. What do we need? Are there **any** eggs?
    A: There are **some**, but I think we need to buy **some** more.
    B: OK. And let's get **some** yogurt, too. We don't have **any**, and I love yogurt for breakfast.
    A: Me, too. Do you see **any** bread in the refrigerator?
    B: Yes there's **some** in the refrigerator.
    A: Great! So we don't need to buy **any** at the store.
    B: That's right. Just eggs and yogurt!

2 Adverbs of frequency

B: I **often** go to a restaurant near work.
A: Do you **ever** eat at your desk?
B: No, I **hardly ever** stay in for lunch.
A: And what do you **usually** have?
B: I **always** have soup and a sandwich.
A: Me, too. I **never** have a big lunch.

Unit 10

1 Simple present Wh-questions

2. **Who do** you go to games with? a
3. **How** often **does** your team play? d
4. **When do** they play? e
5. **Where do** they play? f
6. **What** time **do** the games start? b

2 *Can* for ability

A

2. John can play the piano and the violin.
3. Brad and George can act, but they can't sing.
4. Maria can snowboard, but she can't ice skate.
5. Justin can't upload photos or download a video.
6. Lisa can't write poems but she can tell good jokes.

B

2. Lisa can.   4. Yes, he can.   6. He can act.
3. Yes, she can.   5. Maria can.

Unit 11

1 The future with *be going to*

1. Tomorrow **is going to be** a very exciting day. It's my birthday, and my friends and I **are going to celebrate**. In the morning, Scott and I **are going to drive** to the beach. Our friend Sara **is going to meet** us there. We**'re going to stay** at the beach for a few hours. Then we**'re going to have** lunch at my favorite restaurant. After lunch, Scott **is going to go** to work, and Sara and I **are going to see** a movie. After the movie, we**'re going to go** to our friend Charlie's house. He **is going to cook** dinner for Sara and me.
2. Q: Are Scott and Robert going to take the bus to the beach?
    A: No, they're going to drive to the beach.
4. Q: Are the friends going to have lunch at a restaurant?
    A: Yes, they are.
5. Q: Are Sara and Robert going to go to a museum?
    A: No, they're not. (They're going to see a movie.)
6. Q: Are Sara and Robert going to have dinner at a restaurant?
    A: No, they're not. (They're going to have dinner at Charlie's house.)

2 Wh-questions with *be going to*

A: What **are** you **going to do** this weekend?
B: I**'m going to have** a very busy weekend. My friend Ali **is going to visit** me, and we**'re going to spend** the weekend in the city.
A: That's nice. **Are** you **going to stay** in a hotel?
B: No, we**'re going to stay** with our friend Donna. And Donna **is going to have** a big party on Saturday night.
A: Really? And who**'s going to be** at the party? Do you know any of Donna's friends?
B: No, I don't. But Ali and I **are going to meet** everyone on Saturday night.

Unit 12

1 *Have* + noun; *feel* + adjective

A: **Hi, Chris. How are you?**
B: I'm terrific, thanks. How about you?
A: **I feel awful, actually.**
B: Oh, no! What's the matter?
A: **I think I have a fever.**
B: That's too bad. Do you have a headache?
A: **Yes, I do. And I have a stomachache, too.**
B: Are you going to see a doctor?
A: **Yes. I'm going to call my doctor in a few minutes.**
B: Well, feel better soon.
A: **Thanks.**

2 Imperatives

2. Take two aspirins.
3. Don't work too hard.
4. Don't exercise today or tomorrow.
5. Don't eat any cold food.
6. Take an antacid.

Unit 13

1 Prepositions of place

A: Excuse me. Is there a gas station around here?
B: Yes, there is. It's **on** Third Avenue.
A: Where on Third Avenue?
B: It's **on** the corner of Center Street and Third Avenue.
A: Across **from** Stacy's Department Store?
B: Yes, that's right. It's next **to** the park.
A: Thanks. Oh, and where is the post office?
B: It's on Center Street – **between** the hospital and the bank.

2 Directions

2. You: No, don't turn right on Main Street. Turn left on Main Street.
3. You: No, don't go down First Avenue. Go up First Avenue
   You: No, it's not on the left. It's on the right.

Unit 14

1 Simple past statements: regular verbs and irregular verbs

Hi!
I **didn't do** anything special this weekend, but I **had** a lot of fun. I **didn't go** out on Friday night. I **stayed** home. I **cleaned** my room and **did** laundry. I **helped** my sister with her homework, and then we **watched** TV. On Saturday, my friend Taylor **came** over. She **needed** some new shoes, so we **took** the bus downtown to Harry's Shoe Store. We **shopped** for a long time, but Taylor **didn't like** any of the shoes at Harry's. She **bought** some purple socks, but she **didn't buy** any shoes. On our way back to my house, we **stopped** at the gym and **exercised**. We **didn't exercise** very hard. I **invited** Taylor for dinner, and my dad **cooked** hamburgers in the yard. After dinner, Taylor and I **talked** and **played** video games. She **didn't stay** too late – Mom **drove** her home at around ten. On Sunday, my whole family **visited** my mother's best friend and her family. They have a swimming pool, so my sister and I **went** swimming all afternoon.

2 Simple past yes/no questions

A: **Did** you **enjoy** your vacation?
B: Yes, I **did**. My brother and I **had** a great time.
A: **Did** you **take** a lot of pictures?
B: No, we **didn't**. But we **bought** a lot of postcards.
A: That's good. **Did** you **see** a lot of interesting things?

B: Yes, we **did**. And we **ate** a lot of new foods.
A: How about you? **Did** you **have** a good summer?
B: Well, I **didn't go** anywhere, but I **read** a lot of good books and **saw** some great movies.

Unit 15

1 Past of *be*

1. A: **Were** you here yesterday?
   B: No, I **wasn't**. I **was** home in bed.
   A: Oh, **were** you sick?
   B: No. I **was** just really tired.
2. A: Where **were** you born?
   B: I **was** born here in New York.
   A: Really? What about your parents? **Were** they born here, too?
   B: No, they **weren't**. They **were** born in Brazil – in Salvador.
3. A: Where **was** Yusef last week? **Was** he on vacation?
   B: Yes, he **was**. He and his best friend **were** in Spain. They **were** in Barcelona.
   A: **Was** it a good trip?
   B: Yes, it was. Yusef said it **was** a terrific trip!

2 Wh-questions with *did*, *was*, and *were*

2. A: Where
3. A: How old
4. A: When
5. A: Who
6. A: What
7. A: Why

Unit 16

1 Subject and object pronouns

1. A: Hello. Is Mr. Chin there?
   B: No, **he's** not here right now. Can **I** take a message?
   A: Yes. Please tell **him** to call Rob Taylor.
   B: Does **he** have your number?
   A: No, but please give it to **him**. It's 555-0987.
2. A: Hi. This is Eliza. Is Maria home?
   B: No, **she's** at the mall with her brother. Their dad drove **them** there this morning.
   A: Oh. Well, can I leave **her** a message?
   B: Sure.
   A: Sonia and I are going to see a movie tomorrow. Maybe Maria can go with **us**.
   B: I can ask **her**. And she can call **you** tonight.

2 Invitations; verb + *to*

1. B: Oh, I can't. I **have** to work.
2. A: **Would you like** to play tennis on Saturday?
   B: **I'd like** to, but I **need** to help my parents.
3. A: **I'd like** a job at Mike's store.
   B: You **have** to speak to him.
4. A: **Do you want** to go to a party with me?
   B: **I'd like** to, but I can't. I **need** to study.

Credits

Illustrations

Andrezzinho: 4, 7, 50, 119; **Ilias Arahovitis**: 14, 15 (*top*), 31 (*top*), 60 (*top*), 88 (*bottom*); **Ralph Butler**: 11, 13, 87; **Mark Collins**: v, 52; **Paul Daviz**; 19, 38, 59, 66, 67, 72, 79 (*top*), 106, 108, 110; **Carlos Diaz**: 42, 82, 120, 124; **Tim Foley**: 12; **Travis Foster**: 41 (*bottom*); *Chuck Gonzales*: 9, 27, 75, 92 (*bottom*), 100, 102; **Jeff Grunewald**: 56; **Jim Haynes**: 21, 32, 36 (*bottom*), 37, 44 (*bottom*), 45, 47, 53 (*bottom*), 81, 95; **Dan Hubig**: 31 (*center*); **Randy Jones**: 22, 29, 61; **Trevor Keen**: 33, 74; **Joanna Kerr**: 24, 68; **KJA-artists**: 122; **Bruce MacPherson**: 51; **Monika Melynchuk**: 121; **Karen Minot**: 40, 60 (*bottom*), 64 (*top*), 90, 91; **Wally Neibart**: 88 (*top*); **Ortelius Design**: 30 (*top*); **Rob Schuster**: 25 (*top*), 35, 44 (*top*), 69, 97, 118, 127, 128; **Daniel Vasconcellos**: 30 (*bottom*), 85, 94; **Brad Walker**: 2, 3, 5, 6; **Sam Whitehead**: 16 (*bottom*), 23, 25 (*bottom*), 64 (*bottom*), 89 (*bottom*), 114, 116-117; **James Yamasaki**: 15 (*bottom*), 26, 79 (*bottom*), 101, 115: **Rose Zgodzinski**: 41(*top*), 43, 55, 77, 111, 131; **Carol Zuber-Mallison**: 49, 63, 105, 125

Photos

2 (*left*) © Andrew H. Walker/Staff/Getty Images; (*right*) © Michael Buckner/Staff/Getty Images **8** (*all, top*) © Ken Karp Photography; (*bottom, clockwise*) © Deb Lindsey/The Washington Post/Getty Images; © Joseelias/Veer; © Hemera/Thinkstock; © Gunnar3000/Veer; © iStockphoto/Thinkstock **9** (*middle, left to right*) © iStockphoto/Thinkstock; © Helene Rogers/Art Directors & TRIP/Alamy; © Slobo/iStockphoto; © Comstock/Thinkstock; © Clubfoto/iStockphoto; (*bottom, left to right*) © Handout/MCT/Newscom; © Tiridifilm/iStockphoto; © iStockphoto/Thinkstock; © Alloy Photography/Veer **10** (*all, top*) © Erin Garvey/Getty Images; © Ljupco Smokovski/Fotolia; (*clockwise, middle*) © Valkh/Fotolia; © Antenna Audio, Inc./Getty Images; © Pedro/Veer; © Hemera/Thinkstock; © Hemera/Thinkstock; © Igor Groshev/Fotolia; (*bottom, left to right*) © iStockphoto/Thinkstock; © Ibphoto/Veer **12** (*middle, clockwise*) © Hemera/Thinkstock; © Sergej/Veer; © Sergey Zvyagintsev/Fotolia; © Huimin/Fotolia; © WestLight/iStockphoto; © Stockbyte/Thinkstock; © Hemera/Thinkstock; © Witthaya/iStockphoto; © Kondor83/Fotolia; © PhotoObjects.net/Thinkstock **17** (*top to bottom*) © Steve Vidler/SuperStock; © Imagebroker.net/SuperStock **18** (*left to right*) © Eamonn McCormack/WireImage/Getty Images; © Jon Furniss/WireImage/Getty Images; © Harry How/Getty Images; © AP Photo/Jennifer Graylock; © Matthew Peters/Man Utd./Getty Images **20** (*top to bottom*) © Blue Jean Images/Alamy; © Ty Allison/Photographer's Choice/Getty Images; © Cultura/PunchStock **22** © Ken Karp Photography **25** (*top, clockwise*) © Chad Ehlers/Alamy; © Philip Game/Alamy; © Image Source/Corbis; © Liba Taylor/Robert Harding Travel/Photolibrary **29** © PhotoObjects.net/Thinkstock **32** © Stephen Coburn/Shutterstock **34** (*top, left to right*) © Robin Nelson/PhotoEdit; © Valueline/Thinkstock; © Kyle Sparks/Getty Images; © Moodboard/Corbis; (*middle, left to right*) © Asia Images Group Pte Ltd/Alamy; © John Lund/Annabelle B/age fotostock; © Blend Images/SuperStock; © Fuse/Getty Images; (*bottom, left to right*) © Image Source; © Alamy; © Fancy Photography/Veer; © JGI/Jamie Grill/Blend Images/Getty Images **36** (*top, left to right*) © Blend Images/PunchStock; © Jeff Greenberg/age fotostock; © AP Photo/Mike Grol; © Mark Leibowitz/Masterfile; (*middle, left to right*) © John Pickelle/Stockbyte/Getty Images; © Yellow Dog Productions/The Image Bank/Getty Images; © Ocean/Corbis; © G. Baden/Keepsake/Corbis **39** © Diego Cervo/Veer **40** © Canopy/Corbis **41** (*left to right*) © Blend Images/SuperStock; © Fancy Photography/Veer; © Pholdar Nine/A.Collection/Getty Images **45** (*left to right*) © Walter Bibikow/Photolibrary/Getty Images; © Mixa/PunchStock; © Erika Stone; © Donna Day/Alloy/Corbis **46** (*from top left*) (*arm chairs*) © Michaela Stejskalova/Alamy; (*stove*) © C Squared Studios/Photodisc/Getty Images; (*curtains*) © Flirt/SuperStock; (*pictures*) © Simon Brown/Alamy; (*bed*) © Tiler84/Fotolia; (*table*) © Lawrence Manning/Spirit/Corbis; (*coffee table*) © Mehmetcanturkei/Fotolia; (*microwave oven*) © Elnur Amikishiyev/Veer; (*refrigerator*) © Simple stock shots/PunchStock; (*lamps*) © Skip ODonnell/iStockphoto; © Todd Bates/istockphoto; (*sofa*) © Xmasbaby/Fotolia; (*desk*) © Discpicture/Shutterstock; (*bookcase*) © iNNOCENt/Fotolia; (*dresser*) © D. Hurst/Alamy; (*chairs*) © Ustyujanin/Shutterstock; (*mirror*) © George Diebold/Getty Images; (*rug*) © Selahattin BAYRAM/iStockphoto; (*TV*) © Supertrooper/Veer; (*cupboards*) © Yarik/Shutterstock **48** (*top to bottom*) ©Alan Smith/Stone/Getty Images; © Daniel Dempster Photography/Alamy; © Marc Gerritsen/Sheltered Images/age fotostock; © Skyhobo/iStockphoto **49** (*top to bottom*) © CB2/ZOB WENN Photos/Newscom; © Michael Stravato/The New York Times/Redux Pictures **51** (*left to right*) © Corbis Photography/Veer; © Blend Images/Alamy; © Fuse/PunchStock; © View Stock RF/age fotostock **53** (*left to right*) © Stewart Cohen/Blend Images/Getty Images; © RubberBall/Alamy; © John Birdsall/The Image Works; © Moodboard/Alamy **54** (*middle*) © J.W.Alker/Imagebroker/Alamy; (*bottom*) © Steven Ogilvy **55** (*top, left to right*) © AP Photo/Peter Kramer; © Stewart Cohen/Blend Boost/age fotostock; (*middle left to right*) © Akg-images/PictureContact/The Image Works; © Yoshikazu Tsuno/AFP/Getty Images **57** (*bottom row*) © Bill Sykes/Cultura/Corbis; © Spencer Grant/PhotoEdit; © Fancy Photography/Veer; © Fuse/Getty Images **58** (*all*) (*broccoli, lettuce, noodles, nuts*) © Hemera/Thinkstock; (onions) © Texturis/Shutterstock; (*carrots*) © Pedro Nogueira/Shutterstock; (*apples, cream, rice, fish*) © Ericlefrancais/Shutterstock; (*bananas, pasta, crackers, eggs*) © Travellinglight/iStockphoto; (*oranges, lemons, tomatoes, beef*) © iStockphoto/Thinkstock; (*kiwis*) © Dinostock/Fotolia; (*blueberries*) © Morgan Lane Photography/Shutterstock; (*potatoes*) © Schankz/Shutterstock; (*bread*) © Andrew Dernie/iStockphoto; (*cereal*) © Studiomode/Alamy; (*oil*) © Ivan Bajic/iStockphoto; (*Butter*) © Sir Eagle/Fotolia; (*milk*) © Ts/Veer; (*yogurt*) © Ingram Publishing/age fotostock; (*cheese*) © Gregory Gerber/Shutterstock; (*chicken*) © Photonic 5/Alamy; (*beans*) © Frans Rombout/iStockphoto **59** © Steven Ogilvy **60** (*left to right*) © Eising/StockFood; © Steven Ogilvy; © George Kerrigan **61** © Palladium/age fotostock **62** © Asia Images Group/Getty Images **63** (*clockwise from top left*) © Gapys Krzysztof/Alamy; © Nidz/Fotolia; © Antonio Muñoz Palomares/iStockphoto; © TongRo Image Stock/Alamy; © Lisa Charles Watson/FoodPix/Getty Images **64** (*golf ball*) © Stockbyte/Thinkstock; (*soccer ball, basketball, baseball and bat*) © iStockphoto/Thinkstock ; (*volleyball, football*) ©Hemera/Thinkstock; (*swimming goggles and swimming cap, bicycle, snowboard*) © Comstock/Thinkstock; (*hiking boots*) © Melinda Fawver/Shutterstock; (*hockey puck*) © Shutterstock; (*skating*) © Aksenova Natalya/Shutterstock **65** (*middle*) © iStockphoto/Thinkstock; (*bottom*) © Konrad Wothe/Look/age fotostock **66** © Harry Choi/TongRo Image Stock/Alamy **69** (*left*) © Chris Polk/FilmMagic/Getty Images; (*right*) © AP Photo/Sipa **71** (*left to right*) © Goodshoot/Thinkstock; © Sudheer Sakthan/Shutterstock; © Gina Sanders/Veer; © Ron Levine/Taxi/Getty Images **73** (*clockwise from top to left*) © John Lund/Annabelle Breakey/Blend Images/Getty Images; © Nicho Sodling/Johner Images/Getty Images; © Michael Kevin Daly/Workbook Stock/Getty Images; © Masterfile; © Moodboard/Cultura/Getty Images; © Laoshi/The Agency Collection/Getty Images; © Ryan McVay/Photodisc/Thinkstock; © Blend Images/Hill Street Studios/the Agency Collection/Getty Images **74** (*bottom row*) © RubberBall Productions/The Agency Collection/Getty Images; © DAJ/Amana Images/Getty Images; © Jeff Hunter/Photoghaper's Choice/Getty Images; © Corbis Bridge/Alamy; © Image Source/Alamy; © Vstock LLC/Getty Images **76** (*top, left to right*) © InsideOutPix/age fotostock; © Mixa/Alamy; © iStockphoto; © Kimtaegyeong/Leaf Stock/age fotostock; (*middle,left to right*) © Bertrand Gardel/Terra/Corbis; © Craig Lovell/Corbis; © Radius Images/Alamy; © Harry Choi/TongRo Image Stock/Alamy; (*bottom, left to right*) © Joe Raedle/Getty Images; © Toshiyuki Aizawa/Reuters/Corbis **77** (*clockwise from left*) © Mimi Haddon/Digital Vision/Getty Images; © Glow Asia/Alamy; © Cultura/Twinpix/Getty Images; © Peace/Amana images/Corbis **78** (*sea*) © Nik Wheeler/Alamy; (*man*) © Ken Karp Photography **80** (*top, left to right*) © Glowimages/age fotostock; © Tetra Images/Getty Images; © Image Source/Getty Images; © Creatas/Thinkstock; (*all, bottom*) (*Antacid*) © Jesus Jauregui/iStockphoto; (*muscle cream*) © Olinchuk/Shutterstock; (*cough syrup, spray*) © iStockphoto/Thinkstock; (*cool*) © Studioshots/Alamy; (*cold pills*) © Helen Sessions/Alamy; (*Aspirin*) © Creatas/Thinkstock; (*eyedrops*) © Hemera/Thinkstock **83** (*middle, left to right*) © Tanya Constantine/Digital Vision/Getty Images; © Image Source/Alamy; © Jose Luis Pelaez Inc/Blend Images/Alamy; © Tetra Images/Alamy; (*bottom left*) © Harry Choi/TongRo Image Stock/Corbis; (*bottom right*) © Susanna Blavarg/Johner Images/age fotostock **86** (*top, left to right*) © Gerald Martineau/The Washington Post/Getty Images; © Corbis; (*middle, left to right*) © DreamPictures/Blend Images/age fotostock; © Richard Levine/Alamy; © Stockbyte/Getty Images; (*bottom, left to right*) © Yellow Dog Productions/Digital Vision/Getty Images; © Image Source/Alamy; © Katrina Wittkamp/Lifesize/Getty Images **89** (*clockwise from left*) © Jeremy Woodhouse/Digital Vision/Getty Images; © Peter Adams/The Image Bank/Getty Images; © Richard Nowitz/National Geographic Society/Corbis; © Caspar Benson/Getty Images; © Kord.com/age fotostock; © JLImages/Alamy **91** (*top, left to right*) © John McKenna/Alamy; © Gmsphotography/Flickr/Getty Images; © Richard Alexander/Spoon Cafe Bistro; (*middle, left to right*) © Karl Blackwell/Lonely Planet; © The City of Edinburgh Council; © Lonely Planet/SuperStock **92** (*top left to right*) © Yellow Dog Productions/Getty Images; © allesalltag/Alamy; © Daly and Newton/The Image Bank/Getty Images; © Eric Audras/PhotoAlto Agency RF Collections/Getty Images; (*middle left to right*) © Kevin Wheal Surrey/Alamy; © DTP/Stone/Getty Images; © John Lund/Marc Romanelli/Blend Images/Getty Images; © Martin Lee/Mediablitzimages (*UK*) Limited/Alamy **93** © John Lund/Marc Romanelli/Blend Images/Getty Images **95** © PT Images/Getty Images **96** © Dave and Les Jacobs/Blend Images/Getty Images **97** (*top to bottom*) © Glow Images Inc./Getty Images; © Howard Kingsnorth/Cultura/Getty Images; © Jupiterimages/Comstock Images/Getty Images; © Cavan Images/Photodisc/Getty Images **99** (*top*) © Chris Cooper-Smith/Alamy; (*middle*) © iStockphoto; (*bottom*) © Yagi Studio/Photodisc/Getty Images **100** (*left to right*) © Pierre Verdy/AFP/Getty Images; © Alexander Tamargo/Getty Images; © Jason Merritt/Getty Images; © Ferdaus Shamim/WireImage/Getty Images; © Gustavo Caballero/Getty Images **102** © Denkou Images/Alamy **104** © Elke Van de Velde/Photodisc/Getty Images **105** © Mackenzie Bearup/Sheltering Books Inc. **107** © Shoosh/Form Advertising/Alamy **108** (*top, left to right*) © John Eder/Stone/Getty Images; © Drx/Fotolia; © Ataboy/Stone/Getty Images; (*middle, left to right*) © Tom & Dee Ann McCarthy/Corbis; © Jeff Greenberg/PhotoEdit; © Geraint Lewis/Alamy **109** © Catchlight Visual Services/Alamy **110** © KL Services/Masterfile **111** (*top, left to right*) © Eyal Nahmias/Alamy; © David Livingston/Getty Images; © Mario Anzuoni/Reuters/Corbis; (*middle, left to right*) © David Fairchild/Hermosa Beach Chamber of Commerce; © Minden Pictures/SuperStock **112** (*bottom, left to right*) © Maria Picard/Deborah Betz Collection/Corbis; © Tim Graham/Getty Images; © Fotos International/Moviepix /Getty Images **113** © Comstock/Thinkstock **123** (*beef*) © BW Folsom/Shutterstock; (*grapes*) © Jerryhat/iStockphoto; (*corn chips*) © Iain McGillivray/iStockphoto; (*watermelon*) © Frans Rombout//iStockphoto; (*ice cream, shelled peanuts*) © iStockphoto/Thinkstock; (*cake*) © Christy Thompson/Shutterstock; (*potato chips*) © Photodisc/Thinkstock; (*candy*) © Norman Chan/Veer; (*hot dogs*) © Sawayasu Tsuji/iStockphoto; (*cookies*) © Elena Schweitzer/Shutterstock; (*popcorn*) © Nikola Bilic/iStockphoto; (*pizza*) © Viktor1/Shutterstock; (*pineapple*)© Jiri Miklo/iStockphoto; (*chocolates*) © Mikie11/Shutterstock; (*almonds*) © Roman Antonov/iStockphoto **125** (*top to bottom*) © Dean Turner/iStockphoto; © Phase4Photography/Shutterstock; © AlexStar/iStockphoto; © iStockphoto/Thinkstock; © Thomas Northcut/Photodisc/Thinkstock; © Jonya/iStockphoto; © iStockphoto/Thinkstock; © Skip ODonnell/iStockphoto; © Eltopo/iStockphoto; © Magdalena Jankowska/iStockphoto; © Sarah Lee/iStockphoto **126** (*top, left to right*) © BananaStock/Thinkstock; © Blend Images/PunchStock; (*middle, left to right*) © Fancy Photography/Veer; © Aldo Murillo/iStockphoto; (*bottom, left to right*) © Beijing Eastphoto stockimages Co.,Ltd/Alamy; © StockbrokerXtra/Webstockpro **129** (*clockwise, from top right*) © Pixland/Thinkstock; © Myrleen Ferguson Cate/PhotoEdit; © Westend61/PunchStock; © Juanmonino/iStockphoto **130** (*top, left to right*) © Mel Curtis/Photodisc/Getty Images; © Couperfield/Shutterstock; © Barry Austin Photography/Lifesize/Thinkstock; (*middle, left to right*) © BananaStock/Thinkstock; © Image Source/PunchStock; © Quavondo/iStockphoto; © Hemera Technologies/Photos.com/Thinkstock; © Michael DeLeon/iStockphoto

interchange

Jack C. Richards

Revised by Karen Davy

Intro

VIDEO ACTIVITY WORKSHEETS

CAMBRIDGE
UNIVERSITY PRESS

Credits

Illustration credits

Ralph Butler: 20, 29, 41, 54, 61; Mark Collins: 17, 30, 46, 56; Paul Daviz: 34, 58; Chuck Gonzales: 4, 13, 18, 62; Dan Hubig: 8 (*bottom*), 14, 16, 37, 57, 65; Kja-Artists.com: 5 (*top*), 25, 33, 45, 49; Trevor Keen: 38;

Joanna Kerr: 8 (*top*), 26; Monika Melnychuk/i2iart.com: 6, 9, 28; Karen Minot: 50; Ortelius Design: 10, 12; Robert Schuster: 5 (*bottom*), 36, 47; Russ Willms: 48, 63; James Yamasaki: 2, 22, 53

Photography credits

10 (*left to right*) ©Best View Stock/Age Fotostock; ©Guy Needham/National Geographic My Shot/National Geographic Stock; ©Age Fotostock/SuperStock; 12 ©Leonid Plotkin/Alamy; 24 (*clockwise from top left*) ©Mood Board/Age Fotostock; ©Jin Akaishi/Aflo Foto Agency/Photolibrary; ©Jose Luis Pelaez Inc./Age Fotostock; ©Simon Willms/Lifesize/Getty Images; 36 (*left to right*) ©Bonchan/Shutterstock; ©iStockphoto/Thinkstock; ©Edie Layland/istockphoto; ©iStockphoto/Thinkstock; 40 (*center*) ©Ryan McVay/Stockbyte/Getty Images; (*clockwise from top left*) © Flirt/SuperStock; ©All Canada Photos/SuperStock; ©Aispix/Shutterstock; ©Al Bello/Staff/Getty Images Sport/Getty Images; ©Comstock/Getty Images; ©Jim Cummins/Taxi/Getty Images; ©Imagemore Co., Ltd./Getty Images; 42 (*top row, left to right*) ©Corbis/Photolibrary; ©Age

Fotostock/SuperStock; ©Glowimages/Getty Images; ©Fstockfoto/Shutterstock; (*bottom row, left to right*) ©James Quine/Alamy; ©Lite Productions/Glow Images RF/Photolibrary; ©Gregory Dale/National Geographic Stock; ©Kord/Age Fotostock; 44 (*center*) © Ramon Purcell/Istockphoto; (*clockwise from top left*) ©Jim Loscalzo/EPA/Corbis; ©Alex Wong/Staff/Getty Images; ©The Washington Post/Contributor/Getty Images; ©Stock Connection/SuperStock; ©Jim Young/Reuters/Corbis; ©GlowImages/Age Fotostock; 58 (*left to right*) ©Andrew H. Walker/Getty Images; ©Walter McBride/Retna Ltd/Corbis; ©AP Photo/Julie Jacobson; ©Disney/Joan Marcus/Photofest; ©AP Photo/Stuart Ramson; ©Bruce Glikas/FilmMagic/Getty Images; 59 ©Zoonar/Paul Hakimata/Age Fotostock

Plan of Intro Video

Welcome!

Preview

1 VOCABULARY *People and names*

PAIR WORK Fill in the blanks. Use the words in the box. Then compare with a partner.

> ✓ first   friends   last   student   teacher

1. Hi. My ....*first*.... name is Caroline. My .... call me Carol.

2. Ms. Lee is my .... I'm her .... My name's Alex Sims.

3. Hello. I'm Eduardo. My .... name is Robles.

2 INTRODUCTIONS

A Check (✓) the correct responses. Then compare with a partner.

1. Hello.
   - ☐ Excuse me.
   - ☑ Hi.

2. My name is Molly. What's your name?
   - ☐ I'm Peter.
   - ☐ My friends call me Molly.

3. Hi, Pete. It's nice to meet you.
   - ☐ Nice to meet you, too.
   - ☐ Yes, I am.

4. Hello. I'm Peter Krum.
   - ☐ Hello. What's your name?
   - ☐ Hi, Peter. Nice to meet you.

B **PAIR WORK** Practice the conversations in part A. Use your own names.

3 WHAT DO YOU SEE?

Watch the first 30 seconds of the video with the sound off. Check (✓) the correct answers.

1. Peter is
   - ☐ a student.
   - ☐ a teacher.

2. Molly is
   - ☐ a student.
   - ☐ a teacher.

Watch the video

4 GET THE PICTURE

A Check your answers to Exercise 3.
Are they correct?

B Match. Then compare with a partner.

1. ....c.... Molly

2. .... Peter

3. .... Mrs. Smith

4. .... Miss Taylor

C Match the first names or titles with the last names. Then compare with a partner.

A	B
1. Miss	a. Krum
2. Mrs.	b. Lin
3. Peter	c. Smith
4. Molly	d. Taylor

5 WATCH FOR DETAILS

Check (✓) the correct answers. Then compare with a partner.

1. Peter's nickname is
   ☐ Krum.
   ☑ Pete.

2. Molly's friends call her
   ☐ Molly.
   ☐ Holly.

3. Peter is Molly's
   ☐ friend.
   ☐ classmate.

4. Molly and Peter's class is at
   ☐ 8:00.
   ☐ 9:00.

5. Mrs. Smith
   ☐ is Molly and Peter's teacher.
   ☐ is not Molly and Peter's teacher.

6. Miss Taylor's class is in Room
   ☐ 201.
   ☐ 203.

VIDEO ACTIVITIES

Unit 1 ■ 3

6 DO YOU REMEMBER?

Write the sentences under the correct picture. Then compare with a partner.

He's Molly's classmate.
Her last name is Taylor.
Her room is 201.
✓ She's not a teacher.

She's Peter's teacher.
She's the teacher in Room 203.
His teacher is Miss Taylor.
She's not Molly's teacher.

His class is not in Room 201.
Her last name is Smith.
She's Peter's classmate.
Her teacher is Miss Taylor.

 **1**

 **2**

 **3**

 **4**

She's not a teacher.
....
....

....
....
....

....
....
....

....
....
....

☰ Follow-up

7 NICE TO MEET YOU

A Match.

A
1. It's nice to meet you, Sarah.
2. Hello. I'm Paul Thompson.
3. Are you a student here?

B
a. Yes, I am.
b. Nice to meet you, too.
c. Hi. My name is Sarah Long.

B PAIR WORK Put the sentences in order. Then practice the conversation.

A: Hello. I'm Paul Thompson.

B: Hi. My name is Sarah Long.

A: ....

B: ....

A: ....

B: ....

C CLASS ACTIVITY Now introduce yourself around the class. Use your own information.

Language close-up

8 WHAT DID THEY SAY?

Watch the video and complete the conversation. Then practice it.

Molly and Peter are at school.

Molly: Excuse me. Um, ...hello............ .
Peter: .... !
Molly: .... name is Molly.
What's .... name?
Peter: .... Peter. My .... call me Pete.
Molly: My friends .... me . . . Molly.
Hi, Pete. It's nice to .... you.
Peter: It's nice to meet you, ...
Molly: Are you a .... here?
Peter: .... , I am. My .... is at
nine o'clock with .... Taylor.
Molly: Miss Taylor? .... my teacher. You're in
.... class.
Peter: .... !

9 THE VERB BE *Asking for and giving information*

A Complete the conversations with the correct forms of *be*.
Then practice with a partner.

1. A: Excuse me. ......Are...... you Sam?
   B: No, I .... Luis. Sam .... over there.

2. A: I .... Celia. What .... your name?
   B: My name .... Dan.

3. A: .... this Mrs. Costa's classroom?
   B: No. Her class .... in Room 105.

4. A: What .... your email address?
   B: It .... marymary@email.com.

5. A: What .... your phone number?
   B: It .... (646) 555-7841.

B **PAIR WORK** Practice the conversations again.
Use your own information.

C **GROUP WORK** Now ask five students from
your class for their contact information.

A: What's your phone number, David?
B: It's (201) 555-3192.
A: 555-3182?
B: No, 3192.
A: OK, thanks.

David Chang
(201) 555-3192
dchang@email.com

Unit 1 ▪ **5**

2 My passport!

1 VOCABULARY Prepositions

A Look at the pictures. Where are these things? Circle the correct locations.

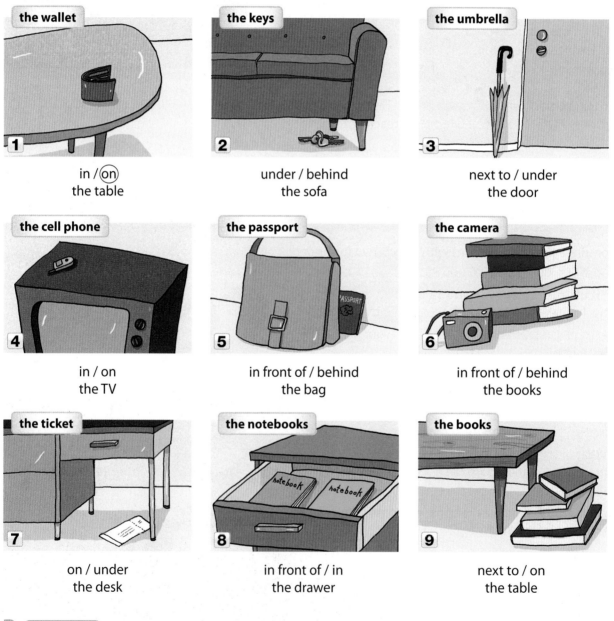

the wallet

1 in / (on)
the table

the keys

2 under / behind
the sofa

the umbrella

3 next to / under
the door

the cell phone

4 in / on
the TV

the passport

5 in front of / behind
the bag

the camera

6 in front of / behind
the books

the ticket

7 on / under
the desk

the notebooks

8 in front of / in
the drawer

the books

9 next to / on
the table

B **PAIR WORK** Ask and answer questions about the things in part A.

A: Where is the wallet?
B: It's on the table.

A: Where are the keys?
B: They're . . .

6 ■ Unit 2

2 WHAT DO YOU SEE?

Watch the video with the sound off. Check (✓) **True** or **False**. Correct the false sentences. Then compare with a partner.

		True	False
1.	The ticket is ~~under~~ ^{on} the TV.	☐	✓
2.	The camera is in a box next to the sofa.	☐	☐
3.	The keys are on the TV.	☐	☐
4.	The passport is behind the desk.	☐	☐

Watch the video

3 GET THE PICTURE

What things do Sofia and Jessica find? Number the things from 1 to 7 in the order they are found. Then compare with a partner.

.... her bag   .... her ticket

.... her camera   .... her umbrella

.... her keys   ....1.... her wallet

.... her passport

4 WATCH FOR DETAILS

Check (✓) the correct answers. Then compare with a partner.

1. At the beginning of the story, it's
   ☐ nine o'clock.
   ✓ ten o'clock.

2. Sofia's flight is at
   ☐ twelve-thirty.
   ☐ two-thirty.

3. Sofia's trip is to
   ☐ Peru.
   ☐ Brazil.

4. Sofia's desk is in the
   ☐ bedroom.
   ☐ living room.

5. Sofia is on a plane to
   ☐ Brazil.
   ☐ Budapest.

5 WHERE IS IT?

A Where are these things in the video? Fill in the blanks. Then compare with a partner.

1. The pen is ....*on*........ the TV.

2. The magazines are .... the coffee table.

3. The lamp is .... the TV.

4. The coffee table is .... the sofa.

B Where are Sofia's things? Complete the sentences. Then compare with a partner.

1. Sofia's wallet is *in her bag* ....
2. Her ticket is on the TV, ...
3. Her camera is ....
4. Her keys are ....
5. Her passport is ....
6. Her bag is ....
7. Her umbrella is ....

Follow-up

6 TRUE OR FALSE?

PAIR WORK Your partner puts some of your things in different places. Can you guess where?

A: My keys are in the desk.
B: True.

A: My ruler is on the desk.
B: False. It's under the desk.

Language close-up

7 WHAT DID THEY SAY?

Watch the video and complete the conversation. Then practice it.

Sofia is looking for her things.

Jessica: Sofia! Where's your ......passport...... ?

Sofia: .... it's . . . maybe it's .... a box!

Jessica: Oh!

Sofia: Maybe it's. . . . It's probably .... the chair.

Jessica: No, ... not here.

Sofia: OK. Maybe it's .... to the ....

Jessica: Sofia! .... this?

Sofia: My .... I'm going to need that. . . .

My .... !

Jessica: Is it .... the books? No.

Sofia: Oh, no!

Jessica: Sofia, are those .... keys, in .... of the TV?

Sofia: Yes, those are .... keys. . . . My passport, Jessica!

Wait a minute. Wait a minute. It's on the .... in the bedroom!

8 PREPOSITIONS OF PLACE *Describing location*

A Complete the sentences about the things in the picture.
Use each preposition only once. Then compare with a partner.

behind	in	in front of	✓next to	on	under

1. The purse *is next to the sofa* .
2. The notebooks ....
3. The wallet ....
4. The lamp ....
5. The sunglasses ....
6. The clock ....

B Write similar sentences about things in your classroom.
Then read your sentences to your partner.

1. ....
2. ....
3. ....
4. ....
5. ....
6. ....

3 Newcomers High School

1 VOCABULARY Countries and regions

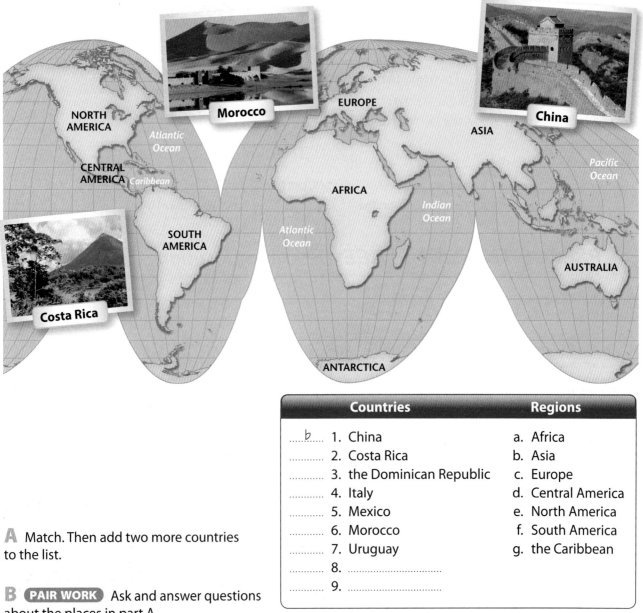

Countries	Regions
...b... 1. China	a. Africa
.... 2. Costa Rica	b. Asia
.... 3. the Dominican Republic	c. Europe
.... 4. Italy	d. Central America
.... 5. Mexico	e. North America
.... 6. Morocco	f. South America
.... 7. Uruguay	g. the Caribbean
.... 8.	
.... 9.	

A Match. Then add two more countries to the list.

B **PAIR WORK** Ask and answer questions about the places in part A.

A: Where's China?
B: It's in Asia. **or**
    I think it's in . . . **or**
    I'm not sure. Is it in . . . ?

2 GUESS THE FACTS

Complete the chart. Use the words in the box.
Then compare with a partner.

Arabic	✓ Casablanca	San José
Cantonese	Hong Kong	Spanish

A: Casablanca is in Morocco.
B: Yes, that's right. **or**
   No, it's not. It's in . . .

B: They speak Spanish in Morocco.
A: No, they speak . . .

	Country	City	Language
1.	Morocco	_Casablanca_	
2.	Costa Rica		
3.	China		

Watch the video

3 GET THE PICTURE

A Check your answers to Exercise 2.

B Where are they from?
Check (✓) the correct answers.

	Fatima	Camilia	Cai
China	☐	☐	☐
Costa Rica	☐	☐	☐
Morocco	✓	☐	☐

4 WATCH FOR DETAILS

Check (✓) the correct answers. Then compare with a partner.

1. Newcomers High School is in
   ☐ Washington, D.C.
   ✓ New York City.

2. The students at Newcomers High School
   ☐ are from the U.S.
   ☐ aren't from the U.S.

3. Morocco is on the
   ☐ ocean.
   ☐ river.

4. Camilia says the rain forest is
   ☐ fun.
   ☐ large.

5. Cai's brother is
   ☐ 20.
   ☐ 22.

6. Cai's brother is
   ☐ talkative.
   ☐ serious.

7. Fatima speaks
   ☐ two languages.
   ☐ three languages.

8. *Ma'a salama* means
   ☐ "Thank you."
   ☐ "Good-bye."

Unit 3 ▪ 11

5 *WHERE IS IT?*

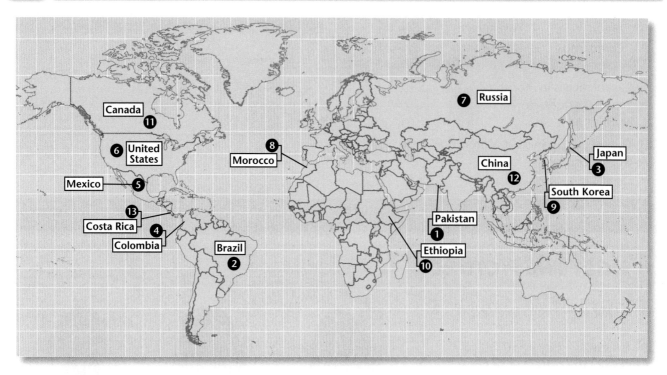

A PAIR WORK Students from Newcomers High School come from these cities. Find the cities on the map.

| Casablanca | Hong Kong | San José |

A: Where's Casablanca?
B: I think it's here, in . . . It's number . . .
A: You're right. **or** No. It's number . . . It's here, in . . .

B PAIR WORK Now take turns finding these cities.

| Addis Ababa | Inchon | Monterrey | Sapporo | Winnipeg |
| Cali | Karachi | San Diego | St. Petersburg | Vitória |

A: Where's Cali?
B: I think it's in Colombia. It's number 4.
A: Yes, that's right. **or** No, it's not. It's here, number . . .

C GROUP WORK Write five cities on five pieces of paper. Mix them up. Pick a city. Where is it?

A: Where's . . . ?
B: I think it's in . . .
A: That's right. **or** No, it's in . . .

Cali, Colombia

Language close-up

6 WHAT DID THEY SAY?

Watch the video and complete the conversation. Then practice it.

Rachel Park is talking to Camilia, a student at Newcomers High School.

Rachel: ....Hello.......... . Where .... you from, Camilia?
Are .... from Morocco, too?

Camilia: No, I'm .... from Costa Rica.

Rachel: .... is Costa Rica, Camilia?

Camilia: .... in Central America.
I'm .... San José, the ....

Rachel: What's San José .... ?

Camilia: It's very .... I like it a lot.

Rachel: What are .... ?

Camilia: These .... photos of the rain forest in my ....
The rain forest is .... and interesting. It's fun, ...

Rachel: It looks fun! .... you, Camilia.

7 PRESENT TENSE OF BE *Countries and regions*

A Complete the conversations. Then practice them.

1. A: How ....are...... you today?
   B: I .... fine, thank you.
   A: Where .... you from, Carlos?
   B: I .... from Mexico. How about you?
   A: I .... from Canada.
   B: Oh, ... you from Montreal?
   A: Yes, I ....

2. A: Where .... Rachel from?
   B: She .... from the U.S.
   A: .... she from New York?
   B: No, she .... not from New York.
   She .... from Chicago originally.

3. A: Where .... Ji-son and Hyo from?
   B: Ji-son .... from Pusan, and
   Hyo .... from Seoul.
   A: Oh, so they .... both from South Korea.
   B: Yes, they ....

Where are you from, Ji-son?

I'm from Pusan. How about you?

I'm from Seoul.

B **CLASS ACTIVITY** Now find out what cities (or countries) your classmates are from.

What are you wearing?

▤ Preview

1 VOCABULARY Clothing

A Find these things in the picture. Match.

1. ....d.... a dark blue suit	5. .... white socks	9. .... a backpack	13. .... a scarf
2. .... a brown tie	6. .... a gray skirt	10. .... boots	14. .... a yellow dress
3. .... black shoes	7. .... a white blouse	11. .... jeans	15. .... a pink hat
4. .... a briefcase	8. .... a blue jacket	12. .... a sweater	16. .... a red shirt

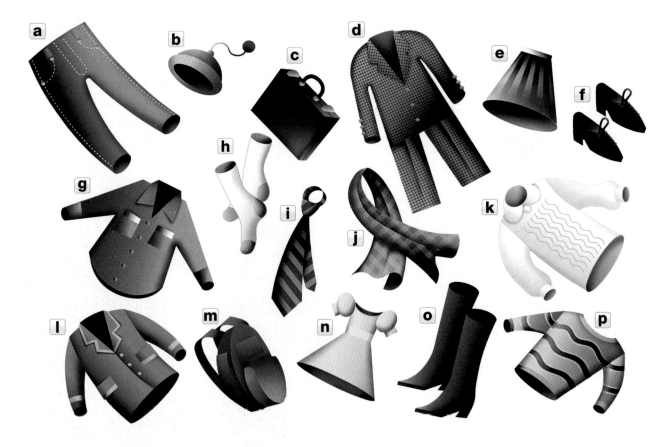

B **PAIR WORK** Cover the words in part A. Then ask about things in the picture.

A: What's this?
B: It's a dark blue suit.
A: What are these?
B: They're black shoes.

2 WHAT DO YOU SEE?

Watch the video with the sound off. Answer the questions.
Check (✓) all correct answers.

1. What is the man wearing and carrying?
   - ☐ a blue suit
   - ✓ a brown tie
   - ☐ brown shoes
   - ✓ a black briefcase

2. What is the uniform for the girl's school?
   - ☐ white socks
   - ☐ a red skirt
   - ☐ a white blouse
   - ☐ a green sweater

3. What are the mother and baby wearing?
   - ☐ sneakers
   - ☐ jeans
   - ☐ a T-shirt
   - ☐ a scarf
   - ☐ yellow pants
   - ☐ a pink hat

4. What is Jamal wearing today?
   - ☐ black pants
   - ☐ a green shirt
   - ☐ a coat

Watch the video

3 GET THE PICTURE

Check your answers to Exercise 2. Then compare with a partner.

4 WATCH FOR DETAILS

Watch the video again. This time, cross out the wrong items in Exercise 2. Write the correct ones. Then compare with a partner.

- ☐ ~~a blue suit~~ *a gray striped suit*
- ✓ a brown tie
- ☐ ~~brown shoes~~ *black shoes*
- ✓ a black briefcase

Check (✓) the correct answers. Then compare with a partner.

1. The season is
   - [ ] spring.
   - [ ] fall.

2. The weather is cool and
   - [ ] cloudy.
   - [ ] sunny.

3. Megan's backpack is yellow, and Jasmin's backpack is
   - [ ] blue.
   - [ ] black.

4. Sheila and Julie are wearing
   - [ ] casual clothes.
   - [ ] formal clothes.

Follow-up

6 **WHAT'S YOUR OPINION?**

A Do you like these people's clothes? Check (✓) your answers.

1. [ ] yes [ ] no

2. [ ] yes [ ] no

3. [ ] yes [ ] no

4. [ ] yes [ ] no

5. [ ] yes [ ] no

6. [ ] yes [ ] no

B **PAIR WORK** Compare your answers to part A.

A: I like his clothes. I like his gray suit.
B: I like his gray suit, and I like his brown tie.

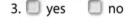

"I like his gray suit, but I don't like his red tie."

> The negative of *like* is *don't like.*

☰ Language close-up

7 WHAT DID THEY SAY?

Watch the video and complete the conversations.

Jamal Greene is asking people about their clothes.

1. Jamal: Excuse me. Hello!
   Man: ....Hello........... there.
   Jamal: .... talking to people about ....
   What are you .... today?
   Man: I'm wearing a .... striped suit,
   brown .... , and black ....
   Jamal: Is it a .... suit?
   Man: .... , it's for cool ....
   It's good for the fall and ....
   Jamal: Very .... , very formal.
   Man: Yes, I'm .... today, so I'm wearing
   formal ....
   Jamal: I ....

2. Jamal: So .... are you wearing .... ?
   Sheila: We're just wearing .... clothes.
   I have on boots and jeans, a .... ,
   a light jacket, and .... sunglasses.
   Jamal: And a very pretty .... scarf.
   Sheila: Thank you.
   Jamal: And what is Julie .... ?
   Sheila: She's wearing blue .... , a white .... ,
   a pink hat. It's her .... hat.

8 PRESENT CONTINUOUS *Asking about and describing clothing*

A Complete these conversations with the present continuous of *wear.*

1. A: ......Are...... you ...wearing... pants today?
   B: No, I .... a skirt.

2. A: What .... our teacher .... today?
   B: She .... a black sweater, a blue blouse, and a gray skirt.

3. A: What color shoes .... you .... ?
   B: I .... white shoes today.

4. A: .... your classmates .... coats today?
   B: No, they .... coats, but they .... sweaters.

5. A: What colors .... you .... today?
   B: I .... yellow, blue, brown, and green.

B **PAIR WORK** Practice the conversations again.
Use your own information.

5 Everybody's having fun.

Preview

1 VOCABULARY Actions

A Write the actions under the pictures. Then compare with a partner.

answering the phone	looking up a phone number	sleeping
babysitting	making popcorn	✓ studying
having dinner together	ordering a pizza	watching movies

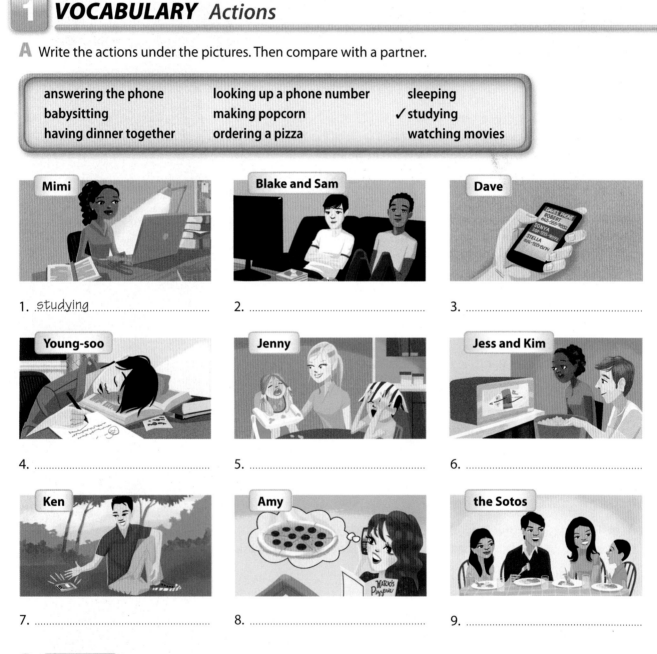

Mimi

Blake and Sam

Dave

1. studying

2. ....

3. ....

Young-soo

Jenny

Jess and Kim

4. ....

5. ....

6. ....

Ken

Amy

the Sotos

7. ....

8. ....

9. ....

B **PAIR WORK** Ask and answer questions about the people in part A.

A: What's Mimi doing?
B: She's studying.
A: What are Blake and Sam doing?
B: They're . . .

2 WHAT DO YOU SEE?

Watch the video with the sound off. Put the pictures in order from 1 to 7.

....

Peter is studying.

....

....

Watch the video

3 GET THE PICTURE

A Check your answers to Exercise 2.

Peter

B Now write the correct description under each picture in Exercise 2. Use the ideas in the box. Then compare with a partner.

Kate

Peter / Kate / Doug / Emi is . . .
answering the phone.   sleeping.
babysitting.   ✓ studying.
calling a friend.   watching movies.
going out.

Doug

Emi

WATCH FOR DETAILS

Check (✓) the correct answers. Then compare with a partner.

1. At the beginning of the video, it's
   - ☐ 6:00.
   - ☑ 7:00.

2. Peter is studying
   - ☐ at home.
   - ☐ in school.

3. Kate thinks babysitting
   - ☐ is fun.
   - ☐ isn't fun.

4. Peter calls Doug at
   - ☐ 8:25.
   - ☐ 7:25.

5. Doug is having dinner
   - ☐ with his grandparents.
   - ☐ at his girlfriend's house.

6. Emi calls Peter at
   - ☐ 9:20.
   - ☐ 8:20.

7. Emi, Ivan, and Carla are at
   - ☐ Carla's place.
   - ☐ Emi's place.

8. Emi, Ivan, and Carla are making
   - ☐ a pizza.
   - ☐ popcorn.

☰ Follow-up

5 **WHAT AM I DOING?**

PAIR WORK Take turns acting out an action and guessing the action.
Use the verbs in the box or your own ideas.

cook	drive	get up	read	shop	study
dance	eat	play	run	sleep	(swim)

A: What am I doing?
B: Are you dancing?
A: No, I'm not.
B: Are you swimming?
A: Yes, I am.

Language close-up

6 WHAT DID THEY SAY?

Watch the video and complete the conversation. Then practice it.

Emi is calling Peter.

Peter: Uh, ...hello......... ?

Emi: Hi, Peter. .... Emi.
Um, ... you OK?

Peter: I'm ....

Emi: .... not studying. You're .... !

Peter: OK, OK. I'm .... But I'm .... ,
too! .... are you doing, Emi?

Emi: I'm hanging out .... Ivan
and Carla.

Peter: .... ? Sounds like fun.

Emi: Yeah. We're .... movies at my place.
.... you busy?

Peter: Well, I'm studying for a test that I have
on ....

Emi: We're .... popcorn.

Peter: What .... is it?

Emi: It's .... after nine. Ivan is .... a pizza.

Peter: OK! I'm ....

7 PRESENT CONTINUOUS *Describing current activities*

A Complete these conversations. Use the correct present continuous
forms of the verbs in parentheses. Then practice with a partner.

1. A: What 's........ Pablo ......doing........... (do)?
   B: He .... (study).

2. A: What .... Mariko .... (read)?
   B: She .... (read) a really good book.

3. A: What .... your family .... (do) right now?
   B: My parents .... (work), and my brother and sister
   .... (talk) on the phone.

4. A: What .... our teacher .... (do)?
   B: He .... (have) lunch.
   A: Really? I .... (get) hungry, too.

5. A: .... you .... (speak) Spanish right now?
   B: No, I .... (speak) English!

B   **PAIR WORK** Now ask and answer similar questions about your classmates,
friends, and family. Use your own information.

6 My life

1 VOCABULARY Daily routines

Look at Vanessa's daily routine. Write the sentences under the pictures.
Then compare with a partner.

I walk to work.	Every night, I write jokes.
✓ Weekdays, I get up at 7:30.	I have breakfast with my parents.
At 5:00, I finish work.	I start work at 9:00.
At 1:30, I take a lunch break.	On Saturdays, I tell my jokes at a comedy club.

1. Weekdays, I get
   up at 7:30.

2. ....

3. ....

4. ....

5. ....

6. ....

7. ....

8. ....

2 GUESS THE FACTS

Look again at the sentences in Exercise 1. Where do you think Vanessa works? Check (✓) your answer.

☐ She works at a school.   ☐ She works in an office.   ☐ She works at home.

3 WHAT DO YOU SEE?

Watch the first minute of the video with the sound off. Check your answer to Exercise 2.

☰ Watch the video

4 GET THE PICTURE

A Complete the description.

On weekdays, Vanessa ...*designs web pages*... all day,
and she .... at night.

B Check (✓) **True** or **False**. Then compare with a partner.

		True	False
1.	Vanessa lives with her brother.	☐	✓
2.	Vanessa's mother is a teacher.	☐	☐
3.	Vanessa's father walks to work.	☐	☐
4.	In the evening, Vanessa writes stories.	☐	☐
5.	On Saturdays, Vanessa goes to a comedy club.	☐	☐
6.	Vanessa gets home early from the club.	☐	☐
7.	On Sundays, Vanessa works all day.	☐	☐

5 WATCH FOR DETAILS

Check (✓) the correct answers. Then compare with a partner.

1. How old is Vanessa?
   - ☐ 25
   - ✓ 22

2. What is Vanessa's brother's name?
   - ☐ Wynton
   - ☐ William

3. What time does Vanessa's mother take the bus?
   - ☐ 8:30 A.M.
   - ☐ 9:00 A.M.

4. What time does Vanessa's father start work?
   - ☐ 9:00 A.M.
   - ☐ 9:30 P.M.

5. What time does the show at the club start?
   - ☐ 8:00 P.M.
   - ☐ 9:00 P.M.

6. When does Vanessa usually go home from the club?
   - ☐ Around 11:00 P.M.
   - ☐ Around 12:00 A.M.

6 DO YOU REMEMBER?

PAIR WORK Complete the chart. Check (✓) the words that describe Vanessa's routine.

	On weekdays	At night	On weekends
Designs web pages	☐	☐	☐
Writes jokes	☐	☐	☐
Tells jokes	☐	☐	☐
Goes downtown	☐	☐	☐

☰ Follow-up

7 A DAY IN THE LIFE

A **PAIR WORK** Choose one of these people. Describe a day in the person's life. Use the ideas in the box below or your own ideas. Your partner guesses the person.

A: He gets up at 1:00 in the afternoon. He starts work at 10:00 at night.
B: I think he's a musician.

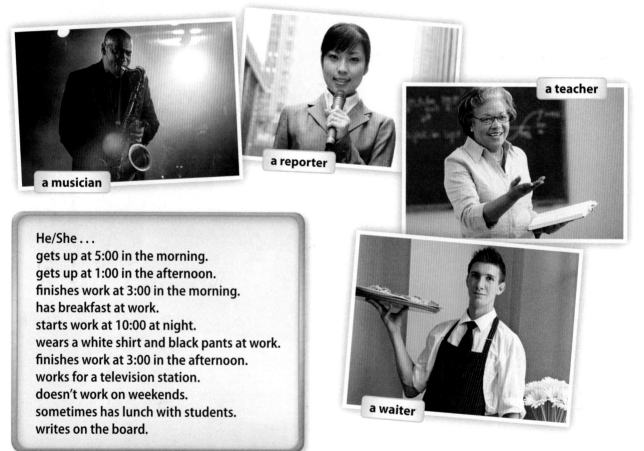

a musician

a reporter

a teacher

a waiter

He/She . . .
gets up at 5:00 in the morning.
gets up at 1:00 in the afternoon.
finishes work at 3:00 in the morning.
has breakfast at work.
starts work at 10:00 at night.
wears a white shirt and black pants at work.
finishes work at 3:00 in the afternoon.
works for a television station.
doesn't work on weekends.
sometimes has lunch with students.
writes on the board.

B **GROUP WORK** Now share your descriptions with another pair. Your partners guess who you're describing.

Language close-up

8 WHAT DID SHE SAY?

Watch the video and complete the descriptions. Then practice it.

Vanessa is talking about her life.

Hi, I'm Vanessa. Welcome to my ....home........ . I live ....
Come on in! This is my .... , and this is my ....
This is my .... , Wynton. He doesn't ....
with us. He has his own .... He's ....
I'm 22, so that makes him .... big brother.

.... , I get up around 7:30. We ....
breakfast at about eight .... , right here. My mom is
a teacher. She .... in the school. She takes the
.... to work. The bus comes at .... , and she gets
home about .... My dad .... to work. He works
.... the clinic. .... a doctor. He starts work at
.... o'clock and gets home at ....

9 SIMPLE PRESENT TENSE *Talking about routines*

A Complete these conversations with the correct verb forms.
Then practice the conversations.

1. A: ....Do........ (Do/Does) you live in the city?
   B: No, I .... (don't/doesn't). I .... (live/lives)
      in the suburbs. My sister .... (live/lives) in the city.
      She .... (have/has) a good job there.

2. A: How .... (do/does) you go to school?
   B: I .... (take/takes) the bus because
      I .... (don't/doesn't) have a car.

3. A: What time .... (do/does) you go to school?
   B: Well, the bus .... (come/comes) at 7:00.

4. A: .... (Do/Does) you have breakfast every day?
   B: Yes, I .... (do/does). My parents ....
      (don't/doesn't) work in the morning, but they ....
      (get up/gets up) early and .... (have/has) breakfast with
      me. Then my father .... (drive/drives) me to the bus.

5. A: Where .... (do/does) you have dinner?
   B: My friends and I .... (go/goes) to a restaurant after class,
      so I .... (don't/doesn't) have dinner with my family.

B PAIR WORK Ask and answer the questions again. Use your
own information.

7 Richdale Street

1 VOCABULARY A new apartment

A Find these places in the picture.
Match. Then compare with a partner.

1. ...f... bathroom
2. ...b... bedroom
3. ...e... closet
4. ...a... kitchen
5. ...c... living room
6. ...d... yard

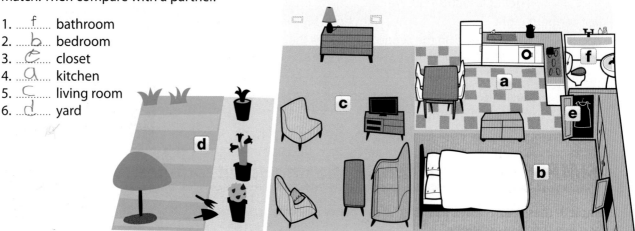

B **PAIR WORK** What do you need in a new apartment? Number
the things from 1 (most important) to 10 (least important).

...1... a bed   ...10... a bookcase   ...5... chairs   ...6... a coffee table   ...4... dishes

...9... a dresser   ...7... a microwave   ...2... an oven   ...3... a refrigerator   ...8... a sofa

C **GROUP WORK** Now compare your answers. Use your own ideas, too.

A: I think you need a refrigerator for the kitchen.
B: And you also need a sofa for the living room.
C: Well, I think you need . . .

2 WHAT DO YOU SEE?

Watch the video with the sound off. What things do the two roommates have? Check (✓) them. Then compare with a partner.

- ✓ a sofa
- ✓ shelves
- ✓ a refrigerator
- ✓ a dresser
- ✓ a coffee table
- ☐ a microwave
- ✓ dishes
- ✓ a bed
- ✓ chairs
- ✓ a stove
- ✓ a coffeemaker
- ✓ a television

Watch the video

3 GET THE PICTURE

Jessica tells her mother about her apartment. What information is true, and what information is false? Check (✓) the correct answers. Then compare with a partner.

	True	False
1. Sofia waves hello to Jessica's mom.	✓	
2. There's no microwave.		✓
3. The kitchen is very sunny.		✓
4. There's a modern refrigerator.		✓
5. The kitchen is clean.		✓
6. The bedroom has a lot of windows.		✓
7. The bedroom has a great view.		✓
8. There's a closet in the bedroom.	✓	
9. They don't have a yard.	✓	
10. The vase is in the living room.	✓	

4 WATCH FOR DETAILS

Check (✓) the correct answers. Then compare with a partner.

1. Who is on the phone?
   - ✓ Jessica's mother.
   - ☐ Sofia's mother.

2. What's the view from Jessica's bedroom?
   - ☐ A park.
   - ✓ A wall.

3. What's the present from Jessica's mother?
   - ☐ A lamp.
   - ✓ A vase.

4. What's Jessica and Sofia's address?
   - ☐ 238 Richdale Street.
   - ✓ 283 Richdale Street.

5. Where is Jessica's mother calling from?
   - ☐ The suburbs.
   - ✓ The city.

6. What does Jessica's mother say about the apartment?
   - ✓ She says it's nice.
   - ☐ She says it's perfect.

Unit 7 ▪ **27**

5 WHAT'S YOUR OPINION?

What important things do you think Jessica and Sofia still need? Check (✔) them.
Then compare with a partner.

☐ an armchair   ☑ a rug   ☐ curtains

☑ a microwave   ☑ a dining table   ☑ pictures

A: I think they need . . .
B: But they don't really need . . .

Follow-up

6 ROLE PLAY

A What questions do you think Jessica's mother asks about the new apartment?
Write six more questions.

1. Do you like your new apartment?
2. How many rooms are there?
3. is the
4. is the Living Room
5. ....
6. ....
7. ....
8. ....

We have an oven,
but we don't have
a microwave.

B **GROUP WORK** Now ask and answer questions.
Two people play the roles of Jessica and Sofia.

A: Do you like your new apartment?
B: Yes, we do.
A: How many rooms are there?
C: There are four rooms.

VIDEO ACTIVITIES

7 WHAT DID SHE SAY?

Watch the video and complete the conversation. Then practice it.

Jessica is talking to her mother on the phone and answering her questions.

Jessica: She's asking about our apartment. . . . Yeah, I ......like...... it.

Well, let me see. There are ......Four...... rooms: the living room, the ......Kitchen...... , and two bedrooms. Oh, and of course, a ......bathrrom......

The ......Living...... room? Well, it's really big. The kitchen is ......nice...... , too.

No, we don't have a ......micro...... . We just ......have...... a regular oven.

Yes, the kitchen is very ......sunny...... . There is a modern ......Refri...... .

Clean? Yeah, of course, ...it is...... clean.

The bedroom? Actually, there are a ......Lot...... of big windows. And the ......view...... is really ......great...... .

8 THERE IS/THERE ARE *Describing a home*

A Complete these sentences with **there's**, **there are**, and **there aren't**.

1. ......There are...... eight rooms in our house, and ......there's...... a garage, too.
2. ......there are...... some trees in the yard, but ......ther are...... any flowers.
3. ......there are...... some armchairs in the living room, and ......ther's...... a large table in the dining room.
4. ......ther arent...... any pictures in the dining room, but ......there...... some in the living room.
5. ......there...... a stove and a refrigerator in the kitchen, but ......ther's...... no microwave oven.
6. ......there...... three bedrooms in the house, and ......ther's...... one bathroom.

B Rewrite the sentences in part A so that they are true for your house or apartment. Then compare with a partner.

8 The night shift

1 VOCABULARY Jobs

A Write the jobs under the pictures. Then compare with a partner.

| ambulance driver | ✓ doctor | taxi driver | waiter |

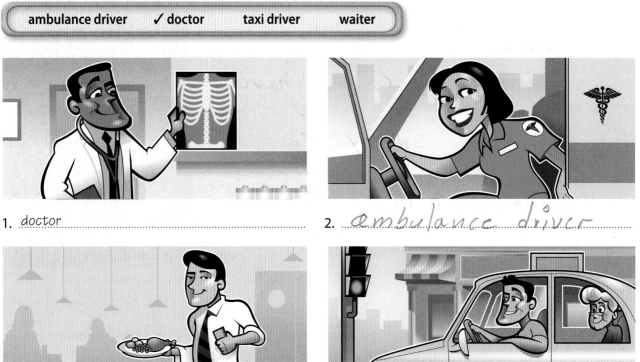

1. doctor

2. ambulance driver

3. waiter

4. Taxi driver

B **PAIR WORK** Choose a job from part A. Say what you do. Use the sentences in the box or your own ideas. Your partner guesses the job.

I take people to the emergency room.	I wear a uniform.
I work at night.	I help sick people.
I sit all day / all night.	I stand all day / all night.
I work in a hospital.	I work in a restaurant.

A: I stand all day.
B: Are you a doctor?
A: No, I'm a waiter.

2 WHAT DO YOU SEE?

Watch the video with the sound off. Write each person's job. Then compare with a partner.

1. ....

2. *amb* ....

3. ....

4. *taxi driber* ....

☰ Watch the video

3 GET THE PICTURE

A Check your answers to Exercise 2. Were they correct?

B These people work at night. What time do they start? What time do they finish?
Write the times. Then compare with a partner.

	Eva	Trey	Dwayne	Gio
Starts	11:00 p.m.	11:Pm	11:Pm	12 am
Finishes	7:A.M	7:am	7:00	12 Ppm

4 WATCH FOR DETAILS

Check (✓) the correct answers. Then compare with a partner.

Eva

1. Eva North thinks her job is ....
   - ☐ dangerous
   - ☑ stressful

2. Eva .... her job.
   - ☑ likes
   - ☐ doesn't like

Trey

3. Trey thinks his job is ....
   - ☐ busy, but interesting
   - ☑ difficult, but exciting

4. Trey works for .... hours, and then he has a breakfast break.
   - ☑ five
   - ☐ seven

Dwayne

5. Dwayne goes to school in the ....
   - ☑ morning
   - ☐ afternoon

6. Dwayne wakes up about ....
   - ☑ 10:00 P.M.
   - ☐ 12:00 P.M.

7. .... is a hard day for Dwayne.
   - ☐ Tuesday
   - ☑ Thursday

Gio

8. Taxi drivers on the night shift often work .... hours.
   - ☐ 10 to 15
   - ☑ 12 to 14

9. It's .... when Rachel speaks to Gio.
   - ☑ 6:00 A.M.
   - ☐ 7:00 A.M.

10. Gio thinks he .... hard.
    - ☐ works
    - ☑ doesn't work

📋 Follow-up

5 ROLE PLAY

PAIR WORK Play the roles of the people in the video. Give your real opinion of the jobs. Use the words in the box.

dangerous	easy	interesting	relaxing	stressful
difficult	exciting	pleasant	safe	unpleasant

A: What do you do, Eva?
B: I'm a doctor.
A: Oh, that's an exciting job!
B: Yes, but it's very stressful.

Language close-up

6 WHAT DID THEY SAY?

Watch the video and complete the conversation. Then practice it.

A reporter is talking to people who work at night.

Rachel: I'm Rachel Park, and I'm ......standing...... in front of
Memorial Hospital with Eva North. She works
.....her..... in the hospital. Eva, ...what.....
do you do?

Eva: I'm a .....a doctos.....

Rachel: .....Were..... do you work, exactly?

Eva: Right here in the emergency .....Room.... .

Rachel: Is it .....busy..... at night?

Eva: Yes, yes, it .....is..... .

Rachel: Really?

Eva: All .....day..... and all night.

Rachel: .....how..... do you like your job?

Eva: It's .....Stressful.. . I work .....Long..... hours – from
11:00 to 7:00. But .....every..... day
in the hospital is different. I .....Like..... it. . . . Oh,
actually, I'm .....Sorry..... . I have to go.

7 SIMPLE PRESENT TENSE *Talking about work and school*

A Complete these conversations. Use the correct forms of the verb. Then practice the conversations.

1. A: .....Does..... Dwayne .....work..... (work) at night?

   B: Yes, he .....Does.... (do). He .....go.s..... (go) to school in the morning
   and .....Does.. (do) his homework in the afternoon.

   A: When .....Does..... he .....Sleep..... (sleep)?

   B: That's a good question!

2. A: Where .....do..... Eva and Trey .....work..... (work)?

   B: They .....work..... (work) at a hospital.

   A: What .....do..... they .....do..... (do), exactly?

   B: Eva .....take..... (take) care of sick people, and Trey
   .....drive..... (drive) an ambulance.

B **PAIR WORK** Now ask your partner these questions.

1. Do you have classes during the day? What time do you go to school?
2. How do you go to school? How do you go home?
3. When do you do your homework? Where do you do it?
4. Do you have a job? Do you work at night?

examen
unidad 6 7 8

Unit 8 ■ **33**

9 At the diner

1 VOCABULARY Brunch

A Find these things in the picture. Match. Then compare with a partner.

1. ....g.... broccoli	6. .... granola	11. .... steak and eggs
2. .... coffee	7. .... a green salad	12. .... tea
3. .... corn	8. .... jam	13. .... toast with butter
4. .... eggs	9. .... orange juice	14. .... yogurt
5. .... a fruit salad	10. .... pancakes with syrup	

a b c d e

f g h i j

k l m n

B GROUP WORK What do your classmates have for breakfast? Ask them.

A: What do you usually have for breakfast?
B: I usually have eggs and toast.
C: I always have coffee and fruit.
D: I never eat breakfast.

2 WHAT DO YOU SEE?

Watch the video with the sound off. Which of these foods do you see? Check (✓) your answers.

- ☐ broccoli and corn
- ✓ coffee
- ☐ eggs
- ☐ fruit salad
- ☐ muffins
- ☐ orange juice
- ☐ pancakes
- ☐ rice
- ☐ steak and eggs
- ☐ tea
- ☐ toast
- ☐ yogurt and granola

☰ Watch the video

3 GET THE PICTURE

Match the people with their brunches. Check (✓) all correct answers.

	1	2	3	4
coffee	☐	☐	☐	☐
eggs	☐	☐	☐	☐
a fruit salad	☐	☐	☐	☐
granola	☐	☐	☐	☐
a green salad	☐	☐	☐	☐
orange juice	☐	☐	☐	☐
pancakes	☐	☐	☐	☐
tea	☐	☐	☐	☐
toast	☐	☐	☐	☐
water	☐	☐	☐	☐
yogurt	☐	☐	☐	☐

4 WATCH FOR DETAILS

Check (✓) the correct answers. Then compare with a partner.

1. The young man .... jam for his toast.
   - ☐ wants
   - ✓ doesn't want

2. The man .... has coffee in the morning.
   - ☐ always
   - ☐ usually

3. The woman .... sugar in her tea.
   - ☐ likes
   - ☐ doesn't like

4. She is visiting from ....
   - ☐ California
   - ☐ Canada

5. The brunch special today at Sunny's is ....
   - ☐ steak and eggs
   - ☐ bacon and eggs

6. The man .... the special.
   - ☐ wants
   - ☐ doesn't want

7. The boy's name is ....
   - ☐ Richie
   - ☐ Ricky

8. The boy likes ....
   - ☐ broccoli
   - ☐ corn

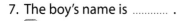

5 WHAT'S YOUR OPINION?

PAIR WORK Which of these meals do you like? Tell your partner why.

A: I like this meal. I love yogurt.
B: Really? I hate yogurt!

6 PLAN A MENU

PAIR WORK You work at the Happy Day Restaurant. Plan eight brunch dishes for the menu. List drinks, too. Then compare menus around the class.

HAPPY DAY RESTAURANT

Open 24 hours
7 days a week

A: Let's serve two eggs with toast.
B: That sounds good. Let's also serve . . .

Language close-up

7 WHAT DID THEY SAY?

Watch the video and complete the conversation. Then practice it.

Jamal Greene is talking to people about brunch.

Student: And I'll have ......*two*...... ......*eggs*...... , some toast with
.... , and some orange juice, ...

Server: Do you want any .... with your toast?

Student: No, ...

Jamal: Hi. I see you're having some .... , too.

Student: Yes, I am.

Jamal: Do you .... have coffee with your meal?

Student: Yes, I do. I .... late at night, and I'm sleepy
in the ....

Jamal: Now, today is .... , and there's a special brunch
menu. Do you ever have .... here on weekdays?

Student: No. On weekdays, I .... breakfast at home.

Jamal: What .... lunch?

Student: I .... have lunch at school with my ....

Jamal: OK. Well, enjoy your ....

Student: Thanks.

8 ADVERBS OF FREQUENCY *Talking about eating habits*

A Complete the sentences. Choose adverbs that are true for you. Then compare
with a partner.

> always   never   seldom   sometimes   usually

I always have a big breakfast.

1. I .... have a big breakfast.
2. People in my country .... eat steak and eggs for breakfast.
3. I .... drink orange juice with my breakfast.
4. I .... drink coffee in the morning.
5. I .... have time for breakfast.
6. On weekends, I .... have a big breakfast.

B **CLASS ACTIVITY** Do you and your partner have the same
or different breakfast habits? Tell the class.

"I seldom have a big breakfast, but Laura always has a big breakfast."

10 What's your sport?

1 VOCABULARY Sports

A Match. Then compare with a partner.

baseball	cricket	handball	tennis
basketball	✓ golf	soccer	

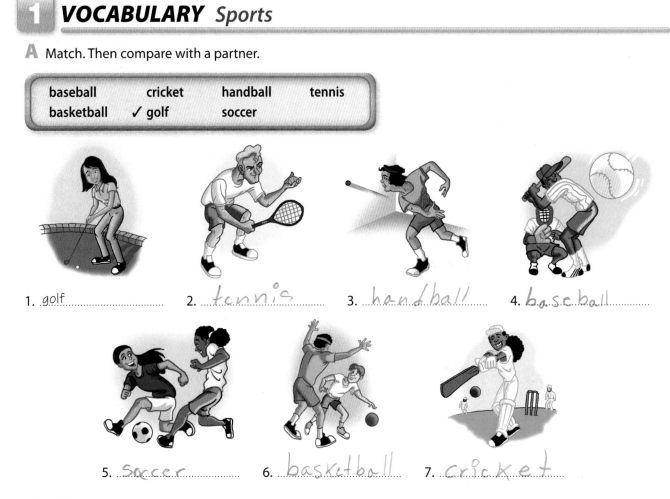

1. golf
2. tennis
3. handball
4. baseball
5. soccer
6. basketball
7. cricket

B PAIR WORK What sports can your partner play? Ask him or her.
Use the words in part A or your own ideas.

A: Can you play baseball?
B: Yes, I can, but not very well. Can you play golf?
A: No, I can't.

2 WHAT DO YOU SEE?

Watch the first minute of the video with the sound off. Which of these
sports do you see? Check (✓) your answers.

✓ baseball	☐ bike riding	☐ golf	✓ soccer
☐ basketball	✓ cricket	☐ hockey	✓ tennis

3 GET THE PICTURE

A What sports do these people enjoy? Check (✓) all correct answers.

	1	2	3	4
cricket	☐	☐	☐	☐
golf	☐	☐	☐	☐
soccer	✓	☐	☐	☐
tennis	☐	☐	☐	☐

B One of the people in part A doesn't play a sport. What does that person say? Complete the sentence.
I don't *play* .... I .... it.

4 WATCH FOR DETAILS

Check (✓) the correct answers. Then compare with a partner.

Omar

1. The players on Omar's team are from the same ....
   ☐ city
   ✓ country
2. They practice every ....
   ✓ day
   ☐ weekend

Ian

3. Ian's sport .... very popular in the U.S.
   ☐ is
   ✓ isn't
4. There are .... people on a cricket team.
   ☐ 7
   ✓ 11

Diane

5. Diane says she .... tennis.
   ☐ likes
   ✓ loves
6. Diane .... tennis.
   ☐ plays
   ✓ doesn't play

Susan

7. Susan's .... takes the kids to the playground.
   ✓ husband
   ☐ sister
8. Susan thinks her favorite sport is *hand ball*
   ✓ relaxing
   ☐ exciting

Unit 10 ▪ **39**

Follow-up

5 ROLE PLAY *A day at the park*

PAIR WORK Choose a partner. Your partner is a reporter. Answer his or her questions.
Use the questions in the box and your own ideas.

> Can you play . . . ?   What sports do you like?
> Who do you play with?   How often do you practice?

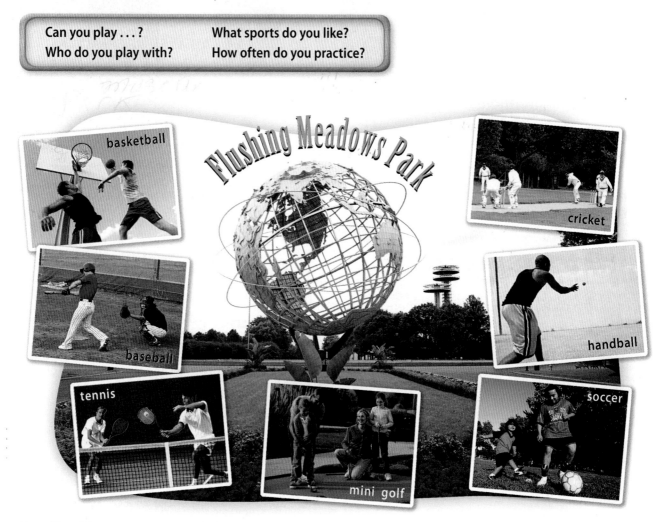

basketball

Flushing Meadows Park

cricket

handball

baseball

tennis

mini golf

soccer

Start like this:
A: Hi. Can I ask you some questions about sports?
B: Sure! What do you want to know?

6 FIND SOMEONE WHO . . .

CLASS ACTIVITY Go around the class. Ask questions and complete the chart with classmates' names.

	Name		Name
Find someone who . . .			
1. plays a sport every week.	....	5. can play tennis.	....
2. doesn't like sports.	....	6. can't swim.	....
3. can play volleyball.	....	7. loves to watch baseball.	....
4. likes to play handball.	....	8. can play soccer well.	....

Language close-up

7 WHAT DID SHE SAY?

Watch the video and complete the information. Then practice it.

Lisa Kim is talking about a popular park in Queens, New York.

Lisa: Flushing Meadows ....*has*............ something for everyone.

And you don't need to ....*play*.......... sports to enjoy the

..........*Park*.......... . You ....*can*.......... also just take it

..........*easy*.......... . There are many ....*beautiful*.......... places to

.... in the park. Like this.

Best of all, you can ....*get*.......... to Flushing Meadows easily on

the ....*subway*.......... from Manhattan. The Number 7 ....*trayn*..........

takes you right to the park.

..........*but*.......... where do you get .... the train? Just

.... for the Unisphere. This giant globe ....

you that you're in Flushing Meadows. .... great,

huh? Flushing Meadows welcomes .... from all

around the world to play sports, ... sports, or just

.... a day in this beautiful park.

8 TALKING ABOUT ABILITIES AND INTERESTS

A Answer these questions with your own information. Choose from the sentences in the box.

Yes, I do.	Yes, I can.
No, I don't.	No, I can't.

Can you ski?

No, I can't!

1. A: Can you ski?
   B: ....

2. A: Do you like basketball?
   B: ....

3. A: Can you do gymnastics?
   B: ....

4. A: Do you play soccer?
   B: ....

5. A: Do you like golf?
   B: ....

6. A: Can you play tennis?
   B: ....

B Write five more questions about sports. Then ask and answer the questions with a partner.

11 A trip to Washington, D.C.

Preview

1 VOCABULARY Sightseeing activities

A Here are some things you can do in Washington, D.C. Match. Then compare with a partner.

1. ...c.... walk around the National Mall
2. ...g.... visit museums
3. ...d.... take a tour of the Capitol
4. ...h.... watch the fireworks on the National Mall
5. ...e.... see the Lincoln Memorial
6. ...a.... go to the top of the Washington Monument
7. ...f.... take a tour of the White House
8. ...b.... get on a sightseeing bus

B **GROUP WORK** What is the most interesting activity? Compare ideas.

A: What are you going to do in Washington, D.C.?
B: I'm going to take a tour of the Capitol.
C: I'm going to . . .

2 WHAT DO YOU SEE?

Watch the video with the sound off. Which activities can you see?
Check (✓) your answers.

✓ take a walk in the park
✓ visit museums
☐ go shopping

✓ see a movie
✓ take a tour of the Capitol
☐ watch the fireworks on the
National Mall

☐ see some monuments
☐ ride the subway
☐ get on a sightseeing bus

Watch the video

3 GET THE PICTURE

What are these people going to do in Washington, D.C.? Check (✓) all correct answers.

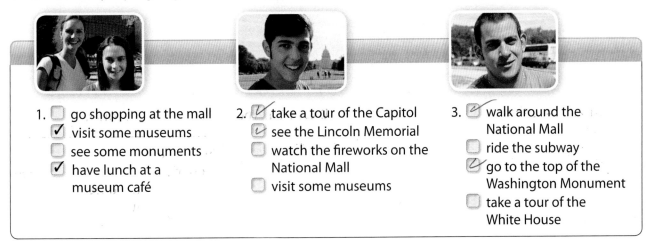

1. ☐ go shopping at the mall
   ✓ visit some museums
   ☐ see some monuments
   ✓ have lunch at a museum café

2. ✓ take a tour of the Capitol
   ✓ see the Lincoln Memorial
   ☐ watch the fireworks on the National Mall
   ☐ visit some museums

3. ✓ walk around the National Mall
   ☐ ride the subway
   ✓ go to the top of the Washington Monument
   ☐ take a tour of the White House

4 WATCH FOR DETAILS

Check (✓) the correct answers. Then compare with a friend.

1. The girl is with her ....
   ☐ aunt
   ✓ mother

2. It's the girl's .... birthday.
   ✓ 16th
   ☐ 17th

3. She wants to be a .... someday.
   ✓ pilot
   ☐ flight attendant

4. The kids think Washington is really ....
   ☐ interesting
   ✓ fun

5. The kids are with their ....
   ☐ family
   ✓ class

6. The fireworks are going to start at ....
   ☐ 9:00
   ✓ 10:00

7. The woman is going to visit some ....
   ✓ monuments
   ☐ museums

8. The man is going to .... to the White House.
   ☐ drive
   ✓ walk

9. Marc is going to ....
   ☐ walk around the National Mall
   ✓ get on a sightseeing bus

5 WHAT THE PEOPLE SAY

What do these people say? Complete the sentences. Then compare with a partner.

1. There are _museums_ _parks_ , famous buildings, and lots of monuments.

2. _I want to visit_ the National Air and Space Museum.

3. I'm an artist, so I want to see the art museum. So, _going to to spend_ the whole day there.

☰ Follow-up

6 A DAY IN WASHINGTON, D.C.

A **GROUP WORK** Plan a day in Washington, D.C. Decide on two things to do in the morning, two things to do in the afternoon, and something to do in the evening.

Take a ride on the Metro.

Eat in a restaurant in Chinatown.

Attend a concert at the Kennedy Center.

Watch the boats at Washington Harbor.

Visit the National Zoo.

Go shopping in Georgetown.

B **CLASS ACTIVITY** Share your plans with the class.

"In the morning, we're going to . . ."
"Then we're going to . . ."

☰ Language close-up

7 WHAT DID THEY SAY?

Watch the video and complete the conversation. Then practice it.

Marc Jones is interviewing people on the National Mall in Washington, D.C.

Marc: And who are you ....*with*.......... ?

Woman: This is my ....*thare*........ . Today's her 16th ....*beysdha*........ . We're .... Washington, D.C., for her birthday.

Marc: Well, ...*Hapy*........ birthday!

Girl: Thanks!

Marc: So, ... are you going to .... ?

Girl: Well, we're going to visit some .... And then, we're going to .... lunch at a café in the museum.

Marc: Nice! .... museum are you going to .... ?

Girl: I want to ....*visit*........ the National Air and Space Museum. I .... to be a pilot someday.

Marc: Great! ....*Hapi*........ , have a good day.

8 FUTURE WITH BE GOING TO *Talking about plans*

A Complete these conversations. Use the correct future with *be going to* forms of the verbs in parentheses.

1. A: ......*Are*...... you ....*going to do*.... (do) anything on Friday night?

   B: Yes, I ...*m see*... (see) a movie.

2. A: What time ...*leave*... you ....*going*........ (leave) school today?

   B: I ...*am go*... (go) home at 7:00 P.M.

3. A: What .... you .... (have) for dinner tonight?

   B: We .... (have) fish.

4. A: .... you .... (study) English tonight?

   B: No. I .... (watch) TV.

B **PAIR WORK** Practice the conversations in part A. Use your own information.

12 Where does it hurt?

☰ Preview

1 VOCABULARY Health problems

A Write the health problems under the pictures. Then compare with a partner.

I feel dizzy.	I have a backache.	✓ I have an earache.
I feel tired.	I have a cough.	I have a fever.

1. I have an earache.

2. ....

3. ....

4. ....

5. ....

6. ....

B PAIR WORK Ask and answer questions about the people in part A.

A: What's the matter with the woman?
B: She has an earache.

2 WHAT DO YOU SEE?

Watch the video with the sound off. Check (✓) all correct answers.

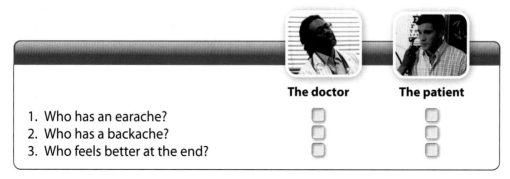

	The doctor	The patient
1. Who has an earache?	☐	☐
2. Who has a backache?	☐	☐
3. Who feels better at the end?	☐	☐

3 GET THE PICTURE

A Check your answers to Exercise 2. Were they correct?

B Complete the doctor's notes about the patient. Then compare with a partner.

Patient Care

Patient's name: **Peter Krum**

Comments:

He swims .... times a week,
and he has an ....
He .... a little dizzy, too.

John J. Smith, MD
University Clinic

R*x*

Take one pill
.... breakfast.
Use the ear drops
every ....
Don't swim for
.... weeks.

4 WATCH FOR DETAILS

Check (✓) the correct answers. Then compare with a partner.

1. When does Peter feel the pain?
   - ☐ Constantly.
   - ☑ From time to time.

2. What is wrong with Peter?
   - ☐ He has extra wax in his ear.
   - ☐ He has a serious fever.

3. When does the doctor's back hurt?
   - ☐ When he stands a lot.
   - ☐ All the time.

4. Why does Peter know how to fix backaches?
   - ☐ His father is a doctor.
   - ☐ His father has the same problem.

5. What does Peter tell the doctor to do first?
   - ☐ Pull his left knee up.
   - ☐ Turn his body to the side.

6. Which way does Peter tell the doctor to turn?
   - ☐ To the right.
   - ☐ To the left.

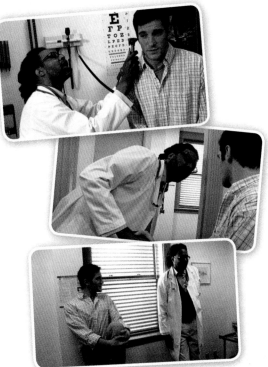

5 DO YOU REMEMBER?

What does the doctor ask the patient? Check (✓) the correct questions.
Then compare with a partner.

- ☐ Why are you here today?
- ☑ How are you feeling today?
- ☐ Do you have a cold?
- ☐ Do you have a headache?
- ☐ Do you have a cough?
- ☐ Do you have a fever?
- ☐ Do you have a sore throat?
- ☐ Do you feel terrible?
- ☐ Do you feel tired?
- ☐ Do you exercise often?
- ☐ Do you go swimming every day?
- ☐ Do you need some medicine?

Follow-up

6 ROLE PLAY *At the doctor's office*

A **PAIR WORK** Take turns playing the roles of the patient and the doctor.
Act out the first part of their conversation. Use the checked questions in Exercise 5.

A: How are you feeling today?
B: Not so good, Doc.

B **PAIR WORK** Talk about your health. Use the problems below or your own ideas.

| **the flu** | **a headache** | **a stomachache** | **sore eyes** | **a toothache** |

A: Do you ever get the flu?
B: I seldom get the flu. What about you? Do you get the flu?
A: Yes, I do, sometimes.

≡ Language close-up

7 *WHAT DID THEY SAY?*

Watch the video and complete the conversation. Then practice it.

Dr. Smith is examining Peter to find out why Peter doesn't feel well.

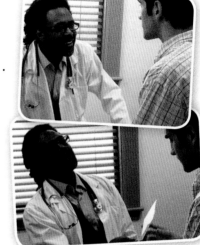

Dr. Smith: So, do you go swimming ......*every*...... ......*day*...... ?

Peter: No, not every day. .... three times a ....

Dr. Smith: I think I .... the problem.

Peter: Is it .... ?

Dr. Smith: Oh, ... You have some ....
wax in your ear, probably .... you swim so much.
I'm going to .... you some .... ,
and you should feel .... in a week.

Peter: OK. .... good.

Dr. Smith: I'm going to give you some .... and
some pills. .... one pill .... breakfast.
Use the ear drops before ....

Peter: One pill .... the morning, ear drops .... night.

Dr. Smith: That's .... !

8 *IMPERATIVES* *Giving advice*

A Complete the conversations. Choose from the advice in the box. Then compare with a partner.

Don't lift heavy things.	Drink a lot of orange juice.	Stay in bed for two days.
Don't try new foods.	✓ Drink hot tea with lemon.	Take two aspirin and close your eyes.

1. A: I have a sore throat.
   B: Drink hot tea with lemon. ....

2. A: I have a headache.
   B: ....

3. A: I have a backache.
   B: ....

4. A: I have the flu.
   B: ....

5. A: I have a stomachache.
   B: ....

6. A: I have a cold.
   B: ....

> I have a sore throat.

> Drink hot tea with lemon.

B Now complete the conversations in part A with your own ideas. Then compare your advice in groups.

 **Across the bridge**

Preview

1 VOCABULARY Directions

Look at the map of the Capilano Suspension Bridge area. Complete the sentences with the words in the box. Then compare with a partner.

across	behind	left	✓ right
around	in front of	past	up

Bridge

Living Forest

Canyon Lookout

Totem Park

Canyon Café

Gift Shop

Tickets

Entrance

1. After you enter the park, turn ...._right_........ . Walk .... the path, ... the Canyon Café. The bridge is on the ....

2. At the bridge, turn to your right and the gift shop is directly .... you. To get to the Canyon Lookout, walk .... the gift shop to the left. The Lookout is .... the gift shop.

3. To visit the Living Forest exhibition, go .... the bridge.

2 GUESS THE FACTS

The Capilano Suspension Bridge is a famous tourist attraction in Canada. What other things do you think visitors can find at the park? Check (✓) your guesses. Then compare with a partner.

- [ ] a gift shop
- [ ] a nature center
- [ ] a rain forest
- [ ] a restaurant
- [ ] a zoo
- [ ] an amusement park
- [ ] an art museum
- [ ] totem poles

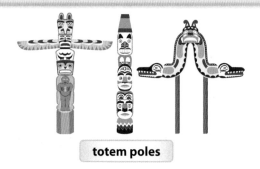

totem poles

3 WHAT DO YOU SEE?

Watch the video with the sound off. Number the pictures in order from 1 to 6.

Ben and Sara arrived at the park.

Watch the video

4 GET THE PICTURE

A Check your answers to Exercise 3. Were they correct?

B Write the correct description under each picture in Exercise 3. Use the ideas in the box. Then compare with a partner.

Ben and Sara looked at the bridge.	✓ Ben and Sara arrived at the park.
Ben helped Sara cross the bridge.	Ben took pictures of Sara.
Sara got scared on the bridge and froze.	Sara took pictures of Ben.

5 WATCH FOR DETAILS

Check (✓) the correct answers. Then compare with a partner.

1. Sara says the bridge is one of .... most popular tourist attractions.
   - ✓ Vancouver's
   - ☐ Seattle's

2. Ben wants to go to the .... first.
   - ☐ totem poles
   - ☐ restaurant

3. The totem poles are .... the gift shop.
   - ☐ next to
   - ☐ across from

4. Sara tells Ben to stand .... two totem poles.
   - ☐ behind
   - ☐ between

5. Ben wants to buy a .... at the gift shop.
   - ☐ present for his mother
   - ☐ picture of the bridge

6. Ben admits that he .... high places.
   - ☐ likes
   - ☐ doesn't like

7. Sara .... angry with Ben.
   - ☐ gets
   - ☐ doesn't get

8. Sara freezes when she looks ....
   - ☐ down from the bridge
   - ☐ across the bridge

Follow-up

6 DIRECTIONS

 Write directions to two places in or near your school. Use the expressions in the box. Then share the directions with another group.

Go right / left . . .	**It's on the corner of . . . and . . .**	**It's next to . . .**
Walk one block . . .	**It's between . . . and . . .**	**It's behind . . .**
Turn right / left . . .	**It's across from . . .**	**It's in front of . . .**

Place 1: ....

....

....

Place 2: ....

....

....

Start like this:

A: How do I get to . . . ?
B: Walk out the door and . . .
C: Then . . .

Language close–up

7 WHAT DID THEY SAY?

Watch the video and complete the conversation. Then practice it.

Ben and Sara are visiting the Capilano Suspension Bridge.

Sara: We got some great ......photos.......... . Now .... go
cross that bridge.

Ben: Oh! I just .... !

Sara: .... ?

Ben: We have to get a .... for my mom.
We ....

Sara: Yeah?

Ben: The gift shop's just .... there. We can get her
something .... nice . . .

Sara: Ben . . .

Ben: . . . and then we can .... to the
restaurant, and we can .... something to eat.

Sara: Ben?

Ben: What?

Sara: What's .... on?

Ben: What do you mean?

Sara: Well, ... you wanted to go to Totem Park. ....
you want to go to the gift shop. What .... the bridge?

Ben: Well, ... , I don't like .... places. I get scared, and I freeze up.

Sara: So you .... want to go .... the bridge?

8 OPPOSITES *Giving directions*

These people need to go the other way. Complete the answers.
Then practice the conversations with a partner.

1. A: Do I walk up this path?
   B: No, not up. Walk .....down...... the path.

2. A: Is the restaurant around the corner on the left?
   B: It's around the corner, but it's on the ....

3. A: Is the restroom in front of the ticket booth?
   B: No, it's .... the ticket booth.

4. A: Are the totem poles far from here?
   B: No, they're really ....

5. A: Do I turn right at the sign?
   B: No, you turn ....

6. A: Is the café two blocks west of the school?
   B: No, it's two blocks .... of the school.

 # How was your vacation?

1 VOCABULARY *Vacation problems*

Look at the problems that people had on vacation. Write the sentences under the pictures. Then compare with a partner.

> *Was* is the past tense of *is.*

I got sunburned.	There was no air-conditioning.	The hotel was too noisy.
✓ I lost my passport.	They canceled my flight.	I didn't like the food.
I was in an accident.	I forgot my camera.	

1. I lost my passport.

2. ....

3. ....

4. ....

5. ....

6. ....

7. ....

8. ....

2 WHAT DO YOU SEE?

Watch the first 40 seconds of the video with the sound off.
Why do you think Hugo's arms and back hurt?

☐ He was in an accident.
☐ He exercised a lot.
☐ He got sunburned.

 Watch the video

3 GET THE PICTURE

A Check your answer to Exercise 2. Was it correct?

B These statements are false. Change one word to correct them. Then compare with a partner.

Evan

Hugo

Hugo
1. ~~Evan~~ was on vacation last week.

2. Evan slaps Hugo's face.

3. The first day, Hugo ran on the beach.

4. Evan and Hugo's co-worker, Harry, is working.

5. The elevator at Hugo's hotel didn't work.

6. Hugo bought a new suitcase for his trip.

7. Hugo remembered to pack his camera.

8. Hugo came back from his vacation on Saturday.

4 WATCH FOR DETAILS

Check (✓) the correct answers. Then compare with a partner.

1. Evan wants to hear about Hugo's ....
   ☐ business trip   ✓ vacation

2. Hugo tells Evan that his vacation was ....
   ☐ great   ☐ OK

3. Hugo went to the beach ....
   ☐ one time   ☐ two times

4. Hugo says that his hotel was really ....
   ☐ hot   ☐ cold

5. Hugo didn't .... well on his vacation.
   ☐ eat   ☐ sleep

6. Hugo didn't take any pictures because he left his camera at ....
   ☐ home   ☐ work

7. Hugo spent Saturday night at the ....
   ☐ hotel   ☐ airport

8. Evan is going to .... tomorrow.
   ☐ Chicago   ☐ Morocco

5 VACATION ACTIVITIES

A Match. Then compare with a partner.

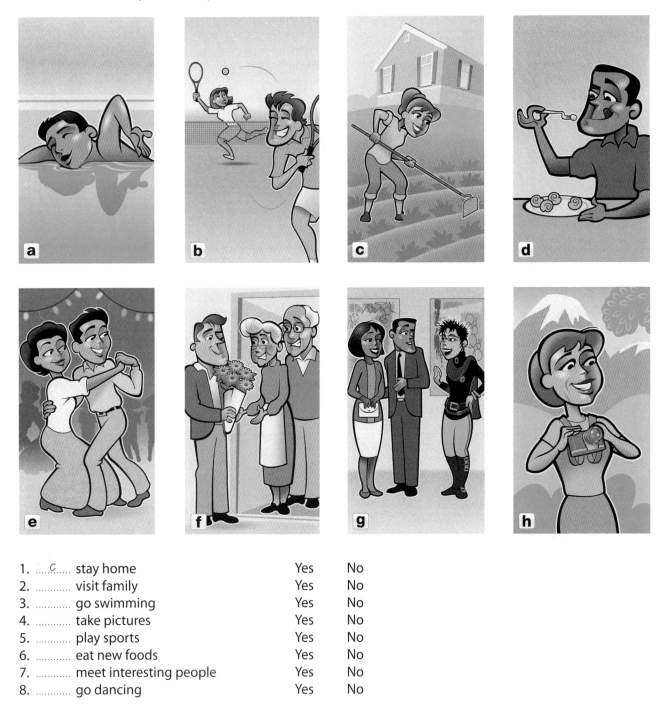

1. ...c... stay home   Yes   No
2. .... visit family   Yes   No
3. .... go swimming   Yes   No
4. .... take pictures   Yes   No
5. .... play sports   Yes   No
6. .... eat new foods   Yes   No
7. .... meet interesting people   Yes   No
8. .... go dancing   Yes   No

B Did you do any of the things in part A on your last vacation? Circle **Yes** or **No**.

C **PAIR WORK** Now ask and answer questions about your last vacation.

A: Did you stay home on your last vacation?
B: Yes, I did. **or** No, I didn't.

Language close-up

6 WHAT DID THEY SAY?

Watch the video and complete the conversation. Then practice it.

Hugo just got back from his vacation.

Hugo: I was really happy when I ....got....... there.
It was .... The water was so .... , and
the sand was .... There were palm ....
and cool breezes. I couldn't wait to hit the ....

Evan: Lucky .... So what did you .... first?

Hugo: Well, the first day I .... relaxed on the beach.
I even fell asleep ....

Evan: Kind of like Harry there?

Hugo: Yeah. Like ....

Evan: So you fell asleep .... the beach. That
sounds ....

Hugo: Yeah, it was, except I didn't use .... sunscreen.

Evan: Uh-oh.

Hugo: And I got sunburned .... over.

Evan: Ouch! So that explains the . . .

Hugo: ....

7 PAST TENSE *Talking about vacations*

A Complete these conversations with the past tense of the verbs
in parentheses. Then practice the conversations.

1. A: ....Did....... you .....visit..... (visit) your family on your vacation?
   B: Yes, I did. I .... (go) home because my sister ....
   (get) married last Saturday. She .... (wear) a beautiful
   white dress.

2. A: .... you .... (go) anywhere interesting on
   your last vacation?
   B: Yes. I .... (go) to Mexico and .... (take) a
   Spanish class.

3. A: .... you .... (have) fun on your vacation?
   B: Yes, we did. We .... (have) a great time. We .... (eat)
   a lot of new foods and .... (meet) some interesting people.

4. A: .... you .... (do) anything interesting on
   your vacation?
   B: No, not really. I .... (stay) home and .... (work)
   around the house. I .... (paint) the front porch and
   .... (clean) the basement. Oh, I .... (see) a few good movies, too.

B **PAIR WORK** Practice the conversations again. Use your own information.

15 On Broadway

▤ Preview

1 VOCABULARY *The theater*

Do you know these theater words?
Match them to the pictures. Then
compare with a partner.

| actor | dancers | musical | musician | ✓play | usher |

1. play

2. _____

3. _____

4. _____

5. _____

6. _____

2 THEATER QUIZ

A PAIR WORK Here are some popular musicals. They began on Broadway and then became popular
around the world. How many do you know? Match.

1. The Lion King
2. Beauty and the Beast
3. Mary Poppins
4. Billy Elliot
5. West Side Story
6. Hairspray

B PAIR WORK Talk about these questions.

1. Did you ever go to the theater to see a play or a musical? If so, what did you see?
2. The musicals in part A are also movies. Which of the movies did you see?
   Did you like each movie? Why or why not?
3. Look again at the musicals in part A. Which one(s) do you think you'd like to
   see – either at the theater or at the movies? Why?

3 WHAT DO YOU SEE?

A *Watch the video with the sound off.* Does each person have a job in the theater?
Circle **Yes** or **No**.

1. Yes   No

2. Yes   No

3. Yes   No

B Where is Broadway?
Check (✓) the correct answer.
Then compare with a partner.

- [ ] Chicago
- [ ] Denver
- [ ] Los Angeles
- [ ] Miami
- [ ] New York
- [ ] San Francisco
- [ ] Seattle

☰ Watch the video

4 GET THE PICTURE

A Check your answers to Exercise 3. Were they correct?

B Where are these people from? Match.

Sylvia

Frank

Andrea

1. .... Sylvia   a. New York

2. .... Frank   b. Mexico

3. .... Andrea   c. Colorado

5 WATCH FOR DETAILS

A Check (✓) all correct answers.

☐ Sylvia came to New York four years ago.

✓ Sylvia came to New York to be an actress.

☐ Before she came to New York, she studied acting.

☐ Her parents were happy when she came to New York.

☐ Her parents thought New York was a big, interesting city.

☐ Her parents love New York now.

☐ Andrea is a musician.

☐ She works five days a week.

☐ There are two shows on Tuesdays.

☐ The theater is closed on Mondays.

☐ Andrea was born and raised in Brazil.

☐ Andrea studied dance in college.

☐ Frank is an actor.

☐ He took this job because he needed the money.

☐ He doesn't like his job.

☐ He meets a lot of nice people.

☐ He came to New York to study acting.

☐ He wants to write movies.

B Look again at the sentences in part A. Correct the false statements. Then compare with a partner.

> five
> Sylvia came to New York ~~four~~ years ago.

C **PAIR WORK** Now ask and answer questions about the people in part A.

A: Did Sylvia come to New York to be an actress?
B: Yes, she did. Is she working as a Spanish teacher?
A: No, she isn't. She's working as a yoga teacher.

Follow-up

6 INTERVIEW

A You're interviewing a young actor. First, match the questions with the answers.
Then, practice the interview with a partner.

1. ...b... When did you come to New York?   a. *Broadway Dreams.*

2. .... Where did you grow up?   b. I came here three years ago.

3. .... Did you study acting in school?   c. In a small town in Arizona.

4. .... What did you do before you came here?   d. No, but I'm studying it now.

5. .... What was the name of your first show?   e. I worked in a restaurant.

B **PAIR WORK** Now interview each other. Use the questions in part A.
Answer with your own ideas.

Language close-up

7 WHAT DID THEY SAY?

Watch the video and complete the conversation. Then practice it.

Rachel Park is interviewing people on Broadway.

Rachel: Times Square. Midtown Manhattan. And the heart and the ....home.......... of the theater
district: Broadway! .... is New York City! And no .... to New York is
complete until you go to a Broadway .... or musical. Broadway
is a .... and exciting place to be. It's .... the dream
of thousands of actors, ..., musicians, and other artists. Let's
.... with some of the people who actually work here on Broadway.

Rachel: Hi, Sylvia.
Sylvia: Hi.
Rachel: .... is Sylvia Santiago. Sylvia, were you ....
in New York?
Sylvia: No. I .... born in Mexico.
Rachel: And when did you .... to New York?
Sylvia: I .... here five years ago. I .... to be an actress.
Rachel: Wow. Do you want to be in a Broadway .... ?
Sylvia: Yes! That's .... dream.
Rachel: Did you study .... before you came to New York?
Sylvia: No, I .... I studied ....

8 PAST TENSE *Giving personal information*

A Complete this interview with a Broadway actor. Use **was, were,
did**, or **didn't**. Then practice the interview with a partner.

A: Where ....did....... you grow up?
B: In Australia.
A: .... you study music when you .... a child?
B: Yes, I .... I studied the violin. Later, I studied acting.
A: .... your parents actors, too?
B: Yes and no. My father .... a professional actor, but my mother
.... a musician. Now they're both teachers.
A: When .... you come to the U.S.?
B: In 2003.
A: .... you get an acting job right away?
B: Yes, I .... I .... lucky. I got a job with the touring company
of a musical. So I .... have to get a day job to support myself, like most actors.

B **CLASS ACTIVITY** Find out about your classmates. Write five more questions.
Then go around the class and ask them.

1. *Where were you born?* ....
2. ....
3. ....
4. ....
5. ....
6. ....

Then he said . . .

1 VOCABULARY *Dating activities*

A **PAIR WORK** What's the perfect date? Add two more activities to the list below.
Then rate each activity from 1 (you like it a lot) to 5 (you don't like it very much).

I like to . . .

a. eat in nice restaurants.

b. go to art fairs.

c. go to sporting events.

d. go to the movies.

e. go to amusement parks.

f. go to dance clubs.

g. go to parties.

h. go to concerts.

Your suggestions: i. .... ☐   j. .... ☐

B **GROUP WORK** Talk about your dating suggestions in part A.

A: I like to . . . on dates.
B: I like to . . .
C: I don't like to . . . on dates. I like to . . .

2 GOOD EXCUSES

A Sometimes people invite us to do something, but we can't accept, or don't want to accept.
Look at these excuses. Number them from 1 (the best excuse) to 8 (the worst excuse).

.... I have to babysit.
.... My family and I have plans.
.... I have an appointment.

.... I need to clean my room.
.... I have dance class.
.... I'm going to study.

.... I'm reading a new book.
.... My grandparents are coming over.

B **PAIR WORK** Take turns choosing an activity from
Exercise 1 and an excuse from part A of Exercise 2.

A: Do you want to go to the movies tonight?
B: I'm really sorry, but I can't. I have to babysit.

3 GUESS THE FACTS

Watch the first 45 seconds of the video with the sound on.
Guess where Abby went on her date. Check (✓) your answer.

She went to . . .

- ☐ a basketball game.
- ☐ an amusement park.
- ☐ an art fair.
- ☐ the movies.

☰ Watch the video

4 GET THE PICTURE

A Check your answer to Exercise 3. Was it correct?

B Put the pictures in order from 1 to 7. Then write the correct sentence under each picture.
Compare with a partner.

1

Abby refused Greg's invitations.

Abby got sick and had to sit down.
✓ Abby refused Greg's invitations.
Abby's family and Greg had lunch.
Abby's sister gave Greg his wallet.

Greg accepted Abby's invitation.
Greg and Abby went on a roller coaster.
Greg bought Abby's sister ice cream.

Check (✓) the correct answers. Then compare with a partner.

Abby

Peter

1. At the beginning of the video, why does Peter want to go outside?
   - ☐ He wants to have lunch with Abby.
   - ☐ He wants to hear Abby's story.
   - ☐ He wants to find Greg.

2. What does Peter mean when he says, "I'm all ears"?
   - ☐ I can't hear you.
   - ☐ I have an earache.
   - ☐ I'm listening.

3. Why did Abby refuse Greg's invitation to the game?
   - ☐ She likes some sports, but she hates basketball.
   - ☐ She likes Greg, but she doesn't want to see him.
   - ☐ She likes Greg, but she doesn't like sports.

4. What day did Abby see Greg?
   - ☐ Friday.
   - ☐ Saturday.
   - ☐ Sunday.

5. When did Greg lose his wallet?
   - ☐ On the roller coaster.
   - ☐ During lunch.
   - ☐ At the ice-cream stand.

6. At the end of the video, why does Abby refuse Greg's invitations?
   - ☐ She's really embarrassed.
   - ☐ She doesn't like him.
   - ☐ She's very busy.

Follow-up

6 **MAKE WEEKEND PLANS**

A Complete the chart with your own ideas. Then compare with a partner.

Weekend activities	Excuses for not accepting an invitation
go to the movies see a ball game go to a dance club	I have to work late. I have a date with a friend. I have to stay in and study.
....	....
....	....
....	....

B **CLASS ACTIVITY** Go around the class and invite people to do something with you this weekend. They should say they can't and give you an excuse.

A: Hi, Sammi. Would you like to go to a dance club with me this weekend?
B: Oh, sorry. I can't. I have a date with a friend.
A: OK. Maybe some other time, then.
B: Sure.

▤ Language close-up

7 WHAT DID THEY SAY?

Watch the video and complete the conversation. Then practice it.

Abby starts to tell Peter about her plans with Greg.

Peter: Great! So you ....<u>went</u>........ to the movies together.

Abby: No, I .... because of my little sister. I had

to babysit. So then he .... if I wanted to

go to the basketball game the .... night.

Peter: Oh, so you .... to the game Saturday night.

Abby: No. I turned him ....

Peter: What? Are you crazy? .... ? What was

your excuse?

Abby: No .... I told him that I like him, but I

.... do not like sports. But, um, he was

really .... about it, and he even asked me

to go to the art fair with him on ....

Peter: So you went to the art fair. I was ...., but I didn't .... you.

Abby: No, we didn't go. I couldn't. On Sunday, I had .... with my family to go

to the amusement park.

Peter: So you .... see him.

Abby: Yes, I ....

Peter: OK, wait a minute. I'm confused. .... did you see him?

8 WANT TO, NEED TO, HAVE TO *Making excuses*

Reply to these invitations, giving your own excuses. Then
practice the conversations with a partner.

1. A: Let's see a movie tonight.
   B: I can't. I have to ....

2. A: Do you want to go downtown after class?
   B: Sorry, I can't. I need to ....

3. A: Do you want to go to a party on Friday night?
   B: Friday night? Oh, I'm not free. I have to ....

4. A: Let's go dancing on Saturday night.
   B: Gee, I can't. I have to .... Sorry. ....

5. A: Do you want to go to a concert on Sunday afternoon?
   B: Sorry, I can't. I need to ....

I can't go. I have
to write a paper
for school.

interchange

FOURTH EDITION

Jack C. Richards

Series Editor: David Bohlke

CAMBRIDGE
UNIVERSITY PRESS

Intro
WORKBOOK

Contents

Credits

Illustrations

Andrezzinho: 28; **Ilias Arahovitis:** 12, 41, 49; **Daniel Baxter:** 71, 92; **Keith Bendis:** 22; **Carlos Diaz:** 44; **Jada Fitch:** 1, 29, 94; **Travis Foster:** 17; **Dylan Gibson:** 19, 64; **Chuck Gonzales:** 2, 23, 76; **Joaquin Gonzalez:** 10, 57, 96; **Dan Hubig:** 14; **Trevor Keen:** 58; **KJA-artists:** 5, 38, 69, 82

Greg Lawhun: 68, 81; **Scott MacNeill:** 37, 74, 77; **Monika Melnychuk:** 11, 51; **Karen Minot:** 31, 34, 62, 72, 78, 80, 87; **Ortelius Design:** 25; **Rob Schuster:** 13, 52, 88; **George Thompson:** 24; **Daniel Vasconcellos:** 6, 15, 21, 36, 63, 67, 79, 84; **James Yamasaki:** 7, 39

Photos

3 © PhotoAlto/SuperStock
4 © amana images inc/Alamy
5 © auremar/Shutterstock
8 *(top, left to right)* © Zakharoff/Shutterstock; © JOAT/Shutterstock; © Brooke Becker/Shutterstock; *(middle, left to right)* © Photodisc/Punchstock; © Tony Rusecki/Alamy; © India Images/Dinodia Photos/Alamy; *(bottom right)* © Britt Erlanson/Stone/Getty Images
9 *(middle right)* © David Malan/Getty Images; *(bottom)* © Radius Images/Alamy
16 © Morrison/Haller/AAD/starmaxinc/NEWSCOM
18 © iStockphoto/Thinkstock
20 © Billy E Barnes/PhotoEdit
26 *(all)* © Hemera/Thinkstock
27 *(top row)* © Stockbyte/Thinkstock; © Aflo Foto Agency/Alamy; © Jessica Peterson/RubberBall/age fotostock; *(middle row)* © MBI/Alamy; © Cultura Limited/SuperStock; © iStockphoto/Thinkstock; *(bottom row)* © Imagemore/PunchStock; © Brand X Pictures/Thinkstock; © Denkou Images/Alamy
30 © Exactostock/SuperStock
32 © Jenny Acheson/Riser/Getty Images
33 *(middle left)* © iStockphoto/Thinkstock; *(middle right)* © GraficallyMinded/Alamy
34 © INSAGO/Shutterstock
35 © Atsushi Sakai/Mixa/Alamy
40 *(top left)* © Fotosearch/Getty Images; *(bottom right)* © photos.com/Thinkstock
43 *(bottom left)* © iStockphoto/Thinkstock; © Image Source/Alamy; © Wendy Hope/Stockbyte/Getty Images; © Jose Luis Pelaez Inc/Blend Images/Alamy; *(right, top to bottom)* © iStockphoto/Thinkstock; © Bob Daemmrich/Alamy; © Comstock Images/Getty Images; © Jack Hollingsworth/Digital Vision/Thinkstock; © Photodisc/PunchStock; © David R. Frazier Photolibrary, Inc./Alamy
45 *(top left)* © Fancy/Alamy; *(middle right)* © Jupiterimages/Polka Dot/Getty Images; *(middle left)* © ampyang/Shutterstock; *(bottom right)* © Sergio Azenha/Alamy
46 *(top right)* © Rayes/Digital Vision/Thinkstock; *(bottom right)* © Creatas/Thinkstock
47 *(top right)* © Digital Vision/thinkstock; *(bottom right)* © Darren Setlow/Built Images/Alamy
48 *(clockwise from top left)* © Image Source/age fotostock; © Fuse/Getty Images; © Tetra Images/SuperStock; *(model, miner)* © iStockphoto/Thinkstock; © speedpix/Alamy
50 *(clockwise from top left)* © Hemera/Thinkstock; © Dan Peretz/Shutterstock; © iStockphoto/Thinkstock; © Foodfolio/the food passionates/Corbis; © iStockphoto/Thinkstock; © Stockbyte/Getty Images; *(middle)* © Amanda Ahn/Dbimages/Alamy
53 *(top right)* © Steve J Benbow/Axiom Photographic Agency/age fotostock; *(bottom right)* © liv friis larsen/Alamy
54 *(bottom, left to right)* © JTB Photo Communications Inc/Alamy © Dan Goldberg/FoodPix/Getty Images; © Steve Cohen/FoodPix/Getty Images
55 *(middle right, clockwise from top left)* © C Squared Studios/Photodisc/Getty Images; © iStockphoto/Thinkstock; © Hemera/Thinkstock;

© PhotoObjects.net/Thinkstock; *(bottom, left to right)* © iStockphoto/Thinkstock; © Digital Vision/PunchStock; © iStockphoto/Thinkstock; © Jules Frazier/Photodisc/Getty Images; © Stockbyte/Thinkstock; © Hemera/Thinkstock
56 *(top right)* © Benis Arapovic/Shutterstock; *(bottom left)* © STR/Stringer/AFP/Getty Images
59 *(top right)* © Michael Cogliantry/Photonica/Getty Images; *(middle right)* © Fancy Collection/SuperStock; *(bottom left)* © Adie Bush/Cultura/age fotostock
60 © Herbert Spichtinger/Corbis
61 *(middle, left to right)* © David Bratley/Alamy; © Siri Stafford/Photodisc/Getty Images; © Radius Images/Corbis; © Ocean/Corbis
65 *(top, left to right)* © Juice Images/Alamy; © Michael Hitoshi/Taxi Japan/Getty Images; © Fuse/Getty Images; *(middle, left to right)* © GoGo Images Corporation/Alamy; © Liam Norris/Cultura/Getty Images; © Altrendo images/Getty Images; *(bottom, left to right)* © Daniel Dempster Photography/Alamy; © Eric Audras/PhotoAlto/Getty Images; © Sonntag/Alloy/Corbis
66 *(top, left to right)* © Steve Kelley/Flickr/Getty Images; © Jeffrey Coolidge/Photodisc/Getty Images; *(middle, left to right)* © Taylor Hinton/istockphoto; © D Hurst/Alamy; *(bottom, left to right)* © Hemera/Thinkstock; © Matt Henry Gunther/Stone/Getty Images
70 *(top right)* *(cough syrup, nasal spray)* © iStockphoto/Thinkstock; *(cold pills)* © Helen Sessions/Alamy; *(antacid)* © Jesus Jauregui/iStockphoto; *(muscle cream)* © Olinchuk/Shutterstock; *(cough drops)* © Studioshots/Alamy; *(eyedrops)* © Hemera/Thinkstock; *(aspirin)* © Creatas/Thinkstock; *(bottom right)* © Altrendo/Getty Images
73 © Richard Walters/iStockphoto
80 © Jack Hollingsworth/Photodisc/Getty Images
83 © Douglas Peebles Photography/Alamy
85 © Walter Bibikow/Photolibrary/Getty Images
86 *(top right)* © Miles Ertman/Canopy/Corbis; *(middle left)* © Elisabeth Pollaert Smith/Photographer's Choice/Getty Images; *(bottom left)* © Jean-Pierre Pieuchot/Stone/Getty Images
87 *(all)* *(clockwise from top left)* © Bloomberg/Getty Images; © Photo File/MLB Photos/Getty Images; © Silver Screen Collection/Moviepix /Getty Images; © Hulton Archive/Getty Images; © Bettmann/Corbis; © Cat's Collection/Corbis
89 © Bill Aron/PhotoEdit
90 *(right, top to bottom)* © Corbis/Blend Images; © Alyson Aliano/Taxi Getty Images
91 *(top, left to right)* © Jonathan Ross/Digital Vision/Getty Images; © Reggie Casagrande/Photodisc/Getty Images
93 © Nick Wright/Photolibrary/Getty Images
94 © Blend Images/Corbis
95 © Manchan/Photodisc/Getty Images

Puzzles

13 Word search puzzle made at WordSearchMaker.net.
55 Crossword puzzle made at CustomPuzzles.com.

iv

1 It's nice to meet you.

1 Complete the conversations. Use the names in the box.

☑ Sandy   ☑ John   ☐ Mr. Valencia   ☐ Ms. Landon

Hi, ___Sandy___ .

Hello, __Johs__ .

It's nice to meet you, _ms. landon_ .

Nice to meet you, too, _mr. Valencia_

2 Complete the conversations. Use **my, your, his,** or **her.**

1. A: Hi. What's ___your___ name?

   B: ___my___ name is Carla. And what's ___his___ name?

   A: ___my___ name is David.

2. A: What's ___your___ name?

   B: ___my___ name is Michael.

   A: And what's ___her___ name?

   B: ___my___ name is Sarah.

1

1. A: Hello, __Mr.__ Jones.
   B: _good_ morning, Susan.
      HOW are you?
   A: _I'm_ OK, thank you.

2. A: Hi. How are _you_ , Mrs. Stein?
   B: I'm just _ok_ , thank you.
      How about _you_ ,
      _mr_ Smith?
   A: Pretty _good_ , thanks.

3. A: How's it _going_ , Tim?
   B: Great. _how_ are you doing?
   A: Pretty good.

4 Choose the correct responses.

1. A: Hi, Daniel.

   B: _Hello._
   - Hello.
   - It's nice to meet you.

2. A: My name is Pam Walker.

   B: _I'm Jake Williams._
   - It's Williams.
   - I'm Jake Williams.

3. A: Hello, Yuko. How's it going?

   B: _Fine, thanks_
   - Fine, thanks.
   - Nice to meet you, too.

4. A: How do you spell your last name?

   B: _R-O-G-E-R-S._
   - R-O-G-E-R-S.
   - It's Rogers.

5. A: I'm Bill Delgado.

   B: _It's nice to meet you_
   - Nice to meet you, too.
   - It's nice to meet you.

5 Complete the crossword puzzle. Spell the numbers.

Across (→)	Down (↓)
a 2	**a** 3
c 8	**b** 1
e 7	**d** 10
g 5	**e** 6
h 0	**f** 9
	g 4

6 *Write the telephone numbers.*

1. two-one-two, five-five-five, six-one-one-five   212-555-6115
2. eight-four-five, five-five-five, nine-three-oh-four   845.555.9304
3. six-oh-four, five-five-five, four-seven-three-one   604 555 4737
4. nine-four-nine, five-five-five, three-eight-oh-two   949 555 3802
5. three-oh-five, five-five-five, five-six-eight-six   305 555 5686
6. seven-seven-three, five-five-five, one-seven-seven-nine   773 555 1779
7. nine-one-four, five-five-five, two-zero-zero-three   914 555 2003
8. five-four-one, five-five-five, eight-one-eight-three   541 555 8183

7 *Complete the conversations. Write 'm, 're, or 's.*

1. A: What __'s__ your name?
   B: I __'m__ Tomiko Mita.
   A: It __'s__ nice to meet you, Tomiko.
2. A: Hello. I __'m__ Josh Evans.
       I __'m__ in your English class.
   B: Yes, and you __'re__ in my math class, too.

3. A: What __'s__ his name?
   B: It __'s__ Steven Hill.
   A: He __'s__ in our English class.
   B: You __'re__ right!

8 Complete the conversations. Use the words in the box.

☑ am •   ☑ he's •   ☑ I'm not •   ☑ it's ✓   ☑ you •
☑ are •   ☐ I'm   ☑ is •   ✓ me   ☑ you're •

1. Debra: Excuse ____me____ . Are ___you___
           James Lawson?
   Kevin: No, _I'm not_ . _he's_ over there.
   Debra: Oh, _you're_ sorry.

2. Debra: Excuse me. ___are___ you James Lawson?
   James: Yes, I _am_ .
   Debra: Hi, James. My name _is_
           Debra Marks.
   James: Oh, ___it's___ in my English class.
   Debra: That's right. ___I'm___ nice to meet you.
   James: Nice to meet you, too.

9 Complete the conversation. Use the questions in the box.

☑ What's your name?   ☑ And what's your email address?
☑ And how do you spell your last name?   ☑ What's your phone number?
✓ Are you Ashley Nevins?   ☑ How do you spell your first name?

A: Hi. <u>Are you Ashley Nevins?</u>

B: No, I'm not.

A: Oh, I'm sorry. _What's your nam?_

B: Kerry Moore.

A: _How do you spell your first name_

B: K-E-R-R-Y.

A: _and how do you spell your las name_

B: M-O-O-R-E.

A: _what's your phone number?_

B: It's 618-555-7120.

A: _and what's your email address?_

B: It's kmoore19@cup.org.

A Complete the conversations. Use the words in parentheses.

1. A: <u>Hi.</u>

    (Hi. / Excuse me.) How are you?

    B: I'm fine, thanks.

2. A: <u>Good-bye</u>

    (Hello. / Good-bye.)

    B: See you tomorrow.

3. A: <u>excuse me</u>

    (Excuse me. / Thank you.) Are you Soo-mi Kim?

    B: Yes, I am.

4. A: <u>Good evening</u>

    (Good evening. / Good night.)

    B: Hello.

B Match the pictures with the conversations in part A.

a. <u>1</u>

b. <u>3</u>

c. <u>4</u>

d. <u>2</u>

2 What's this?

1 What are these things?

A What's in the picture? Write the things.

1. a bag
2. umbrella
3. computer
4. telephone
5. book
6. portfolio
7. hairbrush
8. _____

B What's in the picture? Write sentences.

1. This is a bag.
2. this is a umbrella
3. this is a computer
4. this is a telephone
5. this is a book
6. this is a portfolio
7. this is a hairbrush
8. _____

2 Complete the chart with the words in the box.

☑ bags	☐ briefcases	☐ desks	☐ markers
☑ books	☐ cameras	☐ hairbrushes	☐ stamps
☑ boxes	☐ clocks	☐ keys	☐ watches

/z/	/s/	/ɪz/
bags _____	books _____	boxes _____
_____ _____	_____ _____	_____ _____

3 Complete the questions with **this** or **these**. *Then answer the questions.*

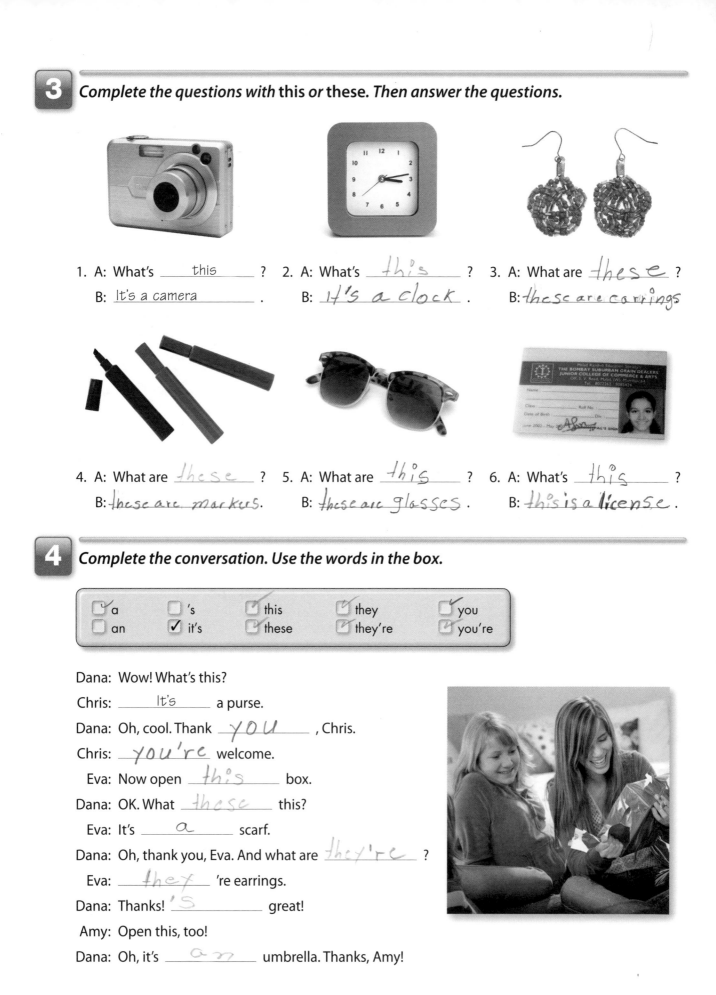

1. A: What's _____this_____ ?
   B: It's a camera _____ .

2. A: What's _____this_____ ?
   B: It's a clock .

3. A: What are _these_ ?
   B: these are earrings

4. A: What are _these_ ?
   B: these are markers.

5. A: What are _this_ ?
   B: these are glasses .

6. A: What's _this_ ?
   B: this is a license .

4 Complete the conversation. Use the words in the box.

| ✔ a | ☐ 's | ✔ this | ✔ they | ✔ you |
| ☐ an | ✔ it's | ✔ these | ✔ they're | ✔ you're |

Dana: Wow! What's this?

Chris: _____It's_____ a purse.

Dana: Oh, cool. Thank _____you_____ , Chris.

Chris: _____you're_____ welcome.

Eva: Now open _____this_____ box.

Dana: OK. What _____these_____ this?

Eva: It's _____a_____ scarf.

Dana: Oh, thank you, Eva. And what are _____they're_____ ?

Eva: _____they_____ 're earrings.

Dana: Thanks! _____'s_____ great!

Amy: Open this, too!

Dana: Oh, it's _____an_____ umbrella. Thanks, Amy!

5 *Complete the conversations. Use the answers in the box.*

☑ Yes, I am.   ☑ Yes, it is.   ☑ Yes, they are.   ☑ It's
☑ No, I'm not.   ☑ No, it's not.   ☑ No, they're not.   ☑ They're

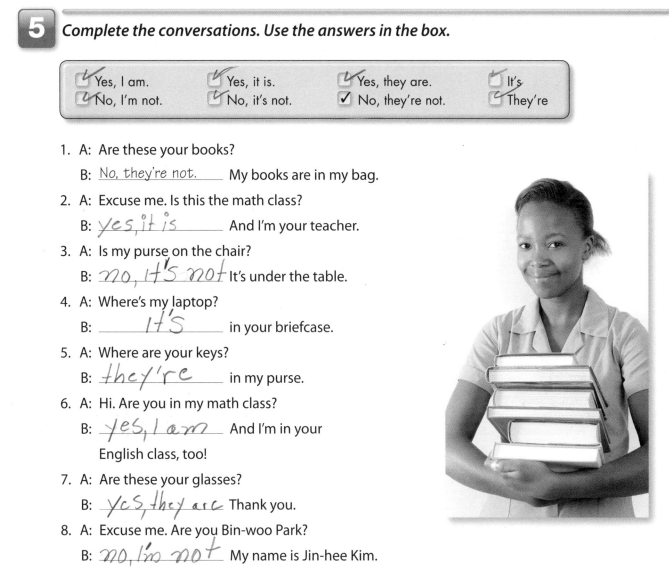

1. A: Are these your books?

   B: <u>No, they're not.</u>   My books are in my bag.

2. A: Excuse me. Is this the math class?

   B: yes, it is   And I'm your teacher.

3. A: Is my purse on the chair?

   B: no, it's not It's under the table.

4. A: Where's my laptop?

   B: It's   in your briefcase.

5. A: Where are your keys?

   B: they're   in my purse.

6. A: Hi. Are you in my math class?

   B: yes, I am   And I'm in your
   English class, too!

7. A: Are these your glasses?

   B: yes, they are Thank you.

8. A: Excuse me. Are you Bin-woo Park?

   B: no, I'm not   My name is Jin-hee Kim.
   Bin-woo isn't in this class.

6 *Complete the conversations.*

1. A: Where ___is___ my English dictionary?

   B: Is _____ in your book bag?

   A: No, it's _____ .

   B: Wait a minute. _____ it on the desk?

   A: Yes, _____ is. Thank you!

2. A: _____ this my newspaper?

   B: No, _____ not.

   It's *my* newspaper.

   A: Sorry. _____ is my newspaper?

   B: Is _____ under your chair?

   A: Oh, yes, it _____ . Thanks.

3. A: Where _____ my glasses?

   B: Are _____ in your purse?

   A: No, they're _____ .

   B: _____ they on your desk?

   A: Hmm. Yes, _____ are. Thanks.

4. A: _____ my pens on

   your desk?

   B: No, _____ not. Sorry.

   A: Hmm. _____ are my pens?

   B: _____ they in your pocket?

   A: Let me see. Yes, they _____ .

   Thank you!

7 **Answer the questions. Use your own information.**

1. Are you a teacher?
    No, I'm not. I'm a student.

2. Is your name William Smith?
    _____

3. Is your workbook on your desk?
    _____

4. Is your phone number 806-555-0219?
    _____

5. Are you in a math class?
    _____

8 **Complete the sentences. Use the prepositions in the box.**

☐ behind   ☑ in   ☐ in front of   ☐ next to   ☐ on   ☐ under

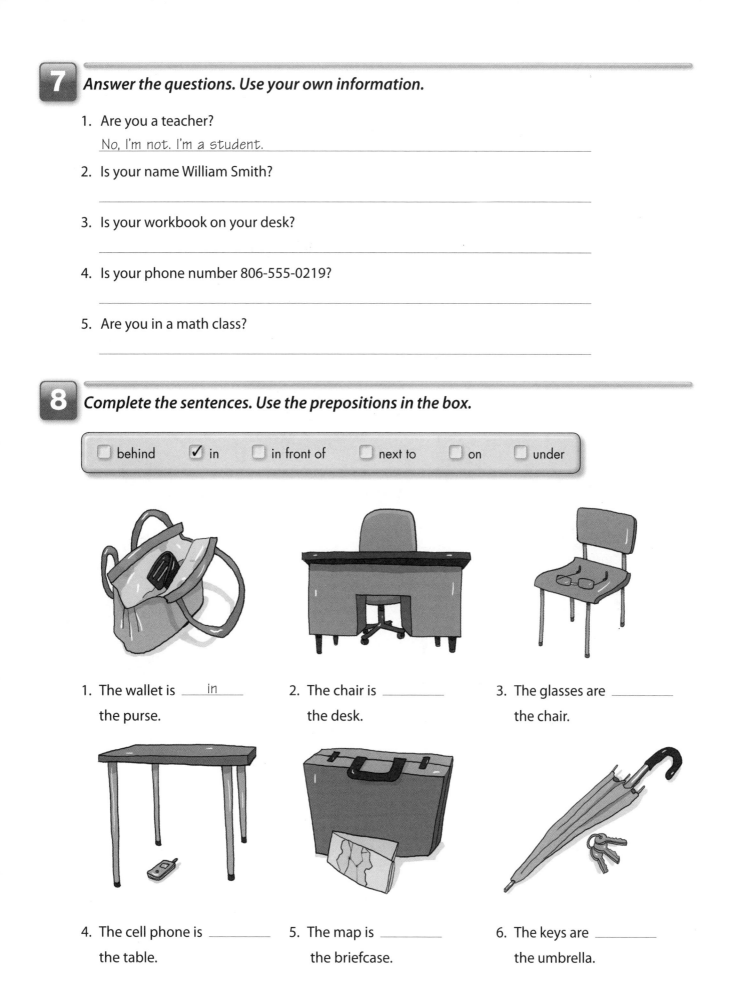

1. The wallet is ___in___ the purse.

2. The chair is _____ the desk.

3. The glasses are _____ the chair.

4. The cell phone is _____ the table.

5. The map is _____ the briefcase.

6. The keys are _____ the umbrella.

9 Where are these things?

A Look at the picture. Write questions and answers about the things in parentheses.

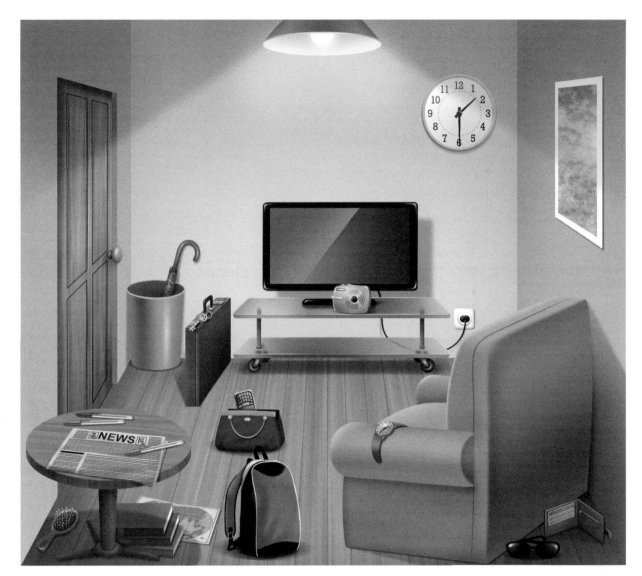

1. A: <u>Where is the briefcase?</u>   (briefcase)

   B: <u>It's next to the television.</u>

2. A: _____ (books)

   B: _____

3. A: _____ (cell phone)

   B: _____

4. A: _____ (keys)

   B: _____

5. A: _____ (camera)

   B: _____

6. A: _____ (sunglasses)

   B: _____

B Write two more questions and answers about the picture.

1. A: _____

   B: _____

2. A: _____

   B: _____

3 Where are you from?

1 Cities and countries

A Find and circle these countries in the puzzle.

- ☑ Argentina
- ☐ Brazil
- ☐ Canada
- ☐ China
- ☐ Colombia
- ☐ India
- ☐ Japan
- ☐ Mexico
- ☐ South Korea
- ☐ Turkey

S	C	M	H	P	F	W	F	B	R
M	O	H	C	J	L	V	P	L	O
E	L	U	I	M	E	X	I	C	O
H	O	S	T	N	X	Z	X	J	F
I	M	K	I	H	A	A	P	A	A
D	B	T	U	R	K	E	Y	P	I
D	I	M	B	I	M	O	C	A	N
C	A	N	A	D	A	S	R	N	D
U	E	P	D	K	Q	S	N	E	I
C	A	R	G	E	N	T	I	N	A

B Where are these cities? Complete the sentences with the countries in part A.

1. Delhi and Mumbai _are in India._

2. Shanghai _____

3. Tokyo _____

4. São Paulo and Rio _____

5. Seoul and Daejeon _____

6. Buenos Aires _____

7. Vancouver and Ottawa _____

8. Istanbul _____

13

2 *Complete the conversations with* am, 'm, are, 're, is, *or* 's.

1. A: __Are__ you and your family from
   South Korea?

   B: No, we _____ not.
   We _____ from China.

   A: Oh, so you _____ from China.

   B: Yes, I _____ . I _____ from Shanghai.

2. A: _____ Brazil in Central America, Dad?

   B: No, it _____ not. It _____ in
   South America.

   A: Oh. _____ we from Brazil, Dad?

   B: Yes, we _____ . We _____ from
   Brazil originally, but we _____
   here in the U.S. now.

3. A: _____ this your wallet?

   B: Yes, it _____ . Thanks.

   A: And _____ these your pictures?

   B: Yes, they _____ .

   A: Well, they _____ very nice pictures.

   B: Thank you!

4. A: _____ your English teacher from
   the U.S.?

   B: No, she _____ not. She _____ from
   Canada. Montreal, Canada.

   A: _____ English her first language?

   B: No, it _____ not. Her first language
   _____ French.

Answer the questions.

1. A: Is he from Brazil?

    B: <u>No, he's not. He's from Ireland.</u>

2. A: Are they from India?

    B: _____

3. A: Is she from Canada?

    B: _____

4. A: Is she in Mexico?

    B: _____

5. A: Are they in Jakarta?

    B: _____

6. A: Are they in Australia?

    B: _____

4 *Spell the numbers.*

1. 11 _eleven_
2. 15 _____
3. 50 _____
4. 101 _____
5. 24 _____

6. 13 _____
7. 70 _____
8. 30 _____
9. 19 _____
10. 90 _____

5 *Complete the conversations with the correct responses.*

1. A: Where are they from?

   B: _She's from the U.S., and he's from the U.K._

   • She's Gwyneth Paltrow, and he's Chris Martin.
   • She's from the U.S., and he's from the U.K.

2. A: Is your first language English?

   B: _____

   • No, it's Japan.
   • No, it's Japanese.

3. A: What are they like?

   B: _____

   • They're very nice.
   • They're in London.

4. A: Who's that?

   B: _____

   • He's the new math teacher.
   • It's my new cell phone.

5. A: Where are Tony and his family?

   B: _____

   • They're in the U.S. now.
   • They're from São Paulo.

6. A: How old is he now?

   B: _____

   • It's twenty-eight.
   • He's twenty-eight.

7. A: What's Marrakech like?

   B: _____

   • It's in Morocco.
   • It's very interesting.

6 Descriptions

A Write sentences about the people in the pictures. Use the words in the box.

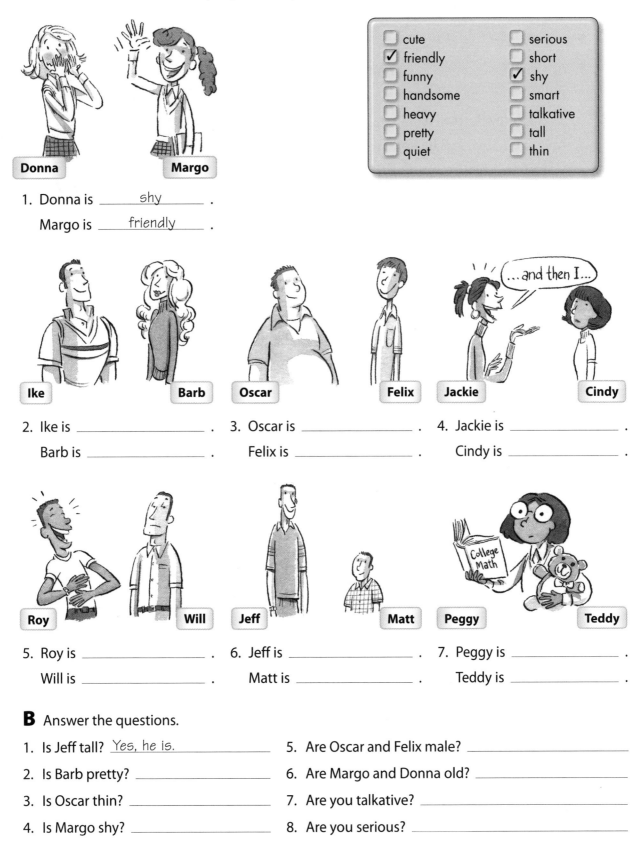

☐ cute	☐ serious
☑ friendly	☐ short
☐ funny	☑ shy
☐ handsome	☐ smart
☐ heavy	☐ talkative
☐ pretty	☐ tall
☐ quiet	☐ thin

Donna **Margo**

1. Donna is _____shy_____ .

   Margo is _____friendly_____ .

Ike **Barb**   **Oscar** **Felix**   **Jackie** ...and then I... **Cindy**

2. Ike is _____ .

   Barb is _____ .

3. Oscar is _____ .

   Felix is _____ .

4. Jackie is _____ .

   Cindy is _____ .

Roy **Will**   **Jeff** **Matt**   **Peggy** College Math **Teddy**

5. Roy is _____ .

   Will is _____ .

6. Jeff is _____ .

   Matt is _____ .

7. Peggy is _____ .

   Teddy is _____ .

B Answer the questions.

1. Is Jeff tall? _Yes, he is._____

2. Is Barb pretty? _____

3. Is Oscar thin? _____

4. Is Margo shy? _____

5. Are Oscar and Felix male? _____

6. Are Margo and Donna old? _____

7. Are you talkative? _____

8. Are you serious? _____

7 Complete the conversations. Use the words in the boxes.

☐ he's ☐ is ☑ what's
☐ his ☐ not ☐ where

1. A: Connie, ___what's___ your boyfriend like?

   B: _____ very nice. _____ name
   is Tommy Ho. I call him Tom.

   A: _____ is he from? _____
   he from China?

   B: No, he's _____ . He's from Singapore.

☐ are ☐ my ☐ we're
☐ her ☐ we ☐ what's

2. A: Marco, are you and Rita from Puerto Rico?

   B: Yes, _____ are. _____ from San Juan.

   A: _____ your first language?

   B: _____ first language is Spanish, but Rita's first
   language is English. _____ parents
   _____ from New York originally.

8 Answer the questions. Use your own information.

1. Where are you from?

   _____

2. What's your first language?

   _____

3. How are you today?

   _____

4. Where is your teacher from?

   _____

5. What is your teacher like?

   _____

6. What are you like?

   _____

4 Whose jeans are these?

1 *Label the clothes. Use the words in the box.*

☐ belt	☐ cap	☐ jacket	☐ shorts	☐ sneakers	☐ swimsuit
☐ blouse	☐ high heels	✓ scarf	☐ skirt	☐ socks	☐ T-shirt

SPORTS CLUB

1. scarf

2. _____

3. _____

4. _____

5. _____

6. _____

7. _____

8. _____

9. _____

10. _____

11. _____

12. _____

2 *What clothes don't belong? Check (✓) the things.*

For work	For leisure	For cold weather	For warm weather
☐ shirt	☐ T-shirt	☐ boots	☐ swimsuit
✓ shorts	☐ shorts	☐ scarf	☐ T-shirt
☐ tie	☐ suit	☐ shorts	☐ boots
☐ belt	☐ sneakers	☐ pants	☐ sneakers
✓ swimsuit	☐ jeans	☐ sweater	☐ shorts
☐ shoes	☐ gloves	☐ gloves	☐ sweater
☐ jacket	☐ high heels	☐ T-shirt	☐ cap

3 *What things in your classroom are these colors? Write sentences.*

light blue	black	green	pink	red	yellow
dark blue	gray	orange	purple	white	brown

1. My desk is brown.
2. Celia's bag is purple.
3. _____
4. _____
5. _____
6. _____
7. _____
8. _____
9. _____
10. _____

4 *Whose clothes are these?*

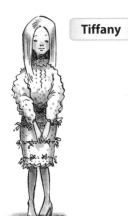 Tiffany    Jade    Daniel

A Complete the conversations.

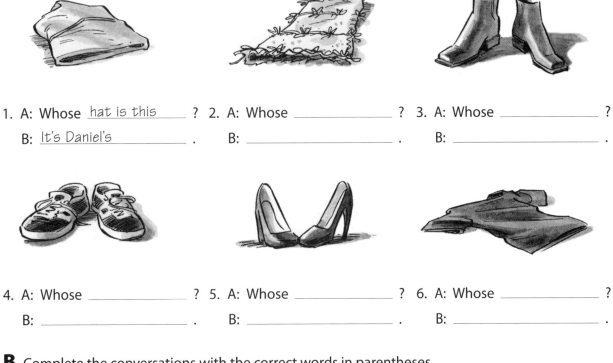

1. A: Whose <u>hat is this</u> ?
   B: <u>It's Daniel's</u> .

2. A: Whose _____ ?
   B: _____ .

3. A: Whose _____ ?
   B: _____ .

4. A: Whose _____ ?
   B: _____ .

5. A: Whose _____ ?
   B: _____ .

6. A: Whose _____ ?
   B: _____ .

B Complete the conversations with the correct words in parentheses.

1. A: _____<u>Whose</u>_____ (Whose / His) T-shirt is this? Is it Lisa's?

   B: No, it's not _____ (her / hers). It's _____ (my / mine).

2. A: Are these _____ (your / yours) jeans?

   B: No, they aren't _____ (my / mine) jeans. Let's ask Keith.
      I think they're _____ (his / he's).

3. A: Are these Annie's and Jennifer's socks?

   B: No, they aren't _____ (their / theirs). They're _____ (your / yours).

   A: I don't think so. These socks are white, and _____ (my / mine) are blue.

5 *What season is it? How is the weather? Write two sentences about each picture.*

1. It's winter.

   It's very cold.

2. _____

3. _____

   _____

4. _____

   _____

5. _____

   _____

6. _____

   _____

6 *Waiting for the bus*

A Write sentences. Use the words in parentheses.

| Todd | Alicia | Chul-woo | Maya | Maggie | Hugo |

1. Hugo is wearing a tie. _____ (tie)
2. Todd and Alicia are wearing boots. _____ (boots)
3. _____ (T-shirt)
4. _____ (skirt)
5. _____ (dress)
6. _____ (sneakers)
7. _____ (scarf)
8. _____ (hats)

B Correct the false sentences.

1. Chul-woo is wearing jeans.
   No, he isn't. / No, he's not. He's wearing shorts. _____

2. Maggie and Hugo are wearing raincoats.
   _____

3. Alicia is wearing a skirt.
   _____

4. Maya is wearing pajamas.
   _____

5. Alicia and Maggie are wearing T-shirts.
   _____

6. Todd and Hugo are wearing shorts.
   _____

7 *Complete the sentences.*

1. My name's Jane. I _'m wearing_
   a T-shirt and shorts. I _____
   sneakers, too. It _____ raining,
   but I _____ a raincoat.

2. It _____ snowing, but Amy
   _____ boots – she _____
   high heels. She _____ gloves, and
   she _____ a hat.

3. It's very hot. Tom and Sue _____
   sweaters today. They _____ pants.
   It's sunny, so Sue _____ a hat,
   and Tom _____ sunglasses.

4. Roger _____ a suit.
   He _____ a belt, but
   he _____ a tie.
   He _____ shoes and socks.
   It's very windy.

8 *Complete these sentences with* **and, but,** *or* **so.**

1. He's wearing jeans and sneakers, ___and___ he's wearing a T-shirt.

2. It's very cold outside, _____ I'm not wearing a coat.

3. Her skirt is blue, _____ her blouse is blue, too.

4. It's raining, _____ I need an umbrella.

5. He's wearing an expensive suit, _____ he's wearing sneakers.

6. It's summer and it's very sunny, _____ it's hot.

5 What are you doing?

1 *Write each sentence a different way.*

1. It's midnight.   It's twelve o'clock at night.

2. It's 4:00 P.M.   _____

3. It's 9:15 A.M.   _____

4. It's 8:00 P.M.   _____

5. It's 10:45 P.M.   _____

6. It's 3:30 P.M.   _____

7. It's 6:00 P.M.   _____

8. It's 12:00 P.M.   _____

2 *What time is it in each city? Write the time in two different ways.*

1. It's 10:00 a.m. in Los Angeles.

    It's ten o'clock in the morning.

2. _____

   _____

3. _____

   _____

4. _____

   _____

5. _____

   _____

6. _____

   _____

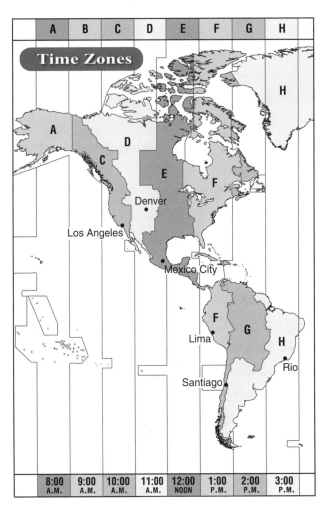

25

3 What time is it? Use the sentences in the box.

☐ It's five-oh-five.
☑ It's twenty after nine.
☐ It's ten to eight.
☐ It's a quarter after one.
☐ It's eight after six.
☐ It's a quarter to three.

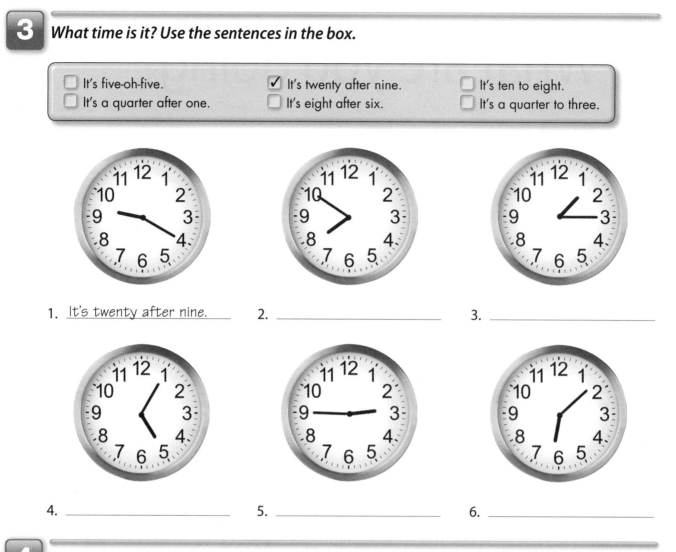

1. It's twenty after nine.   2. _____   3. _____

4. _____   5. _____   6. _____

4 Complete the crossword puzzle. Write each time a different way.

Across (→)

1 It's five in the morning. It's five _____ .

4 It's 4:15. It's a quarter _____ four.

7 It's twelve A.M. It's _____ .

8 It's 8:00 P.M. It's eight in the _____ .

9 It's twelve P.M. It's _____ .

Down (↓)

2 It's 7:00 A.M. It's seven in the _____ .

3 It's 3:30. It's three- _____ .

4 It's 4:00 P.M. It's four in the _____ .

5 It's 1:15. It's one- _____ .

6 It's 3:45. It's a _____ to four.

10 It's 11:00 P.M. It's eleven at _____ .

5 *What are these people doing? Write sentences. Use the words in the box.*

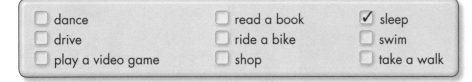

dance	read a book	☑ sleep
drive	ride a bike	swim
play a video game	shop	take a walk

1. She's sleeping.

2. _____

3. _____

4. _____

5. _____

6. _____

7. _____

8. _____

9. _____

6 **Answer these questions.**

1. Is Debbie getting up?

   No, she's not. She's sleeping.

2. Are Kelly and Tony taking a walk?

   No, they're not. They're shopping.

3. Are Dan and Megan studying?

4. Is Carmen driving a car?

5. Is Bill playing tennis?

6. Is Michiko checking her email?

7. Is Claire watching television?

8. What about you? Are you sleeping?

7 *Write questions about these people. Use the words in parentheses.*
Then answer the questions.

1. A: <u>Is Terry wearing shorts?</u>
   (Terry / wear shorts)

   B: <u>No, he's not. He's wearing jeans.</u>

2. A: _____
   (Tai-lin / wear a raincoat)

   B: _____

3. A: _____
   (Maria / talk on the phone)

   B: _____

4. A: _____
   (Terry and Helen / eat)

   B: _____

5. A: _____
   (Pedro and Sonia / watch television)

   B: _____

6. A: _____
   (Tai-lin and Brandon / eat pizza)

   B: _____

7. A: _____
   (Carlos / chat online)

   B: _____

8. A: _____
   (Maria / wear boots)

   B: _____

8 Write questions and answers. Use **What + doing** *and the words in parentheses.*

1. A: <u>What are you and Ricky doing?</u> (you and Ricky)

   B: <u>We're eating pizza.</u> (eat pizza)

2. A: <u>What's Michael doing?</u> (Michael)

   B: <u>He's cooking dinner.</u> (cook dinner)

3. A: _____ (Ron and Lucy)

   B: _____ (take a walk)

4. A: _____ (Julie)

   B: _____ (get up)

5. A: _____ (Mary)

   B: _____ (shop)

6. A: _____ (Belle and Hank)

   B: _____ (watch a movie)

7. A: _____ (Steven)

   B: _____ (study math)

8. A: _____ (you)

   B: _____ (study English)

9. A: _____ (you and Emma)

   B: _____ (have lunch)

10. A: _____ (I)

    B: _____ (finish this exercise)

9 *What are you doing? What are your friends doing? Write sentences.*

1. _____

2. _____

3. _____

4. _____

5. _____

6. _____

6 My sister works downtown.

1 Family

A Jessica is talking about her family. Complete the sentences with the words in the box.

☐ brother	☐ daughters	☐ husband	☑ parents	☐ son
☐ children	☐ father	☐ mother	☐ sister	☐ wife

Family Photos   Search [   ] [Go]   Log Out

Helen and Jack

Pedro and Jessica

Kate, Brad, and Joan

1. Helen and Jack are my ___parents___ . Helen is my _____ , and Jack is my _____ .

2. Pedro is my _____ . I'm his _____ .

3. Kate, Joan, and Brad are our _____ . Kate and Joan are our _____ , and Brad is our _____ . Kate is Joan's _____ , and Brad is her _____ .

B Write four sentences about your family.

1. _____

2. _____

3. _____

4. _____

2 *Complete the conversation with the correct words in parentheses.*

Marta: So, do you live downtown, David?

David: Yes, I ____live____ with my brother.
(live / lives)

He _____ an apartment near here.
(have / has)

Marta: Oh, so you _____ to work.
(walk / walks)

David: Actually, I _____ walk to work in
(don't / doesn't)

the morning. I _____ the bus to work,
(take / takes)

and then I _____ home at night.
(walk / walks)

What about you?

Marta: Well, my husband and I _____ a house
(have / has)

in the suburbs now, so I _____ to work.
(drive / drives)

My husband doesn't _____ downtown.
(work / works)

He _____ in the suburbs near our house,
(work / works)

so he _____ to work by bus.
(go / goes)

3 *Third-person singular -s endings*

A Write the third-person singular forms of these verbs.

1. dance *dances*
2. do *does*
3. go _____
4. have _____

5. live _____
6. ride _____
7. sleep _____
8. study _____

9. take _____
10. use _____
11. walk _____
12. watch _____

B Practice the words in part A. Then add them to the chart.

s = /s/	s = /z/	(e)s = /ɪz/	irregular
_____	_____	*dances*	*does*
_____	_____	_____	_____
_____	_____	_____	_____

4 True or false?

A Are these sentences true for you? Check (✓) True or False.

	True	False		True	False
1. I live in the city.	☐	☐	6. I do my homework alone.	☐	☐
2. I have a car.	☐	☐	7. I ride my bike to school.	☐	☐
3. I live in an apartment.	☐	☐	8. I have sisters / a sister.	☐	☐
4. I live with my parents.	☐	☐	9. I have brothers / a brother.	☐	☐
5. I do my homework at school.	☐	☐	10. I work downtown.	☐	☐

I live in an apartment.

I live in the suburbs.

B Correct the false statements in part A.

I don't live in the city. I live in the suburbs.

5 Write about Brian's weekly schedule. Use the words in parentheses.

	Monday	Tuesday	Wednesday	Thursday	Friday
8:00 A.M.	get up →				→
9:00 A.M.	go to work →				→
10:00 A.M.					
11:00 A.M.					
12:00 P.M.	have lunch →				→
1:00 P.M.					
2:00 P.M.					
3:00 P.M.	drink coffee →				→
4:00 P.M.					
5:00 P.M.	finish work →				→
6:00 P.M.	go to school	play tennis	go to school	play tennis	have dinner with friends

1. <u>He gets up at 8:00 every day.</u> _____ (8:00)

2. _____ (9:00)

3. _____ (noon)

4. _____ (3:00)

5. _____ (5:00)

6. _____ (6:00 / Mondays and Wednesdays)

7. _____ (6:00 / Tuesdays and Thursdays)

8. _____ (6:00 / Fridays)

6 Write something you do and something you don't do on each day.
Use the phrases in the box or your own information.

check email	exercise	have dinner late	sleep late
drive a car	get up early	play video games	talk on the phone
eat breakfast	go to school	see my friends	watch television

1. Monday   <u>I get up early on Mondays. I don't sleep late on Mondays.</u>

2. Tuesday _____

3. Wednesday _____

4. Thursday _____

5. Friday _____

6. Saturday _____

7. Sunday _____

7 Complete these conversations with **at**, **in**, or **on**. *(If you don't need a preposition, write Ø.)*

1. A: Do you go to bed _Ø_ late _on_ weekends?

   B: Yes, I do. I go to bed _____ 1:00 A.M. But I go to bed _____ early _____ weekdays.

2. A: Do you study _____ the afternoon?

   B: No, I study _____ the morning _____ weekends, and I study _____ the evening _____ Mondays and Wednesdays.

3. A: What time do you get up _____ the morning _____ weekdays?

   B: I get up _____ 8:00 _____ every day.

4. A: Do you have English class _____ the morning?

   B: No, I have English _____ 1:30 _____ the afternoon _____ Tuesdays and Thursdays. _____ Mondays, Wednesdays, and Fridays, our class is _____ 3:00.

8 Write questions to complete the conversations.

1. A: _Do you live alone?_

   B: No, I don't live alone. I live with my family.

2. A: _____

   B: Yes, my family and I watch television in the evening.

3. A: _____

   B: Yes, I get up late on Sundays.

   A: _____

   B: I get up at 11:00.

4. A: _____

   B: No, my sister doesn't drive to work.

   A: _____

   B: No, she doesn't take the subway. She takes the bus.

5. A: _____

   B: No, my father doesn't work on weekends.

   A: _____

   B: He works on weekdays.

6. A: _____

   B: Yes, my mother has a job. She's a teacher.

   A: _____

   B: No, she doesn't use public transportation. She drives to work.

7. A: _____

   B: Yes, we have a big lunch on Sundays.

   A: _____

   B: We have lunch at 1:00.

9 Write each sentence a different way. Use the sentences in the box.

☐ He goes to work before noon.
☐ We take the bus, the train, or the subway.
☐ I don't work far from here.
☐ She doesn't get up early on Sundays.
☐ We don't live in the suburbs.
☑ Sarah is Sam's wife.

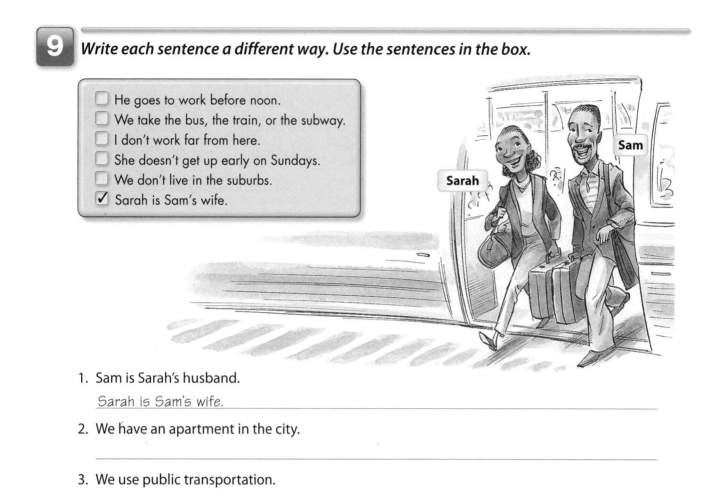

1. Sam is Sarah's husband.
   Sarah is Sam's wife.

2. We have an apartment in the city.
   _____

3. We use public transportation.
   _____

4. He goes to work in the morning.
   _____

5. My office is near here.
   _____

6. She sleeps late on Sundays.
   _____

10 Answer the questions about your schedule.

1. What do you do on weekdays?
   _____

2. What do you do on weekends?
   _____

3. What do you do on Friday nights?
   _____

4. What do you do on Sunday mornings?
   _____

7 Does it have a view?

1 Label the parts of the house.

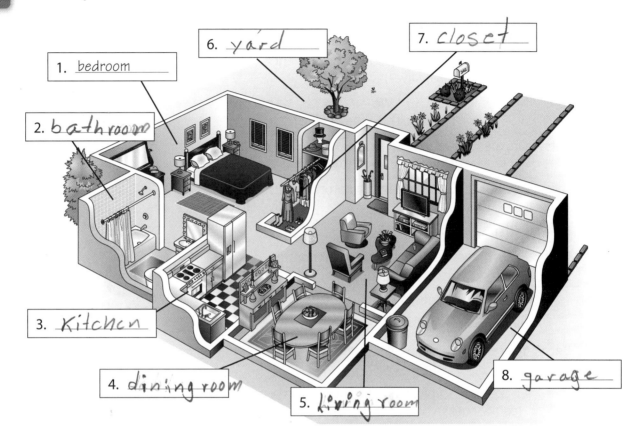

6. yard

7. closet

1. bedroom

2. bathroom

3. kitchen

4. dining room

5. living room

8. garage

2 Complete the conversation. Use the sentences in the box.

- ☐ No, it only has two rooms.
- ☐ Yes, I do. I love it!
- ☐ Yes, it has a great view of the city.
- ☑ No, I live in an apartment.

Simon: Do you live in a house, James?

James: No, I live in an apartment.

Simon: Well, is it very big?

James: no it only has two rooms

Simon: Does it have a view?

James: yes it has a great view of the city

Simon: Oh, that's great! And do you live alone?

James: yes I do I love it

37

3 *Complete the conversation with the correct words in parentheses.*

Betsy: _____Do_____ you _____live_____ near here, Lauren?
(Do / Does) (live / lives)

Lauren: Yes, I _____does_____ . My husband and I
(do / does)

_____Lives_____ on Main Street.
(live / lives)

Betsy: Oh, do you _____Live_____ in an apartment?
(live / lives)

Lauren: No, we _____don't_____ . We _____has_____ a house.
(don't / doesn't) (have / has)

Betsy: Oh, great! _____Do_____ you _____hav_____ children?
(Do / Does) (have / has)

Lauren: No, we _____don't_____ . But my brother _____Lives_____
(don't / doesn't) (live / lives)

with us.

Betsy: Really? Does he do a lot of work at home?

Lauren: Yes, he _____do_____ . In fact, he _____cook_____
(do / does) (cook / cooks)

dinner every night!

Betsy: You're lucky! I _____ alone, and
(live / lives)

I _____ my own dinner.
(cook / cooks)

4 *Answer these questions with your information. Use short answers.*

1. Do you live in an apartment?	<u>Yes, I do. / No, I don't.</u>
2. Do you have a yard?	<u>yes, I do</u>
3. Do you live with your family?	_____
4. Does your city or town have a park?	_____
5. Does your teacher have a car?	<u>yes hi do</u>
6. Do you and your classmates speak English?	_____
7. Do you and your classmates study together?	_____
8. Does your classroom have a view?	_____
9. Does your school have an elevator?	_____
10. Does your city or town have a subway?	_____

5 *What furniture do they have?*

A Answer the questions about the pictures.

1. A: Does she have a television?
   B: <u>Yes, she does.</u>

2. A: Does she need curtains?
   B: no, she does'nt

3. A: Does she need a sofa?
   B: yes she does

4. A: Does she have a chair?
   B: no she does'nt

5. A: Does she have a rug?
   B: yes she does

6. A: Does she need pictures?
   B: no, she does'nt

7. A: Do they have a lamp?
   B: yes they do

8. A: Do they need a table?
   B: yes they do

9. A: Do they have chairs?
   B: no they don't

10. A: Do they need a clock?
    B: no they don't

11. A: Do they have a mirror?
    B: no they don't

12. A: Do they need curtains?
    B: yes they do

B What furniture do you have? What furniture do you need? Write four sentences.

1. _____
2. _____
3. _____
4. _____

6 *Complete the description with 's, are, or aren't.*

balcony

In Roger's house, there **'s** a big living room. There **are** two bedrooms and two bathrooms. There **aren't** no yard, but there **'s** a balcony. He has a lot of books, so there **are** bookcases in the living room and bedrooms. There **aren't** any chairs in the kitchen, but there **'s** a big table with chairs in the dining room. There **'s** no stove in the kitchen, but there **'s** a small microwave oven. There _____ two televisions in Roger's house – there **are** one television in the living room, and there **'s** one television in the bedroom.

7 *Answer these questions with information about your home. Use the phrases in the box.*

there's a . . .	there are some . . .
there's no . . .	there are no . . .
there isn't a . . .	there aren't any . . .

dishwasher

1. Does your kitchen have a dishwasher?

   Yes, there's a dishwasher in my kitchen.

   No, there isn't a dishwasher. / No, there's no dishwasher.

2. Does your kitchen have a clock?

   _____

3. Do you have a television in your living room?

   _____

4. Do you have bookcases in your living room?

   _____

5. Does the bathroom have a mirror?

   _____

6. Do you have pictures in your bedroom?

   _____

7. Does your bedroom have a closet?

   _____

8 *What's wrong with this house?*

A Write sentences about the house. Use *there* and the words in parentheses.

1. <u>There's no stove in the kitchen. / There isn't a stove in the kitchen.</u> (stove / kitchen)
2. <u>there's yes chairs in the dining room.</u> (chairs / dining room)
3. <u>there isn't</u> (stove / living room)
4. _____ (refrigerator / bedroom)
5. _____ (bed / bedroom)
6. _____ (armchairs / bathroom)
7. _____ (clock / kitchen)
8. _____ (bookcases / living room)

B Write four more sentences about the house.

1. _____
2. _____
3. _____
4. _____

9 *Choose the correct responses.*

1. A: My apartment has a view of the river.

   B: _You're lucky._

   - Guess what!
   - You're lucky.

2. A: Do you need bedroom furniture?

   B: _____

   - Yes, I do. I need a bed and a lamp.
   - No, I don't. I need a bed and a lamp.

3. A: I really need a new desk.

   B: _____

   - So let's go shopping on Saturday.
   - That's great!

4. A: Do you have chairs in your kitchen?

   B: _____

   - Yes, I do. I need four chairs.
   - Yes, I do. I have four chairs.

10 *Draw a picture of your home. Then write a description.*
Use the questions in the box for ideas.

Where do you live?	What rooms does your home have?
Do you live in a house or an apartment?	What furniture do you have?

_____

_____

_____

_____

8 What do you do?

1 *Find and circle these jobs in the puzzle.*

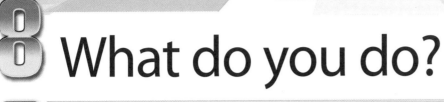

F	E	D	N	V	D	O	C	T	O	R
I	L	T	O	L	F	H	A	N	M	L
R	B	O	S	R	E	B	M	U	L	P
E	S	D	R	C	U	S	R	O	A	G
F	V	B	E	I	L	M	H	I	O	R
I	E	E	P	J	S	F	N	C	E	E
G	N	C	S	N	E	T	R	I	U	H
H	D	O	E	R	E	B	H	G	A	C
T	O	D	L	R	U	S	M	N	F	A
E	R	I	A	E	A	N	U	S	C	E
R	O	H	S	C	I	R	A	N	P	T

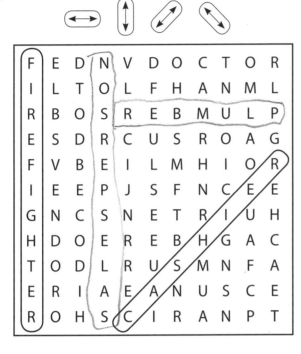

43

What do these people do? Write three sentences about each person.
Use the phrases in the box and your own ideas.

handle money	sit/stand all day	wear a uniform	work inside
help people	talk on the phone	work hard	work outside

1. She's a nurse.
   She helps people.
   She works in a hospital.

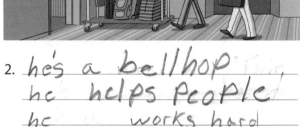

2. he's a bellhop
   he helps people
   he works hard

3. he's a vendor
   he's stands all day
   he's works outside

4. he's a Police oficial
   he wears a uniform
   he works outside

5. he's a receptionist
   he's sits all day
   he's talk on the phone

6. She's a cashier
   his work is heavy
   She's stand all day

3 Complete the questions in these conversations.

1. A: Where _does your brother work_ ?

   B: My brother? He works in a department store.

   A: What _does he do_ ?

   B: He works in the shoe department. He's a salesperson.

2. A: What _do Kelly and Pam do?_

   B: Kelly and Pam are nurses. And they work together, too.

   A: Where _do they work_ ?

   B: At Springfield Hospital.

3. A: Where _work she_ ?

   B: My daughter works in an office.

   A: What _is it_ ?

   B: She's an accountant. _contadora_

4. A: What _do they do_ ?

   B: Joe and I? We fix computers.

   A: How _do they do that_ ?

   B: We like it a lot!

4 *Complete the conversations.*

1. A: _____Do_____ you _____have_____ a job?

   B: Yes, I _____DO_____ .

   A: Oh, what _____Do_____ you _____Do_____ ?

   B: I _____m_____ a server.

   A: Where _____DO_____ you _____work_____ ?

   B: I _____job_____ at Paul's Coffee Shop.

   A: How _____Do_____ you _____Like_____ your job?

   B: I really _____Like_____ it. It's a great job!

   A: What time _____do_____ you start work?

   B: I _____Star_____ work at 8:00 A.M., and
   I _____finish_____ at 3:00 P.M.

2. A: My brother _____has_____ a new job.

   B: Really? Where _____does_____ he _____work_____ ?

   A: He _____work_____ at the new clothing store
   downtown.

   B: What _____does_____ he _____do_____ there?

   A: He _____is_____ a security guard.

   B: How _____does_____ he
   _____Like_____ his job?

   A: Oh, I guess he _____Like_____ it.

   B: What time _____does_____ he
   _____Star_____ work?

   A: He _____Star_____ work at
   10:00 A.M., and he
   _____finish_____ at 6:00 P.M.

5 *Exciting or boring?*

A Match the adjectives.

1. _d_ exciting   a. not stressful
2. _b_ easy   b. not difficult
3. _a_ relaxing   c. not dangerous
4. _c_ safe   d. not boring

B Write each sentence two different ways.

1. A flight attendant's job is exciting.

   A flight attendant has an exciting job.

   A flight attendant doesn't have a boring job.

2. A security guard has a boring job.

   _____

   _____

3. Steven's job is dangerous.

   _____

   _____

4. A front desk clerk's job is stressful.

   _____

   _____

5. Linda has a small apartment.

   _____

   _____

6. Martha's house is big.

   _____

   _____

7. Sarah has a talkative sister.

   _____

   _____

8. My job is easy.

   _____

   _____

6 *Write sentences with your opinion about each job.*

1 reporter

2 pilot

3 carpenter

4 athlete

5 miner

6 model

1. <u>A reporter has an exciting job. / A reporter's job isn't boring.</u>
2. _____
3. _____
4. _____
5. _____
6. _____

7 *Imagine you have a dream job. Write a description. Use the questions in the box for ideas.*

What is the job?	What do you do, exactly?
Where do you work?	What's the job like? (Is it dangerous, relaxing, or . . . ?)

_____

_____

_____

_____

Do we need any eggs?

1 *Write the names of the foods.*

Fruit

1. lemons
2. oranje
3. apple
4. banana

Vegetables

5. letuce
6. Tomato
7. patatoes
8. carrot

Grains

9. rice
10. bread
11. cookies
12. cereal

Fats and oils

13. oil
14. butter

Dairy

15. milk
16. cheese

Meat and other proteins

17. fish
18. chicken
19. beans
20. pcanuts

2 *Complete the sentences with the articles* **a** *or* **an.** *If you don't need an article, write Ø.*

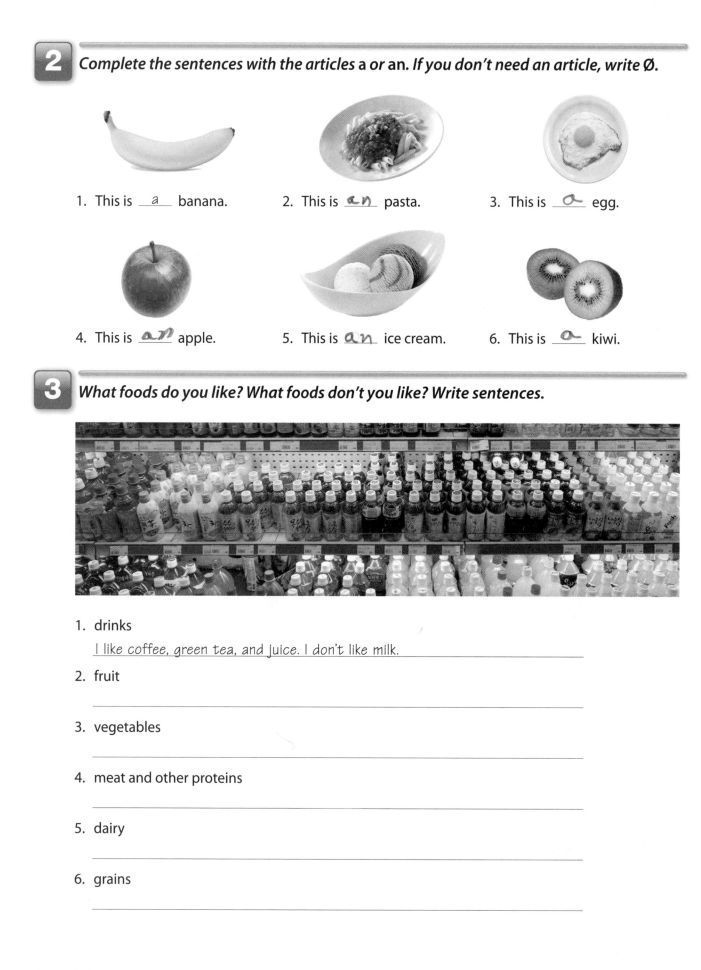

1. This is ___a___ banana.

2. This is _an_ pasta.

3. This is _a_ egg.

4. This is _an_ apple.

5. This is _an_ ice cream.

6. This is _a_ kiwi.

3 *What foods do you like? What foods don't you like? Write sentences.*

1. drinks

   I like coffee, green tea, and juice. I don't like milk.

2. fruit

3. vegetables

4. meat and other proteins

5. dairy

6. grains

4 *Complete the conversations with **some** or **any**.*

1. A: What do you want for dinner?

   B: Let's make ___some___ pasta with tomato sauce.

   A: Good idea. Do we have _____ meat?

   B: Well, we have _____ beef, but I don't want _____ meat in the sauce. Let's get _____ tomatoes and onions.

   A: OK. Do we need _____ green peppers for the sauce?

   B: Yes, let's get _____ peppers. Oh, and _____ garlic, too.

   A: Great. We have _____ spaghetti, so we don't need _____ pasta.

   B: Yeah, but let's get _____ bread. And _____ cheese, too.

2. A: What do you eat for breakfast?

   B: Well, first, I have fruit – _____ grapes or strawberries.

   A: That sounds good. Do you have _____ eggs or meat?

   B: No, I don't eat _____ eggs or meat in the morning.

   A: Really? Do you have anything else?

   B: Well, I usually have _____ bread, but I don't put _____ butter on it.

   A: Do you drink anything in the morning?

   B: I always have _____ juice and coffee. I don't put _____ sugar in my coffee, but I like _____ milk in it.

5 *What do you need to make these foods? What don't you need? Write sentences.*

1. an omelet

   <u>You need some butter, milk, eggs,</u>

   <u>and cheese. You don't need</u>

   <u>any lemons.</u>

2. a chicken sandwich

   _____

   _____

   _____

3. chicken soup

   _____

   _____

   _____

4. a vegetable salad

   _____

   _____

   _____

5. a fruit salad

   _____

   _____

   _____

6. your favorite food

   _____

   _____

   _____

6 Food habits

A Put the adverbs in the correct places.

1. Brazilians make drinks with fruit. (often)

   Brazilians often make drinks with fruit.

2. Some people in Mexico eat pasta. (never)

   _____

3. In China, people put sugar in their tea. (hardly ever)

   _____

4. In England, people put milk in their tea. (usually)

   _____

5. In Japan, people have fish for breakfast. (sometimes)

   _____

6. Americans put cream in their coffee. (often)

   _____

7. In Canada, people have salad for breakfast. (hardly ever)

   _____

8. Some people in South Korea eat pickled vegetables for breakfast. (always)

   _____

B Rewrite the sentences in part A. Use your own information.

1. Brazilians often make drinks with fruit.

   I hardly ever make drinks with fruit. /

   I sometimes make drinks with chocolate.

2. _____
3. _____
4. _____
5. _____
6. _____
7. _____
8. _____

7 *Do you often have these things for dinner? Write sentences. Use the adverbs in the box.*

never	hardly ever	sometimes	often	usually	always

1. cheese   I hardly ever have cheese for dinner.
2. milk
3. coffee
4. eggs
5. beef
6. rice
7. beans
8. cereal

8 *Answer the questions with your own information.*

1. What's your favorite kind of food?

2. What's your favorite restaurant?

3. What do you usually have at your favorite restaurant?

4. Do you ever cook?

5. What's your favorite snack?

Chinese food   Mexican food   Italian food

10 What sports do you play?

1 Sports

A Complete the crossword puzzle. Write the names of the sports.

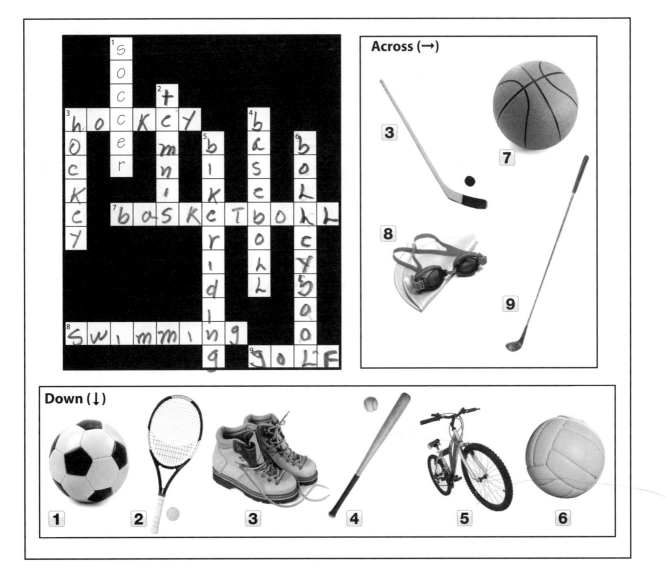

Across (→)

3
7
8
9

Crossword answers:
1 soccer
2 t...
3 hockey
4 b...
5 b...
6 b...
7 basketball
8 swimming
9 golf

Down (↓)

1
2
3
4
5
6

B Which sports in part A follow *go*? Which sports follow *play*? Complete the chart.

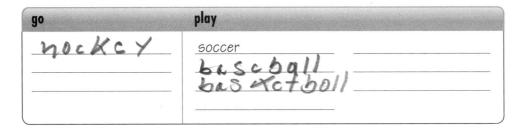

go	play
hockey	soccer
	baseball
	basketball

55

2 *Complete the conversation. Use the questions in the box.*

☐ Who do you practice with?   ☐ Does your sister play volleyball, too?
☑ Do you like sports?   ☐ When do you usually practice?
☐ What sports do you like?

Joe: _Do you like sports?_

Liz: Yes, I do. I like them a lot.

Joe: Really? what sports do you Like?

Liz: Well, I love volleyball.

Joe: who do you practice with?

Liz: On weekends. I'm too busy on weekdays.

Joe: when do you usualy Practice

Liz: I usually practice with my friends from school.

Joe: does your sister play volleyball, too

Liz: No, she doesn't like sports. She thinks they're boring.

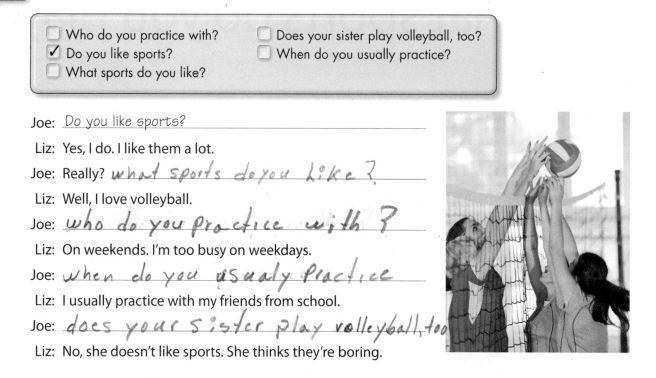

3 *Unscramble the questions. Then answer with your own information.*

1. you   do   like   baseball
   Do you like baseball?
   _____

2. sports   what   do   watch   you
   2   1   3   5   4
   _____

3. you   play   sports   what   do
   _____

4. snowboarding   do   you   how often   go
   _____

5. do   with   who   sports   you   play
   _____

4 *Write questions and answers about these people.*

Andrew

1. Can Andrew fix a car?

   No, he can't.

Chris and Nick

2. can chris and Nick swimming

   yes they can

Kenji

3. Can Kenji yoga

   yes he can

Juliet

4. _____

   _____

Erica

5. _____

   _____

Natasha

6. _____

   _____

5 *Write sentences about these people. Use* can, can't, *and* but.

1. She can play the guitar, but
   she can't play the piano.

2. he can play the sing
   he can't play the dancing

3. she can play the soccer
   she can't play the golf

4. He can play the

6 *Choose the correct responses.*

1. A: Do you like the guitar?

   B: No, I don't.
   - Yes, I can.
   - No, I don't.

2. A: Who do you play tennis with?

   B: my sister
   - I do.
   - My sister.

3. A: Who can fix a computer?

   B: I can
   - I can.
   - Yes, I can.

4. A: Where do you go snowboarding?

   B: in the mountains
   - In winter.
   - In the mountains.

7 Can or can't?

A Can you do these things? Check (✓) can or can't.

	can	can't
1. cook	☐	☐
2. dance	☐	☐
3. drive a car	☐	☐
4. play chess	☐	☐
5. play the piano	☐	☐
6. snowboard	☐	☐
7. speak two languages	☐	☐
8. swim	☐	☐
9. tell good jokes	☐	☐
10. upload photos	☐	☐

B Write sentences about the things in part A.

1. _I can't cook at all._
2. _I can dance really well._
3. _____
4. _____
5. _____
6. _____
7. _____
8. _____
9. _____
10. _____

8 *Write each sentence a different way. Use the sentences in the box.*

> ☑ I hardly ever go hiking.   ☑ I love it.   ☑ He can play sports well.
> ☑ She tells good jokes.   ☑ He can't sing at all.   ☑ She has many talents.

1. He's a great athlete.
   He can play sports well.

2. I don't go hiking very often.
   I hardly ever go hiking.

3. She has a lot of abilities.
   She has many talents

4. I really like it.
   I love it

5. He's a terrible singer.
   He can't sing at all

6. She's very funny.
   She tells good jokes.

9 *Answer these questions with short answers. Use your own information.*

Puedes hablar bien ingles
1. Can you speak English well?   a Litle
Pu hablar espanal
2. Can you speak Spanish?   iF I speak
andar en bicicleta
3. Can you ride a bike?   I dont know
te gusta el deporte
4. Do you like sports?   yes I Like it
eres un buen estudiante
5. Are you a good student?   yes I am
te gusta tu clase de ingles
6. Do you like your English class?   iF I Like it very much
Puedes Tocar un instrumento musical
7. Can you play a musical instrument?   I can not touch
alguna vez vas a patinar sobre nielo
8. Do you ever go ice-skating?   I have never done it
alguna vez juegas baloncesto
9. Do you ever play basketball?   I can not do it
Puedes descargar un video
10. Can you download a video?   yes I can do it

10 *What can your friends and family do? What can't they do? Write sentences.*

1. _____
2. _____
3. _____
4. _____

11 What are you going to do?

1 Months and dates

A Put the months in the box in time order.

☐ April	☐ December	☑ January	☐ June	☐ May	☐ October
☐ August	☐ February	☐ July	☐ March	☐ November	☐ September

1. January _____
2. _____
3. _____
4. _____

5. _____
6. _____
7. _____
8. _____

9. _____
10. _____
11. _____
12. _____

B When are the seasons in your country? Write the months for each season.

Spring	Summer	Fall	Winter
_____	_____	_____	_____
_____	_____	_____	_____
_____	_____	_____	_____

C Write each date a different way.

1. March 12th   March twelfth _____
2. April 11th _____
3. January 16th _____
4. February 9th _____

5. October 1st _____
6. May 22nd _____
7. July 3rd _____
8. August 30th _____

2 It's January first. How old are these people going to be on their next birthdays? Write sentences.

	Alex	Anita	Peggy and Patty	You
Age now	76	25	18	_____
Birthday	March 15th	July 27th	September 6th	_____

1. Alex is going to be seventy-seven on March fifteenth. _____

2. _____

3. _____

4. _____

3 Read Beth's calendar. Write sentences about her plans. Use the words in parentheses.

CALENDAR	Sunday	Monday	Tuesday	Wednesday	Thursday	Friday	Saturday
◀ **June** ▶	1	2 play golf after work	3 have lunch with Tony	4	5	6	7 go shopping with Julie
June 1 2 3 4 5 6 7	8 meet John for dinner	9	10	11 work late	12	13 go to Sam's party	14
8 9 10 11 12 13 14 15 16 17 18 19 20 21	15	16 see a movie with Tony	17	18	19	20	21 have a family picnic
22 23 24 25 26 27 28 29 30	22	23	24 buy Paula's birthday present	25 go to Paula's birthday dinner	26	27	28
🖨 Print ✉ Email							

1. On June second, she's going to play golf after work. _____ (June 2nd)

2. _____ (June 3rd)

3. _____ (June 7th)

4. _____ (June 8th)

5. _____ (June 11th)

6. _____ (June 13th)

7. _____ (June 16th)

8. _____ (June 21st)

9. _____ (June 24th)

10. _____ (June 25th)

4 *Complete these sentences. Use the correct form of* **be going to** *and the verbs in parentheses.*

1. This __is going to be_____ (be) a very busy weekend.

2. On Friday, my friend Ben and I _____ (see) a movie. After the movie, we _____ (eat) dinner at our favorite Thai restaurant.

3. On Saturday morning, my parents _____ (visit). They _____ (drive) into the city, and we _____ (go) to the art museum. I think my mother _____ (love) it, but my father _____ (not like) it. Later, we _____ (watch) a football game on TV. My parents _____ (go) home after dinner.

4. On Sunday, I _____ (sleep) late. Then I _____ (read) the newspaper. On Sunday afternoon, I _____ (take) a walk. In the evening, my friend Jill and I _____ (study) together.

5 *Complete these conversations. Write questions with* **be going to.**

1. Eric: <u>What are you going to do this</u>
           <u>weekend?</u>

    Sarah: This weekend? I'm going to go to the
            country with my brother.

    Eric: That's nice. _____
            _____

    Sarah: We're going to stay at our friend
            Marjorie's house. She lives there.

    Eric: Really? _____
            _____

    Sarah: I think we're going to go mountain
            climbing.

    Eric: _____
            _____

    Sarah: No, Marjorie isn't going to go with
            us. She's going to go bike riding.

2. Scott: I'm going to have a birthday party for
            Tara next Saturday. Can you come?

    Emily: Sure. _____
            _____

    Scott: It's going to be at my house. Do you
            have the address?

    Emily: Yes, I do. And _____
            _____

    Scott: It's going to start at seven o'clock.

    Emily: _____
            _____

    Scott: No, Bob isn't going to be there.

    Emily: That's too bad. _____
            _____

    Scott: No, I'm not going to bake a cake.
            I can't bake! I'm going to buy one.

    Emily: OK. Sounds good. See you on Saturday.

64 ▪ *Unit 11*

6 Next weekend

A What are these people going to do next weekend? Write sentences.

1. <u>They're going to go to the gym.</u>

2. _____

3. _____

4. _____

5. _____

6. _____

7. _____

8. _____

9. _____

B What are you going to do next weekend? How about your family and friends? Write sentences.

1. _____

2. _____

3. _____

4. _____

7 Are you going to do anything special on these holidays or special occasions? Write sentences. Use the phrases in the box or your own information.

dance	go to a parade	sing songs
eat special food	go to a restaurant	stay home
give gifts	have a party	stay out late
go on a picnic	play games	watch fireworks
go out with friends	play music	wear special clothes

New Year's Eve

New Year's Day

1. I'm not going to have a party. I'm going to watch fireworks with my friends, but we're not going to stay out late.

2. _____

Your next birthday

Your best friend's birthday

3. _____

4. _____

Valentine's Day

The last day of class

5. _____

6. _____

12 What's the matter?

1 *Label the parts of the body. Use the words in the box.*

- [ ] arm
- [ ] ear
- [ ] elbow
- [ ] eye
- [ ] fingers
- [ ] foot
- [✓] hair
- [ ] hand
- [ ] leg
- [ ] mouth
- [ ] neck
- [ ] nose
- [ ] shoulder
- [ ] stomach
- [ ] teeth
- [ ] toes

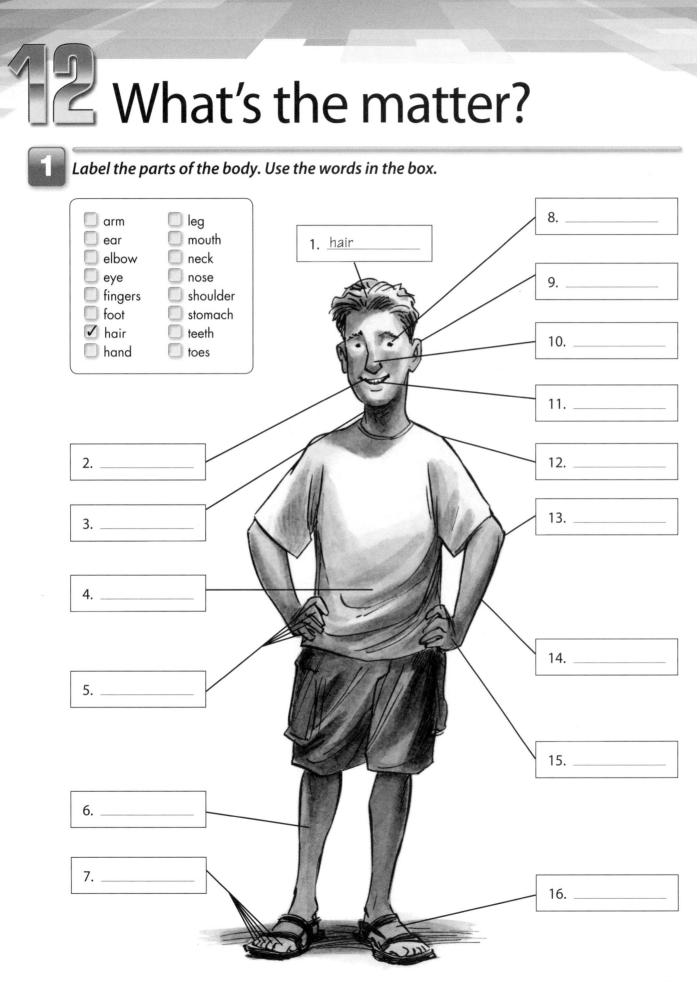

1. hair

2. _____

3. _____

4. _____

5. _____

6. _____

7. _____

8. _____

9. _____

10. _____

11. _____

12. _____

13. _____

14. _____

15. _____

16. _____

What's wrong with these people? Write sentences.

1. <u>He has an earache.</u>

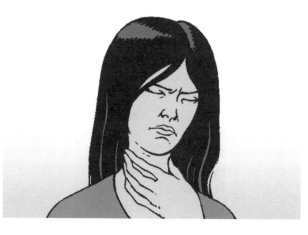

2. _____

3. _____

4. _____

5. _____

6. _____

3 *Complete the conversations. Use the questions and sentences in the box.*

☐ I'm glad to hear that.
☐ How do you feel tonight?
☑ I'm fine, thanks. How about you?
☐ That's too bad. Are you going to see a doctor?

☐ What's wrong?
☐ Great. See you tomorrow.
☐ OK. Get some rest.
☐ So, are you going to go to school tomorrow?

In the afternoon

1. Jason: Hi, Lisa. How are you?

   Lisa: <u>I'm fine, thanks. How about you?</u>

   Jason: Not so good. Actually, I feel really awful.

   Lisa: _____

   Jason: I think I have the flu.

   Lisa: _____

   Jason: No, I'm going to go home now.

   Lisa: _____

   Jason: OK. Thanks.

In the evening

2. Lisa: _____

   Jason: I feel much better.

   Lisa: _____

   Jason: Thanks.

   Lisa: _____

   Jason: Yes, I am.

   Lisa: _____

In the afternoon

In the evening

4 *Complete the sentences with the correct medications.*

1. Her eyes are very tired. She needs some _____eyedrops_____ .

2. Your cough sounds terrible. Buy some _____
   or some _____ .

3. I have a headache, so I'm going to take
   some _____ .

4. My arm is sore. I'm going to put some
   _____ on my arm.

5. Kristina has a stomachache, so I'm going
   to give her some _____ .

6. Suzie has a terrible cold. She's going to take
   some _____ .

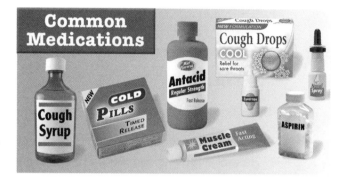

5 *Write each sentence a different way. Use the sentences in the box.*

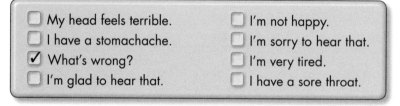

☐ My head feels terrible.   ☐ I'm not happy.
☐ I have a stomachache.   ☐ I'm sorry to hear that.
☑ What's wrong?   ☐ I'm very tired.
☐ I'm glad to hear that.   ☐ I have a sore throat.

1. What's the matter?
   What's wrong? _____

2. I feel sad.
   _____

3. That's too bad.
   _____

4. My stomach hurts.
   _____

5. My throat is sore.
   _____

6. I have a headache.
   _____

7. That's good.
   _____

8. I'm exhausted.
   _____

6 *Give these people advice. Use the phrases in the box.*

☐ drink some water	☐ go to the grocery store	☐ have a hot drink	☐ stay up late
☐ go home early	☐ lift heavy things	☐ go outside	☑ work too hard

1. <u>Don't work too hard.</u> 2. _____

3. _____ 4. _____

5. _____ 6. _____

7. _____ 8. _____

7 *Write two pieces of advice for each problem.*

1. I have a cold.   Don't go to school today. Take a cold pill.
2. I have a toothache.   _____
3. I have a sore throat.   _____
4. I have an earache.   _____
5. I have a stomachache.   _____
6. I have a backache.   _____
7. I have sore eyes.   _____
8. I have a fever.   _____

8 *Health survey*

A How healthy and happy are you? Complete the survey.

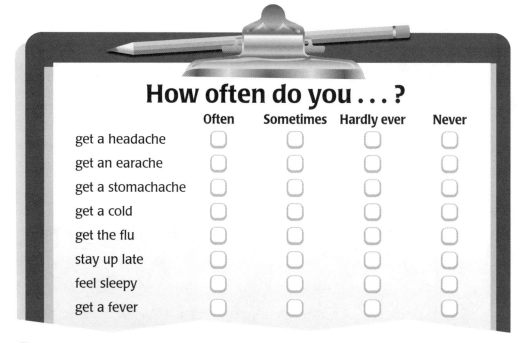

How often do you . . . ?

	Often	Sometimes	Hardly ever	Never
get a headache	☐	☐	☐	☐
get an earache	☐	☐	☐	☐
get a stomachache	☐	☐	☐	☐
get a cold	☐	☐	☐	☐
get the flu	☐	☐	☐	☐
stay up late	☐	☐	☐	☐
feel sleepy	☐	☐	☐	☐
get a fever	☐	☐	☐	☐

B Write four sentences about your health. Use the information from the survey in part A.

Examples:

I hardly ever get a headache, an earache, or a stomachache.

I often stay up late on weekends, but I never stay up late on weekdays.

1. _____
2. _____
3. _____
4. _____

13 You can't miss it.

1 Places

A Complete these sentences with the correct places.
Write one letter on each line.

1. We need gasoline for the car. Is there a

   _g_ _a_ _s_   _s_ _t_ _a_ _t_ _i_ _o_ _n_ near here?

2. I'm going to go to the ___ ___ ___ ___ . I need some traveler's checks.

3. I work at a ___ ___ ___ ___ ___ ___ ___ ___ ___ . I love books, so it's a great job.

4. Are you going to the ___ ___ ___ ___   ___ ___ ___ ___ ___ ___ ? I need some stamps.

5. We don't have anything for dinner. Let's buy some food at the

   ___ ___ ___ ___ ___ ___ ___ ___ ___ ___ ___ .

6. Tomorrow we're going to go to Paris for five days. We're going to stay

   at an expensive ___ ___ ___ ___ ___ .

7. I have a stomachache. Can you buy some antacid at the ___ ___ ___ ___ ___ ___ ___ ___ ___ ?

8. Let's go out for lunch. There's a great Mexican ___ ___ ___ ___ ___ ___ ___ ___ ___ ___ downtown.

B Find and circle the places in part A in the puzzle.

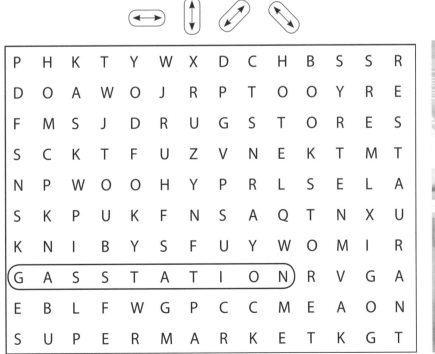

P	H	K	T	Y	W	X	D	C	H	B	S	S	R
D	O	A	W	O	J	R	P	T	O	O	Y	R	E
F	M	S	J	D	R	U	G	S	T	O	R	E	S
S	C	K	T	F	U	Z	V	N	E	K	T	M	T
N	P	W	O	O	H	Y	P	R	L	S	E	L	A
S	K	P	U	K	F	N	S	A	Q	T	N	X	U
K	N	I	B	Y	S	F	U	Y	W	O	M	I	R
G	A	S	S	T	A	T	I	O	N	R	V	G	A
E	B	L	F	W	G	P	C	C	M	E	A	O	N
S	U	P	E	R	M	A	R	K	E	T	K	G	T

2 Look at the map. Complete the sentences with the prepositions in the box.

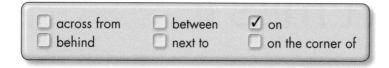

☐ across from	☐ between	☑ on
☐ behind	☐ next to	☐ on the corner of

1. The English school is ___on___ Catherine Street.

2. The hospital is _____ the hotel.

3. The Mexican restaurant is _____ Beatrice Street and Fourth Avenue.

4. The bank is on Barbara Street, _____ Sixth and Seventh Avenues.

5. The bookstore is _____ the English school.

6. The coffee shop is _____ the park.

3 Where is it?

A Look at the map in Exercise 2 again. Where is each place? Write two sentences.

1. bookstore   <u>The bookstore is on the corner of Catherine Street</u>
                                  <u>and Fifth Avenue. It's next to the English school.</u>

2. supermarket

3. department store

4. gas station

5. Chinese restaurant

6. hotel

7. post office

8. drugstore

B Where is your school? Draw a map. Then write two sentences.

4 *Complete the conversation. Use the sentences and questions in the box.*

> ☐ Next to the café?
> ☐ Is there a post office around here?
> ☐ Thanks a lot.
>
> ☑ Excuse me. Can you help me?
> ☐ Where on Diane Street?

Rachel: _Excuse me. Can you help me?_

Man: Sure.

Rachel: _____

Man: Yes, there is. It's on Diane Street.

Rachel: _____

Man: It's on the corner of Diane Street and Seventh Avenue.

Rachel: _____

Man: Yes, that's right. It's right next to the café.

Rachel: _____

Man: You're welcome.

5 *Complete the sentences with the opposites.*

1. Don't turn *right* on Fifth Avenue. Turn ____left____ .

2. The Waverly Hotel isn't *in front of* the concert hall. It's _____ it.

3. Don't walk *down* Columbus Avenue. Walk _____ Columbus Avenue.

4. The museum isn't on the *left*. It's on the _____ .

5. The Empire State Building is *far* from here, but Central Park is _____ here. You can walk there.

6 *Look at the map. Give these people directions. Use the phrases and sentences in the box.*

Walk up/Go up . . . Street/Avenue.	Walk down/Go down . . . Street/Avenue.
Turn left on . . . Street/Avenue.	Turn right on . . . Street/Avenue.
Walk to . . . Street/Avenue.	It's on the left/right.

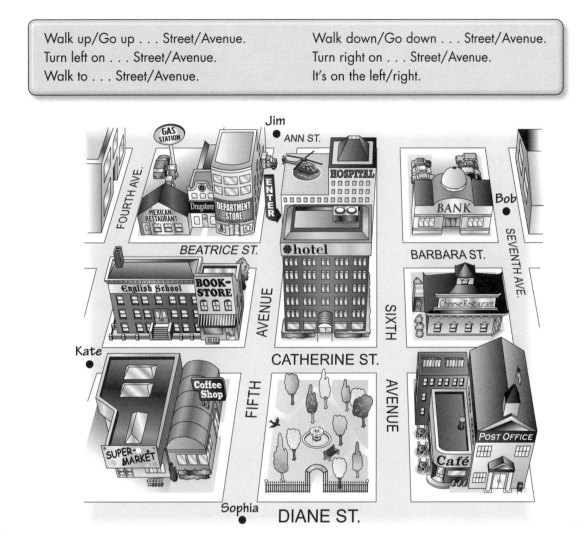

1. Sophia is looking for the Mexican restaurant.

   Go up Fifth Avenue. Turn left on Beatrice Street.

   Walk to Fourth Avenue. It's on the right.

2. Kate is looking for the post office.

3. Bob is looking for the supermarket.

4. Jim is looking for the bank.

7 *Imagine you're going to have a party. Complete the invitation. Then draw a map and write directions to the party from your school.*

PARTY!

Date: _____

Time: _____

Place: _____

Map to the party

Directions to the party

Start at the school. Then _____

_____

_____

_____

14 Did you have fun?

1 *Last Saturday*

A What did these people do last Saturday? Write sentences.

1 pay bills

2 vacuum

3 wash clothes

4 exercise

5 dust

6 work in the yard

7 shop for groceries

8 cook

1. _She paid bills._
2. _____
3. _____
4. _____
5. _____
6. _____
7. _____
8. _____

B What did you do last Saturday? Write three sentences.

1. _____
2. _____
3. _____

2 *Ben is writing his blog. Complete the sentences. Use the simple past form of the verbs in parentheses.*

Just Another Day

Friday, April 7
Fun with friends

What a great day! This afternoon, I ____invited____ (invite) some friends over after school. We _____ (stop) at the video arcade, but we _____ (not stay) long. We _____ (play) basketball and _____ (listen) to music. Mom _____ (cook) some hamburgers for dinner. After dinner, we _____ (watch) TV.

Posted by Ben at **9:27 P.M.**   2 comments

Saturday, April 8
Party time

This morning, Kelly _____ (call). She _____ (invite) me to her sister's birthday party. I _____ (need) a present for the party, so I _____ (walk) to the mall. The party _____ (start) at 7:00 and _____ (end) at 10:00. Kelly and I _____ (dance) and _____ (talk) all evening. She's really cool.

Posted by Ben at **10:15 P.M.**   5 comments

Sunday, April 9
Helping at home

I _____ (study) this morning. In the afternoon, Mom, Dad, and I _____ (shop) for some clothes for me. Then I _____ (help) Mom with dinner. After dinner, I _____ (clean) my room. In the evening, I _____ (call) Kelly, but we _____ (not talk) very long. Time for bed!

Posted by Ben at **11:01 P.M.**   3 comments

About me

**Ben
Boston,
Massachusetts,
U.S.**

Blog Archive
► March
► February
► January
► December
► November
► October
► September
► August

3 *Carol and Max did different things last weekend. Write sentences about them.*

1. study   Carol studied. Max didn't study.

2. clean the kitchen _____

3. play golf   _____

4. cook   _____

5. listen to music _____

6. walk in the park _____

7. watch TV   _____

4 *Complete the chart.*

Present	Past	Present	Past
buy	_bought_	go	_____
come	_____	have	_____
do	_____	read	_____
_____	ate	_____	rode
feel	_____	_____	saw
_____	got up	sit	_____

5 *Complete the conversation. Use the simple past forms of the verbs in parentheses.*

Kevin: So, Megan, _____did_____ you _____have_____ (have) a good summer?

Megan: Well, I _____ (have) an interesting summer. My sister

and her family _____ (visit) for two weeks.

Kevin: That's nice.

Megan: Yes and no. My sister _____ (not feel)

well, so she _____ (sit) on the sofa

and _____ (watch) TV.

She hardly ever _____ (get up).

Kevin: Oh, well. _____ her husband and kids

_____ (have) a good time?

Megan: I think so. They _____ (play) volleyball

and _____ (ride) their bikes every day.

Kevin: _____ you _____ (go out) to

any restaurants?

Megan: No, I _____ (cook) breakfast, lunch,

and dinner every day. They _____ (eat)

a lot of food, but they _____ (not wash)

any dishes.

Kevin: That's too bad. _____ you

_____ (relax) at all last summer?

Megan: Yes. My sister and her family finally

_____ (go) home, and then I

_____ (relax). I just _____ (read)

some books and _____ (see) some movies.

6 *Unscramble the questions about last summer. Then answer with your own information.*

Last summer, . . . ?

1. go   interesting   anywhere   you   did

   A: <u>Did you go anywhere interesting?</u>

   B: <u>Yes, I did. I went to Hawaii. / No, I didn't. I just stayed home.</u>

2. any   take   did   you   pictures

   A: _____

   B: _____

3. buy   you   did   anything   interesting

   A: _____

   B: _____

4. did   eat   you   foods   any   new

   A: _____

   B: _____

5. games   did   you   any   play

   A: _____

   B: _____

6. you   did   sports   play   any

   A: _____

   B: _____

7. you   did   interesting   meet   any   people

   A: _____

   B: _____

8. did   any   books   you   read   good

   A: _____

   B: _____

9. any   see   you   did   movies   good

   A: _____

   B: _____

7 Summer activities

A Greg and Grant did different activities last summer. Write sentences about them.

1. Greg got up early every day.
2. _____
3. _____
4. _____
5. _____
6. _____
7. _____
8. _____

B Write sentences about your activities last summer.

1. _____
2. _____
3. _____
4. _____

15 Where did you grow up?

1 *Complete the conversation. Use the sentences in the box.*

- [ ] I was sixteen.
- [x] No, I wasn't. I was born in the Caribbean.
- [ ] I came here to study English.
- [ ] I was born in Santo Domingo.
- [ ] No, it wasn't. I loved it.
- [ ] No, I'm from the Dominican Republic.
- [ ] I moved here in 2007.
- [ ] Yes, they were. We were all born there.

Melissa: Were you born here in the U.S., Luis?

Luis: _No, I wasn't. I was born in the Caribbean._

Melissa: Oh, were you born in Cuba?

Luis: _____

Melissa: Really? What city were you born in?

Luis: _____

Melissa: Were your parents born in Santo Domingo, too?

Luis: _____

Melissa: And why did you come to the U.S.?

Luis: _____

Melissa: So when did you move here?

Luis: _____

Melissa: Really? How old were you then?

Luis: _____

Melissa: Was it scary?

Luis: _____

2 *Complete these conversations with* **was, wasn't, were,** *or* **weren't.**

1. Peter: I called you on Saturday, but you ___weren't___ home.

   David: No, I _____ . I _____ in the mountains all weekend.

   Peter: That's nice. How _____ the weather there?

   David: It _____ beautiful.

   Peter: _____ your parents there?

   David: No, they _____ . I _____ alone. It _____ great!

the mountains

Chicago

2. Sue: _____ you born in the U.S., Pat?

   Pat: Yes, I _____ . My brother and I _____ born here in New York.

   Sue: I _____ born here, too. What about your parents? _____ they born here?

   Pat: Well, my father _____ . He _____ born in China, but my mother _____ born in the U.S. – in Chicago.

   Sue: Chicago? Really? My parents _____ born in Chicago, too!

Nice

3. Nancy: _____ you in college last year, Chuck?

   Chuck: No, I _____ . I graduated from college two years ago.

   Nancy: So where _____ you last year?

   Chuck: I _____ in France.

   Nancy: Oh! _____ you in Paris?

   Chuck: No, I _____ . I _____ in Nice. I had a job there.

   Nancy: What _____ the job?

   Chuck: I _____ a front desk clerk at a hotel.

3 *Write four sentences about each person.*

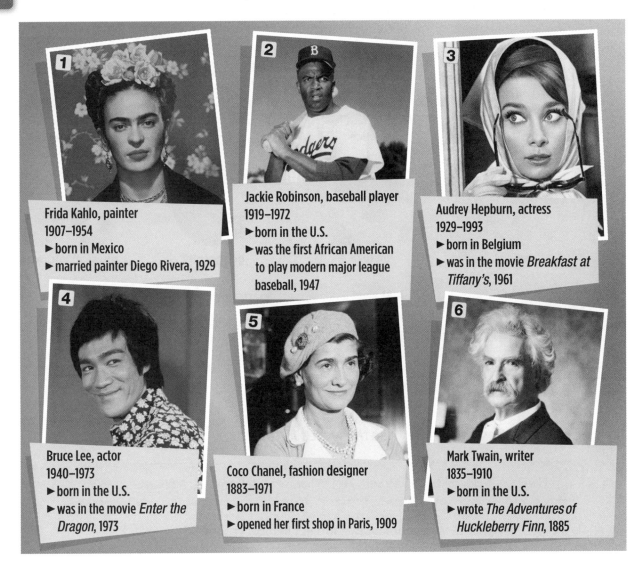

1
Frida Kahlo, painter
1907–1954
► born in Mexico
► married painter Diego Rivera, 1929

2
Jackie Robinson, baseball player
1919–1972
► born in the U.S.
► was the first African American
to play modern major league
baseball, 1947

3
Audrey Hepburn, actress
1929–1993
► born in Belgium
► was in the movie *Breakfast at
Tiffany's*, 1961

4
Bruce Lee, actor
1940–1973
► born in the U.S.
► was in the movie *Enter the
Dragon*, 1973

5
Coco Chanel, fashion designer
1883–1971
► born in France
► opened her first shop in Paris, 1909

6
Mark Twain, writer
1835–1910
► born in the U.S.
► wrote *The Adventures of
Huckleberry Finn*, 1885

1. Frida Kahlo was a painter. She was born in 1907 in Mexico.
She married painter Diego Rivera in 1929. She died in 1954.

2. _____

3. _____

4. _____

5. _____

6. _____

4 Do you think these classes are easy, difficult, interesting, or boring? Complete the chart. Then add one more class to each column.

math

science

drama

computer lab

art

history

geography

physical education

Easy	Difficult	Interesting	Boring

5 Complete these questions. Use the words in the box.

☐ How   ☐ How old   ☑ What   ☐ When   ☐ Where   ☐ Who   ☐ Why

1. A: _____What_____ was your favorite subject in high school?

   B: It was math.

2. A: _____ was your favorite teacher?

   B: My math teacher, Mrs. Stone.

3. A: _____ did you graduate from high school?

   B: In 2006.

4. A: _____ did you go to college?

   B: I went to Boston University.

5. A: _____ did you study geography?

   B: Because I wanted to travel!

6. A: _____ were your professors in college?

   B: They were great.

7. A: _____ were you when you graduated?

   B: I was 22 years old.

6 *Unscramble the questions about your elementary school days. Then answer with your own information.*

1. was   your   of   school   how   first   day

   A: _How was your first day of school?_

   B: _____

2. your   was   teacher   who   favorite

   A: _____

   B: _____

3. favorite   was   your   what   class

   A: _____

   B: _____

4. your   who   best   were   friends

   A: _____

   B: _____

5. spend   did   your   where   you   free time

   A: _____

   B: _____

6. finish   did   when   you   elementary school

   A: _____

   B: _____

7 *Childhood memories*

A Complete the questions with *did*, *was*, or *were*. Then answer the questions. Use short answers.

1. A: _____Were_____ you born here?

   B: Yes, I was. / No, I wasn't.

2. A: _____ you grow up in a big city?

   B: _____

3. A: _____ you live in an apartment?

   B: _____

4. A: _____ your home near your school?

   B: _____

5. A: _____ you walk to school?

   B: _____

6. A: _____ you a good student?

   B: _____

7. A: _____ your teachers nice?

   B: _____

8. A: _____ you have a lot of friends?

   B: _____

9. A: _____ your best friend live near you?

   B: _____

10. A: _____ both your parents work?

    B: _____

B Write sentences about your childhood.

1. _____
2. _____
3. _____
4. _____
5. _____
6. _____

Can she call you later?

1 *Make a phone conversation. Use the sentences and questions in the box.*

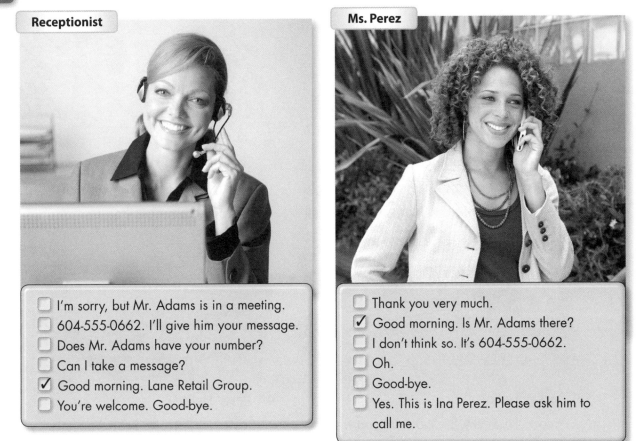

Receptionist

- ☐ I'm sorry, but Mr. Adams is in a meeting.
- ☐ 604-555-0662. I'll give him your message.
- ☐ Does Mr. Adams have your number?
- ☐ Can I take a message?
- ☑ Good morning. Lane Retail Group.
- ☐ You're welcome. Good-bye.

Ms. Perez

- ☐ Thank you very much.
- ☑ Good morning. Is Mr. Adams there?
- ☐ I don't think so. It's 604-555-0662.
- ☐ Oh.
- ☐ Good-bye.
- ☐ Yes. This is Ina Perez. Please ask him to call me.

Receptionist: *Good morning. Lane Retail Group.* _____

Ms. Perez: *Good morning. Is Mr. Adams there?* _____

Receptionist: _____

Ms. Perez: _____

Receptionist: _____

Ms. Perez: _____

Receptionist: _____

Ms. Perez: _____

Receptionist: _____

Ms. Perez: _____

Receptionist: _____

Ms. Perez: _____

2 *Scott called his friends yesterday. Where were they? Complete the conversations. Use the words in the box.*

☐ class   ☐ hospital   ☐ mall   ☐ shower   ☐ vacation   ☑ work

1. Susan: Hello?

    Scott: Hello, Susan? It's Scott.

    Susan: Oh, hi, Scott. Listen. I can't talk right
    now. I'm ____at work____ . Call
    me later?

2. Kurt: Hello?

    Scott: Hey, Kurt. It's –

    Kurt: Scott. Sorry, can you call me in
    20 minutes? I'm

    _____ .

3. Becky: Hello?

    Scott: Hi, Becky. It's Scott. Do you want to
    see a movie tonight?

    Becky: I'd love to, but I can't. I'm

    _____ with my

    parents.

4. Pete: Hello?

    Scott: Hi, Pete. It's Scott. You know, you
    sound terrible. Are you OK?

    Pete: Not really. I'm _____ .
    But it's nothing serious.

5. Lori: Hello?

    Scott: Hello, Lori? It's Scott. It sounds noisy
    there. Where are you?

    Lori: Oh, I'm _____ .

6. Mark: Hello?

    Scott: Hey, Mark. Do you have a minute?

    Mark: Not really. I'm _____ .
    Call me in ten minutes.

3 *Subject and object pronouns*

A Complete the chart.

Subjects	Objects
I	me
_____	you
he	_____
she	_____
we	_____
_____	them

B Complete the sentences with the correct words in parentheses.

1. Please give it to _____ (he / him).

2. _____ (She / Her) isn't here right now.

3. Can _____ (I / me) help you?

4. Please leave _____ (we / us) a message.

5. _____ (They / Them) are in the library.

4 *Jim is checking his voice-mail messages. Complete the messages with the correct pronouns.*

Bob's message

Hi, Jim. This is Bob. My sister Olivia is visiting _____me_____ .
Do you remember _____ ? Well, _____ 're
going to have lunch at Carol's Café tomorrow. Can you
meet _____ there? Please call _____ today.

Allie's message

Hey, Jim. It's Allie. I'm sorry _____ missed your call
this morning. Listen, my friends and I are going to go out
to a great pizza restaurant after work. Would you like to
join _____ ? Give _____ a call!

Derek's message

Hi, Jim. It's Derek. I'm in your math class with Mr. Stevens.
Did _____ give a homework assignment today?
_____ missed the class. Can _____ call
_____ ? My number is 608-555-9914. Thanks!

5 *Complete the phone conversation. Use the words in the box.*

☐ at	☐ call	☐ does	☐ her	☐ please
☐ but	✔ can	☐ have	☐ in	☐ this

Sam: Hello?

Ray: Hello. _____Can_____ I speak to

Monica, _____ ?

Sam: I'm sorry, _____

she's _____ a meeting.

Can I give _____ a message?

Ray: Yes. _____ is Ray Santos.

Please ask her to _____ me.

I'm _____ work.

Sam: Does she _____ your number?

Ray: Yes, she _____ .

6 *Complete the excuses. Use your own ideas.*

1. A: Can you cook dinner for me this evening?

   B: I'm sorry, but I have to _____ work late. _____

2. A: Do you want to go to the library this weekend?

   B: I'd like to, but I need to _____

3. A: Can you feed my cat on Sunday?

   B: I'm sorry, but I can't. I have to _____

4. A: Can you help me with my homework tonight?

   B: I'm sorry, but I can't. I have to _____

5. A: Would you like to go bike riding on Saturday?

   B: I'd like to, but I need to _____

6. A: Can you play golf this weekend?

   B: I'm sorry, but I have to _____

7 *Imagine your friends invite you to do these things. Accept or refuse their invitations. Use the phrases and sentences in the chart.*

Accepting	Refusing and making excuses
I'd love to.	I'm sorry, but I can't. I have to / need to / want to . . .
I'd like to.	I'd like to, but I have to / need to / want to . . .

1. A: Do you want to go to the art gallery this afternoon?

   B: _____

2. A: Do you want to have dinner with me tomorrow night?

   B: _____

3. A: Do you want to watch the game at my house next Wednesday?

   B: _____

4. A: Do you want to go dancing with me on Saturday night?

   B: _____

5. A: Do you want to go hiking with me this weekend?

   B: _____

8 *Write each sentence a different way. Use the sentences in the box.*

☑ Hi, this is Amy.   ☐ I'm busy.   ☐ Do you want to see a movie?
☐ Is Barbara there?   ☐ I'd like to go to the movies.   ☐ Can I take a message?

1. Hi, it's Amy.

   Hi, this is Amy.

2. Can I speak with Barbara?

   _____

3. Would you like to go to the movies?

   _____

4. I want to go to the movies.

   _____

5. I already have plans.

   _____

6. Do you want to leave a message?

   _____

9   *Answer the questions. Write sentences with* **like to,** *want to,* **and** **need to.**

Example: What are two things you need to do tomorrow?

<u>I need to buy groceries.</u>

<u>I need to clean my room.</u>

1. What are two things you like to do often?

_____

_____

2. Where are two places you want to visit?

_____

_____

3. Who are two famous people you want to meet?

_____

_____

4. What are two things you need to do this week?

_____

_____

5. Where are two places you like to go on weekends?

_____

_____

6. What are two things you like to do after class?

_____

_____

7. What are two things you want to do in your next class?

_____

_____